SHAW ON SHAKESPEARE

SHAW ON SHAKESPEARE

An Anthology of Bernard Shaw's Writings
on the Plays and Production
of Shakespeare

ข

Edited, and with an Introduction,

by

EDWIN WILSON

Essay Index Reprint Series

 BOOKS FOR LIBRARIES PRESS
FREEPORT, NEW YORK

ACKNOWLEDGMENTS AND OTHER COPYRIGHTS

The editor and publishers of this volume are grateful to the following publishers and literary executors for permission to include copyright material:

The Estate of Elbridge L. Adams, Max Reinhardt, Ltd. and G. P. Putnam's Sons for extracts from *Ellen Terry and Bernard Shaw: A Correspondence.* Copyright, 1931, by Bernard Shaw and Elbridge L. Adams.

Harper & Brothers for extracts from *G. B. S.: A Full Length Portrait* by Hesketh Pearson. Copyright, 1942, by Hesketh Pearson.

The Bobbs-Merrill Company for an extract from *Confessions of an Actor* by John Barrymore. Copyright, 1926, by The Bobbs-Merrill Company.

Alfred A. Knopf, Inc. and Curtis Brown, Ltd. for extracts from *Bernard Shaw and Mrs. Patrick Campbell: Their Correspondence.* Copyright, 1952, by Alfred A. Knopf, Inc.

Appleton-Century-Crofts, Inc. for extracts from *Bernard Shaw: Playboy and Prophet* by Archibald Henderson. Copyright, 1932, by D. Appleton and Company.

Appleton-Century-Crofts, Inc. for extracts from *George Bernard Shaw: Man of the Century* by Archibald Henderson. Copyright, 1932, by D. Appleton and Company. Copyright, ©, 1956, by Archibald Henderson.

Roy Publishers, A. N., New York and Gerald Duckworth, Ltd. for extracts from *Bernard Shaw: A Chronicle* by R. F. Rattray. Copyright, 1951, by Roy Publishers, A. N., New York.

INTERNATIONAL STANDARD BOOK NUMBER:
0-8369-2175-5

LIBRARY OF CONGRESS CATALOG CARD NUMBER:
77-134134

PRINTED IN THE UNITED STATES OF AMERICA

CONTENTS

INTRODUCTION

FOR MANY PEOPLE Bernard Shaw's writing on Shakespeare began as a joke. When he became drama critic of *The Saturday Review* in the 1890's Shaw attacked Shakespeare with an impudence that had not been seen before, nor is likely to be seen again: he called *Othello* a melodrama, said that *Cymbeline* was "for the most part stagey trash of the lowest melodramatic order," argued that Shakespeare "never thought a noble life worth living or a great work worth doing," and insisted that he was "for an afternoon, but not for all time."

Shaw had a serious purpose in mind with all this, but to the worshipers of Shakespeare, which included practically everyone except Shaw, it was pure sacrilege. Since to take it seriously would be heresy, the only alternative was to regard it as a joke, and not a very good one at that.

As a character in *John Bull's Other Island* remarks, "every jest is an earnest in the womb of time," and while there are still those who think Shaw's Shakespearean criticism flippant, those who have bothered to look at it closely realize that Shaw's wit, like that of the fools in Shakespeare, is often a mask for wisdom.

Shaw has several real assets as a Shakespearean critic, some of them unique. One is his knowledge of Shakespeare. "When I was twenty," he wrote, "I knew everybody in Shakespear, from Hamlet to Abhorson, much more intimately than I knew my living contemporaries." There is no reason to doubt this, or his further claim that he knew several plays virtually by heart. In addition to the plays Shaw was thoroughly familiar with Shakespearean criticism. He was active in scholarly debates of his day and took part in such organizations as the New Shakespeare Society. It should come as no surprise that among Shakespearean critics his favorite was Dr. Johnson.

Another asset is Shaw's own dramatic ability. Next to

Shakespeare's his plays form the most impressive body of dramatic works in English. This dramatic talent by itself would mean very little, however, had Shaw not also possessed great critical perception.

The critical faculty is just as illusive as the artistic: men either have it or they do not. As with his plays, Shaw's criticism, not only of drama, but of music and other arts as well, speaks for itself. Shaw himself explained the advantage of being both critic and dramatist:[1]

> The advantage of having a play criticized by a critic who is also a playwright is as obvious as the advantage of having a ship criticized by a critic who is also a master shipwright. Pray observe that I do not speak of the criticism of dramas and ships by dramatists and shipwrights who are not also critics; for that would be no more convincing than the criticism of acting by actors. Dramatic authorship no more constitutes a man a critic than actorship constitutes him a dramatic author; but a dramatic critic learns as much from having been a dramatic author as Shakespear or Mr. Pinero from having been actors.

There can be no doubt that in being both a critic and a dramatist Shaw has an advantage which very few Shakespearean commentators can claim.

Another of Shaw's assets is his brilliant prose style. In any worthwhile criticism there comes a time when, in order for it to achieve distinction and provide genuine insight, it must have merit of its own quite apart from that of its subject matter. In theatre criticism, for example, it is necessary to re-create the magic the dramatist has created, to suggest the power of his verse, to discuss the production of his works, and this is impossible unless the critic has special talents of his own. These Shaw possessed in abundance, and he gave freely of them in his writings on Shakespeare.

The fact remains that in spite of his assets Shaw has not been universally recognized as a Shakespearean critic. There are several reasons for this. One is the mere fact

---

[1] *Our Theatres in the Nineties* (London, 1931), I, 260-261. Notes are for passages not found elsewhere in this volume and not otherwise identified.

that his Shakespearean material is widely dispersed. Although the bulk of his criticism was written in the years following his debut with *The Saturday Review,* it actually covers a period of more than sixty years. One of his first Shakespearean pieces, a review of *Love's Labour's Lost,* appeared in a little-known magazine in 1886. The magazine was called *Our Corner,* and among its other achievements it published several of Shaw's novels in serial form. Shaw's last work on Shakespeare, a puppet show entitled "Shakes Versus Shav," was written in 1949.

In addition to being written at different times, the material is scattered in such diverse places as reviews of productions, letters to actors, parts of prefaces to his own plays, letters to *The Times Literary Supplement,* and even obituaries for actors and producers. This should not be an insurmountable problem; if Shaw's criticism is not well organized neither is that of many Shakespearean critics—Coleridge, for instance. Even so, it is necessary to bring it together, and that is one of the purposes of this volume.

When the material is collected there is a further objection, raised by a few, that it is too casual in tone, too journalistic, to be given serious consideration. Informality, however, also seems to be more the rule than the exception with Shakespearean criticism, a fact which led E. E. Stoll to observe: "In Shakespearean criticism, as in most things Anglo-Saxon save sport, there has been little professionalism . . . our critics, like our soldiers, have won their Waterloos on cricket fields." [2]

A more formidable problem is that of Shaw's prejudice. It was this which prompted Eric Bentley to say in his introduction to *Shaw on Music* that if he had attempted to compile a "book on the drama" from Shaw's theatre articles, he would have found himself in a difficulty not faced with the music articles. "The dramatic pieces are all *arrière-pensée,* the campaign oratory of a critic who wishes to be elected playwright. Now it is all very well to believe, as Shaw did, that all criticism is prejudiced, but, with Shaw's dramatic criticism, the prejudice is more important than anything else . . ."

There is no question that Shaw was prejudiced; he

[2] *Shakespeare Studies* (New York, 1927), p. 403.

admitted it in his "Author's Apology" to his collected drama reviews: "I postulated as desirable a certain kind of play in which I was destined ten years later to make my mark (as I very well foreknew in the depth of my own unconsciousness); and I brought everybody: authors, actors, managers, and all, to the one test: were they coming my way or staying in the old grooves?"

Before we can determine the importance of Shaw's prejudice we must see just what it is. It turns out to be not one prejudice but several. The most obvious is Shaw's predilection for the "new drama" of Ibsen and, of course, Shaw. Anything which impeded the acceptance of the "new drama" was its natural enemy, and this included Shakespeare. On one level it was simply that Shakespeare got in the way. He was popular fare with the actor-managers of the late nineteenth century; to the extent that they concentrated on Shakespeare they could not concentrate on the "new drama." It was necessary, therefore, to fight both the actor-managers and Shakespeare.

On a deeper level, however, Shakespeare was a symbol of old, outworn ideas. Shaw wrote to Ellen Terry, "My capers are part of a bigger design than you think: Shakespear, for instance, is to me one of the towers of the Bastille, and down he must come." [3] One of Shaw's methods in this campaign was to compare Shakespeare with Ibsen, in which comparison Ibsen invariably came out with "a double-first-class," and Shakespeare "hardly anywhere." Until Ibsen's arrival, Shaw wrote, "Shakespear had been conventionally ranked as a giant among psychologists and philosophers. Ibsen dwarfed him so absurdly in those aspects that it became impossible for the moment to take him seriously as an intellectual force."

Shaw reiterated this theme endlessly: Ibsen was a "thinker of extraordinary penetration, and a moralist of international influence," while Shakespeare's ideas were "platitudinous fudge." Bringing himself into the picture Shaw wrote: "With the single exception of Homer, there is no eminent writer, not even Sir Walter Scott, whom

[3] *Ellen Terry and Bernard Shaw: A Correspondence*, ed. Christopher St. John (New York, 1931), p. 110.

I can despise so entirely as I despise Shakespear when I measure my mind against his."

Let us examine what Shaw meant by all this. When he speaks of Shakespeare's lack of philosophy he is not referring to philosophy in a general sense but to something far more restricted: a concern for contemporary social, political, and moral problems. Shaw felt it was the business of the dramatist to deal with such problems, using his plays as a forum. Thus when he takes Shakespeare to task for a deficiency of ideas, what he is really saying is that he cannot take the plays of Shakespeare and write a "Quintessence of Shakespearism" comparable to his "Quintessence of Ibsenism."

Obviously this is a totally irrelevant basis on which to judge Shakespeare. Because the plays lack the meaning Shaw seeks in them it does not follow that they lack all meaning; for most people they have more than enough. Not only is Shaw's criticism spurious; it is often ambivalent as well. Sometimes he blames Shakespeare for failing to anticipate the social problems of the nineteenth century, for writing *Macbeth* instead of an Elizabethan *Ghosts;* at other times he does not blame Shakespeare but the times in which he lived: "anybody may now have things to say that Shakepear did not say, and outlooks on life and character which were not open to him." [4]

A corollary to Shaw's narrowly conceived notion of a dramatist's intellectual obligations is his premise that the purpose of drama is to teach. In answer to the argument that art should never be didactic Shaw insisted that it "should never be anything else." [5] He called the theatre "a most powerful instrument for teaching the nation how and what to think and feel." [6] Of course, this too is no basis on which to criticize Shakespeare. Shaw himself exposed the fallacy in his position and the extremes to which his theories carried him in one of his frequent comparisons: "A 'Doll's House' will be as flat as ditch water when 'A Midsummer Night's Dream' will still be fresh as paint; but it will have done more work in the

[4] In Frank Harris's *Contemporary Portraits, Second Series* (New York, 1919), p. 323.

[5] *Prefaces* (London, 1934), p. 773.

[6] *Prefaces*, p. 414.

world; and that is enough for the highest genius, which is always intensely utilitarian." [7]

In addition to his argument about social philosophy Shaw also quarrelled with Shakespeare about his fundamental view of life. Shakespeare wrote tragedies; Shaw, on the other hand, was essentially antitragic. This is an important difference; to men of feeling the two views are not easily reconciled. Dr. Johnson could hardly bring himself to read the last act of *King Lear;* he even expressed a preference for Nahum Tate's ending for the play. Goethe once wrote in a letter, "I do not really understand myself enough to know if I could write a true tragedy; I am terrified just by this undertaking and am almost convinced that I might destroy myself in the mere attempt." [8]

Shaw was on the side of Johnson and Goethe: *Saint Joan* was not complete without an epilogue showing the Maid alive. Being unable to accept the tragic view, Shaw was bound to be at odds with Shakespeare over his "barren pessimism." Shaw admitted that this pessimism never crushed Shakespeare: still he could never forgive the outlook expressed in "Out, out brief candle," and "As flies to wanton boys are we to the gods." Shakespeare was one of those Shaw had in mind when he wrote, "the lot of the man who sees life truly and thinks about it romantically is despair." He went on to say that in choosing between despair and giving up the "trumpery moral kitchen scales" by which romanticists weigh the world, men should give up the scales. The answer was to face problems and solve them. In this regard Shaw compared Shakespeare and Molière to Brieux: "The reason why Shakespear and Molière are always well spoken of and recommended to the young is that their quarrel is really a quarrel with God for not making men better. If they had quarrelled with a specified class of persons with incomes of four figures for not doing their work better, or for doing no work at all, they would be denounced as seditious, impious, and profligate corrupters of morality.

[7] "The Problem Play," *The Humanitarian,* VI (May, 1895), 351.

[8] Translation by B. Chabrowe, from *Briefwechsel zwischen Schiller und Goethe in den Jahren 1794 bis 1805* (Stuttgart und Augsburg, 1856), I, 414.

Brieux wastes neither ink nor indignation on Providence.
. . . His fistcuffs are not aimed heavenward: they fall on
human noses for the good of human souls."

Again Shaw is not altogether consistent. Having indicated that the problems posed by tragedy are capable of
solution, he later altered his argument. In the preface to
Man and Superman he wrote, "we may as well make up
our minds that Man 'will return to his idols and cupidities, in spite of all 'movements' and all revolutions, until
his nature is changed." One might ask, is this not one
of the basic assumptions of tragedy? Is it not a quarrel
with God for not making men better?

Still another prejudice of Shaw's, affecting his Shakespearean criticism, is his puritanism, which leads him to
oppose any romantic treatment of glory, war, or physical
love. For Shaw, *Hamlet* is not properly solved by
speeches about flights of angels: such pretty talk only
served as a smoke screen. The adulation of war and
jingoism in *Henry V* is inexcusable. The glorification of
sexual infatuation in *Antony and Cleopatra* is unforgive-
able: "to ask us to subject our souls to its ruinous glamor,
to worship it, deify it, and imply that it alone makes our
life worth living, is nothing but folly gone mad erotically."

Having looked at Shaw's prejudices we can return to
the question of their ultimate effect on his Shakespearean
criticism. It is important to realize, first of all, that Shaw's
way of presenting a prejudice often makes it loom larger
than it really is. Shaw was a fighter, a propagandist, who
would go to any lengths to make a point. As he explained
it, "It is always necessary to overstate a case startlingly
to make people sit up and listen to it, and to frighten
them into acting on it. I do this myself habitually and
deliberately." [9] This may be deceptive and unfair but it
should not mislead any but the most naïve. Besides, it is
partly responsible for Shaw's style, a style that makes it
more delightful and sometimes more enlightening to read
Shaw when he is wrong than certain other critics when
they are right.

Another consideration with Shaw's prejudices is that
they are not without precedent. Mention has been made
of critics sharing his antitragic view. A number of crit-

[9] *Everybody's Political What's What* (London, 1944), p. 49.

ics, again Dr. Johnson being one, have also shared his
ideas on didacticism and moral purpose in writing.
Johnson criticized Shakespeare for sacrificing "virtue to
convenience" and for being "more careful to please than
to instruct." [10] Bias alone, then, should not lead us to
eliminate Shaw's criticism. We certainly do not dismiss
the criticism of others whose point of view we question.
At the same time Shaw's prejudices offer certain definite advantages. For one, Shaw is not the victim of blind
hero worship. Critics from Dryden to Johnson treated
Shakespeare as a quite fallible dramatist: his faults were
criticized as quickly as his virtues were praised. He was
a human genius, not a divine one. After Johnson, however, a sort of adoration set in and Shakespeare was
looked on as more a god than a man. He was no longer
criticized, he was deified. This continued unabated until Shaw came along; and today, seventy-five years later,
there are still remnants of it.

Shaw's word for the worship of Shakespeare was Bardolatry. He put it this way: "We are disposed to agree
that we are making too much of a fetish of our Swan.
He was the greatest intellect we have produced, but the
tendency to regard him as above criticism is bad. Shakespear is supreme because he embodied most completely
the whole range of emotions. But they were human emotions, and his greatness is due to that fact. It is false
admiration to worship him as an infallible demi-god." [11]
Writing at the same time, Walter Raleigh said practically the same thing: "We are idolaters of Shakespeare,
born and bred. Our sin is not indifference, but superstition—which is another kind of ignorance. . . . His
poetry has been cut into minute indigestible fragments,
and used like wedding cake, not to eat, but to dream
upon." [12]

It was Shaw's lack of superstition that led John Middle-
ton Murry to say that Shaw was a better critic of Shakespeare than either Goethe or Coleridge. [13] Shaw knew

[10] *Johnson on Shakespeare,* ed. Walter Raleigh (London, 1929),
pp. 20-21.
[11] *The Daily News,* April 13, 1905.
[12] *Shakespeare* (London, 1907), pp. 3-4.
[13] *Pencillings* (London, 1923), p. 95.

that his attitude was anything but detrimental to Shake-speare; he even claimed that he had done him a great favor: in his last review as a regular drama critic he wrote, "when I began to write, William was a divinity and a bore. Now he is a fellow-creature."

There are other positive effects of Shaw's prejudice. The same bias which made him disparage some of the more popular plays made him approve of the "problem comedies": *All's Well That Ends Well, Measure for Measure,* and *Troilus and Cressida.* In these plays Shaw felt Shakespeare held the mirror up to nature and made an attempt to "pursue a genuinely scientific method in his studies of character and society." Until Shaw's time these plays were either treated with great diffidence or ignored altogether; since then they have been interpreted in much the same way that Shaw interpreted them.

Shaw's irreverent attitude reaped benefits also in his approach to Shakespeare's characters. In the nineteenth century critics invariably treated characters from Shake-speare's plays as real people, not as dramatic creations. While not so widespread today, this too is a tendency which has continued.

Shaw knocked this concept into a cocked hat: he called Enobarbus in *Antony and Cleopatra* "bogus character-ization"; he said that Mercutio was inconsistent, being a "wit and fantasist of the most delicate order" in his first scene and a "detestable and intolerable cad" in his sec-ond; he termed Imogen in *Cymbeline* not one woman but two; and of Iago he wrote, "the character defies all consistency."

In telling us what Shakespeare did not do with his characters, however, Shaw also explained what he did do. He describes the portrayal of character through lan-guage: "the individualization which produces that old-established British specialty, the Shakespearean 'delinea-tion of character,' owes all its magic to the turn of the line, which lets you into the secret of its utterer's mood and temperament, not by its commonplace meaning, but by some subtle exaltation, or stultification, or slyness, or delicacy, or hesitancy, or what not in the sound of it."

In another place Shaw explained how a dramatic char-acter like Lady Macbeth functions: "if you want to know the truth about Lady Macbeth's character, she hasn't one. There never was no such person. She says things that will set people's imaginations to work if she says them in the right way: that is all. I know: I do it myself."

All this is not to say that Shaw's prejudices are inconsequential: far from it; but they are not "more important than anything else." If they limit his criticism in some respects they offer advantages in others, and to throw out Shaw's Shakespearean criticism because it is sometimes capricious or biased would certainly be to throw out the baby with the bath water, or, perhaps, the champagne with the cork. Shaw himself supplied the answer in a postscript to his collected theatre reviews when he wrote, "a certain correction should be made, especially in reading my onslaught on Shakespear."

No correction need be made when we come to the more positive aspects of Shaw's criticism, those matters in which he takes Shakespeare's side wholly and unreservedly. Oddly enough, Shaw's affirmative criticism stems from another of his prejudices, as narrow and as firmly held as any of the others: his conviction that in drama, as in all art, form is one thing and content another, that they are entirely separable, and that of the two content is the more important.

For William Archer the "new drama" meant that the old dramatic conventions, the disguise, the aside, the soliloquy, had to be done away with; for Shaw the "new drama" meant nothing of the sort, it meant only that the old ideas had to be replaced. Dramatic conventions were not the issue. This distinction is made clear in Shaw's statement, "it is the philosophy, the outlook on life, that changes; not the craft of the playwright."

Herein lies one of the keys to Shaw's Shakespearean criticism: by separating form and content so completely he was free to praise the one while criticizing the other, which is precisely what he did with Shakespeare. Shaw is forever juxtaposing manner and matter in his discussions of Shakespeare. Referring to *As You Like It*, Shaw insists that he himself had never written anything "half so bad in matter," but goes on to say, "in manner

and art nobody can write better than Shakespear, because, carelessness apart, he did the thing as well as it
can be done within the limits of human faculty."

The same distinction is made in his essay "Better Than
Shakespear?". Shaw denounces Shakespeare's attitude to-
ward the characters of Cleopatra, Caesar, and Antony in
the bitterest terms, then hastens to add: "It does not
follow, however, that the right to criticize Shakespear
involves the power of writing better plays. And in fact
—do not be surprised at my modesty—I do not profess
to write better plays." The question mark in the title,
"Better Than Shakespear?", simply means that Shaw feels
that *what* he says is better than Shakespeare, but not his
way of saying it.

Another denunciation of Shakespeare, the outburst in
which Shaw says he despises Shakespeare's mind and
would like to dig him up and throw stones at him, is
also followed by a qualification: "but I am bound to
add," Shaw writes, "that I pity the man who cannot
enjoy Shakespear. He has outlasted thousands of abler
thinkers, and will outlast a thousand more."

This separation of content and form explains why
Shaw can despise the pessimism of *King Lear* and turn
around to say "no man will ever write a better tragedy
than Lear." It also explains why, in spite of his prejudices, Shaw could write with complete objectivity and
approval when it came to Shakespeare's dramatic art.

Probably his most effective criticism in this regard is
his discussion of what he called Shakespeare's "word-
music." It was Shaw's contention that the magic of
Shakespeare's language owes more to the music of the
verse, the sheer sound of the words, than to its meaning
or even its imagery. Shakespeare gains his effects through
pauses, rhythm, the color of the vowels, the mixture of
vowels and consonants, and the flow or interruption in
the line.

While still a music critic Shaw had observed: "there
is a great deal of feeling, highly poetic and highly dramatic, which cannot be expressed by mere words—because words are the counters of thinking, not of feeling
—but which can be supremely expressed by music. The

poet tries to make his words serve his purpose by arranging them musically." [14] It is safe to say that Shaw felt
Shakespeare more successful at this than any writer in
the English language; his power, Shaw wrote, "lies in
his enormous command of word-music."

Shaw distinguished between the earlier and later verse
in Shakespeare. The earlier has a sing-song pattern that
is both melodious and rhythmic, "full of the naïve delight of pure oscillation, to be enjoyed as an Italian enjoys a barcarolle, or a child a swing, or a baby a rocking
cradle." In the later verse Shakespeare left the simple,
appealing songs for more complex compositions: "Marlowe's line was not 'mighty': blank verse did not become
mighty until the lines had grown together into the great
symphonic movements of Shakespear's final manner." [15]

It is in his criticism of Shakespeare's word-music that
Shaw's own command of language comes to the fore.
Just as there are things which the poet cannot express
in ordinary language, so there are qualities in Shakespeare which cannot be described except in a style as
masterly as Shaw's. What other Shakespearean commentator can give us the feeling of the language in
Julius Caesar the way Shaw does in this passage from a
review:

What is missing in the performance, for want of specific Shakespearean skill, is the Shakespearean music. When we come to
those unrivalled grandiose passages in which Shakespear turns
on the full organ, we want to hear the sixteen-foot pipes booming, or, failing them (as we often must, since so few actors are
naturally equipped with them), the ennobled tone, and the
tempo suddenly steadied with the majesty of deeper purpose.
You have, too, those moments when the verse, instead of opening up the depths of sound, rises to its most brilliant clangor,
and the lines ring like a thousand trumpets.

Who can match Shaw's description of the language in
Othello: "it remains magnificent by the volume of its passion and the splendor of its word-music, which sweep the

[14] *Music in London 1890-94* (London, 1931), III, 140.
[15] *London Music in 1888-89 as Heard by Corno di Bassetto (Later
Known as Bernard Shaw)* (New York, 1937), p. 391.

scenes up to a plane on which sense is drowned in sound.
The words do not convey ideas: they are streaming ensigns and tossing branches to make the tempest of passion
visible."

It was in terms of word-music that Shaw frequently
discussed acting, another area in which he proved a great
friend to Shakespeare. Shaw paid a great deal of attention to the way Shakespeare should be played; in letters
to actors and in reviews he frequently discussed specific
scenes and even individual lines. Invariably his descriptions of Shakespearean acting, both good and bad, are
vivid and perceptive. He speaks of an actress playing
Cleopatra, "curving her wrists elegantly above Antony's
head as if she were going to extract a globe of goldfish
and two rabbits from behind his ear." Of a girl Augustin
Daly had cast as Puck, Shaw writes, "she announces her
ability to girdle the earth in forty minutes in the attitude
of a professional skater, and then begins the journey . . .
in the opposite direction to that in which she indicated
her intention of going."

When it came to acting Shaw was always on Shakespeare's side. To an actor playing Mercutio in a slovenly
manner he offered the admonition, "Shakespear never
leaves me in any doubt as to when he means an actor
to play Sir Toby Belch and when to play Mercutio, or
when he means an actor to speak measured verse and
when slip-shod colloquial prose." Approving of Forbes
Robertson's Shakespearean acting he wrote: "He does
not utter half a line; then stop to act; then go on with
another half line; then stop to act again, with the clock
running away with Shakespear's chances all the time.
He plays as Shakespear should be played, on the line
and to the line, with the utterance and acting simultaneous, inseparable and in fact identical."

Related to his concern for acting is Shaw's interest in
production. In Shaw's day Shakespeare's plays were performed as if they were contemporary drawing room
dramas with elaborate settings, involved scene shifts and
musical interludes. Shaw understood how antithetical
this was to Shakespeare and spoke up against it at every
opportunity. Those familiar with Shakespearean production of the past seventy-five years know that Shaw,

along with William Poel and Harley Granville-Barker, is one of those most responsible for a return to the Elizabethan-type production with its respect for the integrity of Shakespeare. Margaret Webster called Shaw "the prophet of the new scholarship and the new stagecraft." [16]

Shaw argued against cutting lines, rearranging scenes, and altering roles, but he went deeper than that: he discussed the principles behind Shakespeare's dramatic technique. A good example is his review of William Poel's production of *The Tempest*. For a ship Poel had used an unadorned singing gallery which made no pretense of being the real thing. This, Shaw pointed out, allowed the spectator to conjure up his own ship. In contrast to this, Henry Irving, if he had produced the play, would have provided "an expensive and absurd stage ship." Shaw explained the error in the Irving approach: "if our imagination is to create a ship, it must not be contradicted by something that apes a ship so vilely as to fill us with denial and repudiation by its imposture." All you need to see the ship at sea are Shakespeare's words. In the one line, "What care these roarers for the name of king?" Shaw points out, "you see the white horses and billowing green mountains playing football with crown and purple."

There is one final value in Shaw's Shakespearean writings which has more to do with Shaw than with Shakespeare. This is the insight it gives us into Shaw himself. With Shakespeare Shaw had a subject that challenged him to the utmost. In writing about his illustrious predecessor Shaw revealed a great deal about his own dramatic theory and practice, as well as his ideas on the theatre and life in general.

Thus Shaw on Shakespeare affords us provocative material not only on our greatest dramatist, but on his nearest rival as well. And, thanks to Shaw's wit, it provides us with a good deal of fun in the bargain.

[16] *Shakespeare Without Tears* (New York, 1957), p. 19.

EDITOR'S NOTE

Bernard Shaw's theatre reviews which appeared in *The Saturday Review* between January, 1895 and May, 1898 are collected in three volumes under the title *Our Theatres in the Nineties*.

With a few exceptions the spelling and usages in this volume, such as Shaw's spelling of "Shakespear," conform to those found in *The Standard Edition of the Works of Bernard Shaw* published by Constable & Company, Ltd., London.

SHAW ON SHAKESPEARE

PROLOGUE

In the spring of 1905 Shaw made a speech on Shakes-peare which aroused a good deal of controversy. In order to clarify his position he wrote to The Daily News *of* London *in April, 1905, giving a twelve-point summary of his views. These twelve points form a credo on which Shaw based most of his Shakespearean criticism.*

1. That the idolatry of Shakespear which prevails now existed in his own time, and got on the nerve of Ben Jonson.

2. That Shakespear was not an illiterate poaching laborer who came up to London to be a horseboy, but a gentleman with all the social pretensions of our higher *bourgeoisie*.

3. That Shakespear, when he became an actor, was not a rogue and a vagabond, but a member and part proprietor of a regular company, using, by permission, a nobleman's name as its patron, and holding itself as exclusively above the casual barnstormer as a Harley Street consultant holds himself above a man with a sarsaparilla stall.

4. That Shakespear's aim in business was to make money enough to acquire land in Stratford, and to retire as a country gentleman with a coat of arms and a good standing in the county; and that this was not the ambition of a *parvenu,* but the natural course for a member of the highly respectable, though temporarily impecunious, family of the Shakespears.

5. That Shakespear found that the only thing that paid in the theatre was romantic nonsense, and that when he was forced by this to produce one of the most effective samples of romantic nonsense in existence—a feat which he performed easily and well—he publicly disclaimed any responsibility for its pleasant and cheap false-

3

hood by borrowing the story and throwing it in the face of the public with the phrase As You Like It.

6. That when Shakespear used that phrase he meant exactly what he said, and that the phrase What You Will, which he applied to Twelfth Night, meaning 'Call it what you please,' is not, in Shapespearean or any other English, the equivalent of the perfectly unambiguous and penetratingly simple phrase As You Like It.

7. That Shakespear tried to make the public accept real studies of life and character in—for instance—Measure for Measure and All's Well That Ends Well; and that the public would not have them, and remains of the same mind still, preferring a fantastic sugar doll, like Rosalind, to such serious and dignified studies of women as Isabella and Helena.

8. That the people who spoil paper and waste ink by describing Rosalind as a perfect type of womanhood are the descendants of the same blockheads whom Shakespear, with the coat of arms and the lands in Warwickshire in view, had to please when he wrote plays as they liked them.

9. Not, as has been erroneously stated, that I could write a better play than As You Like It, but that I actually have written much better ones, and in fact, never wrote anything, and never intend to write anything, half so bad in matter. (In manner and art nobody can write better than Shakespear, because, carelessness apart, he did the thing as well as it can be done within the limits of human faculty.)

10. That to anyone with the requisite ear and command of words, blank verse, written under the amazingly loose conditions which Shakespear claimed, with full liberty to use all sorts of words, colloquial, technical, rhetorical, and even obscurely technical, to indulge in the most far-fetched ellipses, and to impress ignorant people with every possible extremity of fantasy and affectation, is the easiest of all known modes of literary expression, and that this is why whole oceans of dull bombast and drivel have been emptied on the head of England since Shakespear's time in this form by people who could not have written Box and Cox to save their lives. Also (this on being challenged) that I can write

blank verse myself more swiftly than prose, and that, too, of full Elizabethan quality plus the Shakespearean sense of the absurdity of it as expressed in the lines of Ancient Pistol. What is more, that I have done it, published it, and had it performed on the stage with huge applause.

11. That Shakespear's power lies in his enormous command of word music, which gives fascination to his most blackguardly repartees and sublimity to his hollowest platitudes.

12. That Shakespear's weakness lies in his complete deficiency in that highest sphere of thought, in which poetry embraces religion, philosophy, morality, and the bearing of these on communities, which is sociology. That his characters have no religion, no politics, no conscience, no hope, no convictions of any sort. That there are, as Ruskin pointed out, no heroes in Shakespear. That his test of the worth of life is the vulgar hedonic test and that since life cannot be justified by this or any other external test, Shakespear comes out of his reflective period a vulgar pessimist, oppressed with a logical demonstration that life is not worth living, and only surpassing Thackeray in respect to being fertile enough, instead of repeating Vanitas vanitatum at second hand to work the futile doctrine differently and better in such passages as Out, out, brief candle.

THE PLAYS

All's Well That Ends Well

While writing drama criticism for The Saturday Review *Shaw saw a performance of* All's Well That Ends Well *by a non-commercial group, the Irving Dramatic Club. His review appeared on February 2, 1895.*

WHAT A PITY it is that the people who love the sound of Shakespear so seldom go to the stage! The ear is the sure clue to him: only a musician can understand the play of feeling which is the real rarity in his early plays. In a deaf nation these plays would have died long ago. The moral attitude in them is conventional and secondhand: the borrowed ideas, however finely expressed, have not the overpowering human interest of those original criticisms of life which supply the rhetorical element in his later works. Even the individualization which produces that old-established British speciality, the Shakespearean "delineation of character," owes all its magic to the turn of the line, which lets you into the secret of its utterer's mood and temperament, not by its commonplace meaning, but by some subtle exaltation, or stultification, or slyness, or delicacy, or hesitancy, or what not in the sound of it. In short, it is the score and not the libretto that keeps the work alive and fresh; and this is why only musical critics should be allowed to meddle with Shakespear—especially early Shakespear. Unhappily, though the nation still retains its ears, the players and playgoers of this generation are for the most part deaf as adders. Their appreciation of Shakespear is sheer hypocrisy, the proof being that where an early play of his is revived, they take the utmost pains to suppress as much of it as possible, and disguise the rest past recognition, relying for success on extraordinary scenic attractions; on very popular performers, including, if possible, a famously

7

beautiful actress in the leading part; and, above all, on Shakespear's reputation and the consequent submission of the British public to be mercilessly bored by each of his plays once in their lives, for the sake of being able to say they have seen it. And not a soul has the hardihood to yawn in the face of the imposture. The manager is praised; the bard is praised; the beautiful actress is praised; and the free list comes early and comes often, not without a distinct sense of conferring a handsome compliment on the acting manager. And it certainly is hard to face such a disappointment without being paid for it. For the more enchanting the play is at home by the fireside in winter, or out on the heather of a summer evening —the more the manager, in his efforts to realize this enchantment by reckless expenditure on incidental music, colored lights, dances, dresses, and elaborate rearrangements and dislocations of the play—the more, in fact, he departs from the old platform with its curtains and its placards inscribed "A street in Mantua," and so forth, the more hopelessly and vulgarly does he miss his mark. Such crown jewels of dramatic poetry as Twelfth Night and A Midsummer Night's Dream, fade into shabby colored glass in his purse; and sincere people who do not know what the matter is, begin to babble insufferably about plays that are meant for the study and not for the stage.

Yet once in a blue moon or so there wanders on to the stage some happy fair whose eyes are lodestars and whose tongue's sweet air's more tunable than lark to shepherd's ear. And the moment she strikes up the true Shakespearean music, and feels her way to her part altogether by her sense of that music, the play returns to life and all the magic is there. She may make nonsense of the verses by wrong conjunctions and misplaced commas, which shew that she has never worked out the logical construction of a single sentence in her part; but if her heart is in the song, the protesting commentator-critic may save his breath to cool his porridge: the soul of the play is there, no matter where the sense of it may be. We have all heard Miss Rehan perform this miracle with Twelfth Night, and turn it, in spite of the impossible Mr. Daly, from a hopelessly ineffective actress show into something like the exquisite poem its author left it. All I can remember of the last performance I witnessed of A Mid-summer Night's Dream is that Miss Kate Rorke got on the stage somehow and began to make some music with Helena's lines, with the result that Shakespear, who had up to that moment lain without sense or motion, imme-diately began to stir uneasily and shew signs of quicken-ing, which lasted until the others took up the word and struck him dead.

Powerful among the enemies of Shakespear are the commentator and the elocutionist: the commentator be-cause, not knowing Shakespear's language, he sharpens his reasoning faculty to examine propositions advanced by an eminent lecturer from the Midlands, instead of sensitizing his artistic faculty to receive the impression of moods and inflexions of feeling conveyed by word-music; the elocutionist because he is a born fool, in which ca-pacity, observing with pain that poets have a weakness for imparting to their dramatic dialogue a quality which he describes and deplores as "sing-song," he devotes his life to the art of breaking up verse in such a way as to make it sound like insanely pompous prose. The effect of this on Shakespear's earlier verse, which is full of the naïve delight of pure oscillation, to be enjoyed as an Italian enjoys a barcarolle, or a child a swing, or a baby a rocking-cradle, is destructively stupid. In the later plays, where the barcarolle measure has evolved into much more varied and complex rhythms, it does not mat-ter so much, since the work is no longer simple enough for a fool to pick to pieces. But in every play from Love's Labour Lost to Henry V, the elocutionist meddles simply as a murderer, and ought to be dealt with as such without benefit of clergy. To our young people studying for the stage I say, with all solemnity, learn how to pronounce the English alphabet clearly and beautifully from some person who is at once an artist and a phonetic expert. And then leave blank verse patiently alone until you have experienced emotion deep enough to crave for poetic expression, at which point verse will seem an absolutely natural and real form of speech to you. Meanwhile, if any pedant, with an uncultivated heart and a theoretic ear, proposes to teach you to recite, send instantly for the police.

Among Shakespear's earlier plays, All's Well That Ends
Well stands out artistically by the sovereign charm of the
young Helena and the old Countess of Rousillon, and
intellectually by the experiment, repeated nearly three
hundred years later in A Doll's House, of making the
hero a perfectly ordinary young man, whose unimagina-
tive prejudices and selfish conventionality make him cut
a very fine mean figure in the atmosphere created by the
nobler nature of his life. That is what gives a certain
plausibility to the otherwise doubtful tradition that
Shakespear did not succeed in getting his play produced
(founded on the absence of any record of a performance
of it during his lifetime). It certainly explains why
Phelps, the only modern actor-manager tempted by it,
was attracted by the part of Parolles, a capital study of
the adventurous yarn-spinning society-struck coward,
who also crops up again in modern fiction as the hero of
Charles Lever's underrated novel, A Day's Ride: a Life's
Romance. When I saw All's Well announced for performance by the Irving Dramatic Club, I was highly interested, especially as the performers were free, for once,
to play Shakespear for Shakespear's sake. Alas! at this
amateur performance, at which there need have been
none of the miserable commercialization compulsory at
the regular theatres, I suffered all the vulgarity and absurdity of that commercialism without its efficiency. We
all know the stock objection of the Brixton Family Shakespear to All's Well—that the heroine is a lady doctor, and
that no lady of any delicacy could possibly adopt a profession which involves the possibility of her having to
attend cases such as that of the king in this play, who
suffers from a fistula. How any sensible and humane person can have ever read this sort of thing without a deep
sense of its insult to every charitable woman's humanity
and every sick man's suffering is, fortunately, getting
harder to understand nowadays than it once was. Nevertheless All's Well was minced with strict deference to it
for the members of the Irving Dramatic Club. The rule
for expurgation was to omit everything that the most
pestiferously prurient person could find improper. For
example, when the non-commissioned officer, with quite
becoming earnestness and force, says to the disgraced

Parolles: "If you could find out a country where but women were that had received so much shame, you might begin an impudent nation," the speech was suppressed as if it were on all fours with the obsolete Elizabethan badinage which is and should be cut out as a matter of course. And to save Helena from anything so shocking as a reference to her virginity, she was robbed of that rapturous outburst beginning

> There shall your master have a thousand loves—
> A mother and a mistress and a friend, etc.

But perhaps this was sacrificed in deference to the opinion of the editor of those pretty and handy little books called the Temple Shakespear, who compares the passage to "the nonsense of some foolish conceited player"—a criticism which only a commentator could hope to live down.

The play was, of course, pulled to pieces in order that some bad scenery, totally unconnected with Florence or Rousillon, might destroy all the illusion which the simple stage directions in the book create, and which they would equally have created had they been printed on a placard and hung up on a curtain. The passage of the Florentine army beneath the walls of the city was managed in the manner of the end of the first act of Robertson's Ours, the widow and the girls looking out of their sitting-room window, whilst a few of the band gave a precarious selection from the orchestral parts of Berlioz's version of the Rackoczy March. The dresses were the usual fancy ball odds and ends, Helena especially distinguishing herself by playing the first scene partly in the costume of Hamlet and partly in that of a waitress in an Aerated Bread shop, set off by a monstrous auburn wig which could by no stretch of imagination be taken for her own hair. Briefly, the whole play was vivisected, and the fragments mutilated, for the sake of accessories which were in every particular silly and ridiculous. If they were meant to heighten the illusion, they were worse than failures, since they rendered illusion almost impossible. If they were intended as illustrations of place and period, they were ignorant impostures. I have seen poetic plays performed without costumes before a pair of curtains by ladies and gentlemen in evening dress with twenty times the effect:

nay, I will pledge my reputation that if the members of
the Irving Dramatic Club will take their books in their
hands, sit in a Christy Minstrel semicircle, and read the
play decently as it was written, the result will be a vast
improvement on this St. George's Hall travesty.

Perhaps it would not be altogether kind to leave these
misguided but no doubt well-intentioned ladies and gentlemen without a word of appreciation from their own
point of view. Only, there is not much to be said for
them even from that point of view. Few living actresses
could throw themselves into the sustained transport of
exquisite tenderness and impulsive courage which makes
poetry the natural speech of Helena. The cool young
woman, with a superior understanding, excellent manners, and a habit of reciting Shakespear, presented before
us by Miss Olive Kennett, could not conceivably have
been even Helena's thirty-second cousin. Miss Lena Hei-
nekey, with the most beautiful old woman's part ever
written in her hands, discovered none of its wonderfully
pleasant good sense, humanity, and originality: she
grieved stagily all through in the manner of the Duchess
of York in Cibber's Richard III. Mr. Lewin-Mannering
did not for any instant make it possible to believe that
Parolles was a real person to him. They all insisted on
calling him *parole,* instead of Parolles, in three syllables,
with the *s* sounded at the end, as Shakespear intended:
consequently, when he came to the couplet which cannot
be negotiated on any other terms:

> Rust, sword; cool, blushes; and, Parolles, thrive;
> Theres place and means for every man alive,

he made a desperate effort to get even with it by saying:

> Rust, rapier; cool, blushes; and *parole, thrive,*

and seemed quite disconcerted when he found that it
would not do. Lafeu is hardly a part that can be acted:
it comes right if the right man is available: if not, no
acting can conceal the makeshift. Mr. Herbert Everitt
was not the right man; but he made the best of it. The
clown was evidently willing to relish his own humor if
only he could have seen it; but there are few actors who
would not have gone that far. Bertram (Mr. Patrick

Munro), if not the most intelligent of Bertrams, played the love scene with Diana with some passion. The rest of the parts, not being character studies, are tolerably straightforward and easy of execution; and they were creditably played, the king (Mr. Ernest Meads) carrying off the honors, and Diana (Mrs. Herbert Morris) acquitting herself with comparative distinction. But I should not like to see another such performance of All's Well or any other play that is equally rooted in my deeper affections.

In The Saturday Review *of November 13, 1897, Shaw compared J. M. Barrie's characters in* The Little Minister *with Shakespeare's more mature character studies in* All's Well.

. . . Mr. Barrie is a born storyteller; and he sees no further than his stories—conceives any discrepancy between them and the world as a shortcoming on the world's part, and is only too happy to be able to rearrange matters in a pleasanter way. The popular stage, which was a prison to Shakespear's genius, is a playground to Mr. Barrie's. At all events he does the thing as if he liked it, and does it very well. He has apparently no eye for human character; but he has a keen sense of human qualities, and he produces highly popular assortments of them. He cheerfully assumes, as the public wish him to assume, that one endearing quality implies all endearing qualities, and one repulsive quality all repulsive qualities: the exceptions being comic characters, who are permitted to have "weaknesses," or stern and terrible souls who are at once understood to be saving up some enormous sentimentality for the end of the last act but one. Now if there is one lesson that real life teaches us more insistently than another, it is that we must not infer one quality from another, or even rely on the constancy of ascertained qualities under all circumstances. It is not only that a brave and good-humored man may be vain and fond of money; a lovable woman greedy, sensual, and mendacious; a saint vindictive; and a thief kindly; but these very terms are made untrustworthy by the facts that the man who is brave enough to venture on personal combat with a prizefighter or a tiger may be abjectly afraid of ghosts, mice, women, a dentist's forceps, public opinion, cholera epidemics, and a dozen other things that many timorous mortals face resignedly enough; the man who is stingy to miserliness with coin, and is the despair of waiters and cabmen, gives thousands (by cheque) to public institutions; the man who eats oysters by the hundred and legs of mutton by the dozen for wagers, is in many matters temperate, moderate, and even abstemious; and men and women alike, though they behave with the strictest conventional propriety when tempted by advances from people whom they do not happen to like, are by no means so austere with people whom they do like. In romance, all these "inconsistencies" are corrected by replacing human nature by conventional assortments of qualities. When Shakespear objected to this regulation, and wrote All's Well in defiance of it, his play was not acted. When he succumbed, and gave us the required assortment "as we like it," he was enormously successful. Mr. Barrie has no scruples about complying.

ANTONY AND CLEOPATRA

Shaw discusses Antony and Cleopatra, *along with other plays, in his introductory essay to* Caesar and Cleopatra *entitled "Better Than Shakespear?" found elsewhere in this volume. During his days as a critic Shaw reviewed a production of the play by Louis Calvert in Manchester in* The Saturday Review *of March 20, 1897.*

SHAKESPEAR is so much the word-musician that mere practical intelligence, no matter how well prompted by dramatic instinct, cannot enable anybody to understand his works or arrive at a right execution of them without the guidance of a fine ear. At the great emotional climaxes we find passages which are Rossinian in their reliance on symmetry of melody and impressiveness of march to redeem poverty of meaning. In fact, we have got so far beyond Shakespear as a man of ideas that there is by this time hardly a famous passage in his works that is considered fine on any other ground than that it sounds beautifully, and awakens in us the emotion that originally expressed itself by its beauty. Strip it of that beauty of sound by prosaic paraphrase, and you have nothing left but a platitude that even an American professor of ethics would blush to offer to his disciples. Wreck that beauty by a harsh, jarring utterance, and you will make your audience wince as if you were singing Mozart out of tune. Ignore it by "avoiding sing-song"—that is, ingeniously breaking the verse up so as to make it sound like prose, as the professional elocutionist prides himself on doing —and you are landed in a stilted, monstrous jargon that has not even the prosaic merit of being intelligible. Let me give one example: Cleopatra's outburst at the death of Antony:

> Oh withered is the garland of the war,
> The soldier's pole is fallen: young boys and girls
> Are level now with men: the odds is gone,

And there is nothing left remarkable
Beneath the visiting moon.

This is not good sense—not even good grammar. If you ask what does it all mean, the reply must be that it means just what its utterer feels. The chaos of its thought is a reflection of her mind, in which one can vaguely discern a wild illusion that all human distinction perishes with the gigantic distinction between Antony and the rest of the world. Now it is only in music, verbal or other, that the feeling which plunges thought into confusion can be artistically expressed. Any attempt to deliver such music prosaically would be as absurd as an attempt to speak an oratorio of Handel's, repetitions and all. The right way to declaim Shakespear is the sing-song way. Mere metric accuracy is nothing. There must be beauty of tone, expressive inflection, and infinite variety of *nuance* to sustain the fascination of the infinite monotony of the chanting.

Miss Janet Achurch, now playing Cleopatra in Manchester, has a magnificent voice, and is as full of ideas as to vocal effects as to everything else on the stage. The march of the verse and the strenuousness of the rhetoric stimulate her great artistic susceptibility powerfully: she is determined that Cleopatra shall have rings on her fingers and bells on her toes, and that she shall have music wherever she goes. Of the hardihood of ear with which she carries out her original and often audacious conceptions of Shakespearean music I am too utterly unnerved to give any adequate description. The lacerating discord of her wailings is in my tormented ears as I write, reconciling me to the grave. It is as if she had been excited by the Hallelujah Chorus to dance on the keyboard of a great organ with all the stops pulled out. I cannot—dare not—dwell on it. I admit that when she is using the rich middle of her voice in a quite normal and unstudied way, intent only on the feeling of the passage, the effect leaves nothing to be desired; but the moment she raises the pitch to carry out some deeply planned vocal masterstroke, or is driven by Shakespear himself to attempt a purely musical execution of a passage for which no other sort of execution is possible, then—well then, hold on tightly to the elbows of your stall, and bear it

like a man. And when the feat is accompanied, as it
sometimes is, by bold experiments in facial expression
which all the passions of Cleopatra, complicated by sev-
enty-times-sevenfold demoniacal possession, could but
faintly account for, the eye has to share the anguish of the
ear instead of consoling it with Miss Achurch's beauty. I
have only seen the performance once; and I would not
unsee it again if I could; but none the less I am a broken
man after it. I may retain always an impression that I
have actually looked on Cleopatra enthroned dead in her
regal robes, with her hand on Antony's, and her awful
eyes inhibiting the victorious Cæsar. I grant that this
"resolution" of the discord is grand and memorable; but
oh! how infernal the discord was whilst it was still un-
resolved! That is the word that sums up the objection to
Miss Achurch's Cleopatra in point of sound: it is dis-
cordant.

I need not say that at some striking points Miss
Achurch's performance shews the same exceptional in-
ventiveness and judgment in acting as her Ibsen achievements did, and that her energy is quite on the grand scale
of the play. But even if we waive the whole musical question—and that means waiving the better half of Shakespear—she would still not be Cleopatra. Cleopatra says
that the man who has seen her "hath seen some majesty,
and should know." One conceives her as a trained professional queen, able to put on at will the deliberate artificial dignity which belongs to the technique of court
life. She may keep it for state occasions, like the unaffected Catherine of Russia, or always retain it, like Louis
XIV, in whom affectation was nature; but that she should
have no command of it—that she should rely in modern
republican fashion on her personal force, with a frank
contempt for ceremony and artificiality, as Miss Achurch
does, is to spurn her own part. And then, her beauty is
not the beauty of Cleopatra. I do not mean merely that
she is not "with Phœbus' amorous pinches black," or
brown, bean-eyed, and pickaxe-faced. She is not even the
English (or Anglo-Jewish) Cleopatra, the serpent of old
Thames. She is of the broad-browed, column-necked,
Germanic type—the Wagner heroine type—which in
England, where it must be considered as the true racial

heroic type, has given us two of our most remarkable
histrionic geniuses in Miss Achurch herself and our
dramatic singer, Miss Marie Brema, both distinguished
by great voices, busy brains, commanding physical energy,
and untameable impetuosity and originality. Now this
type has its limitations, one of them being that it has not
the genius of worthlessness, and so cannot present it on
the stage otherwise than as comic depravity or masterful
wickedness. Adversity makes it superhuman, not sub-
human, as it makes Cleopatra. When Miss Achurch
comes on one of the weak, treacherous, affected streaks in
Cleopatra, she suddenly drops from an Egyptian warrior
queen into a naughty English *petite bourgeoise,* who carries off a little greediness and a little voluptuousness by a
very unheroic sort of prettiness. That is, she treats it as a
stroke of comedy; and as she is not a comedian, the stroke
of comedy becomes in her hands a bit of fun. When the
bourgeoise turns into a wild cat, and literally snarls and
growls menacingly at the bearer of the news of Antony's
marriage with Octavia, she is at least more Cleopatra;
but when she masters herself, as Miss Achurch does, not
in gipsy fashion, but by a heroic-grandiose act of self-
mastery, quite foreign to the nature of the "triple turned
wanton" (as Mr. Calvert bowdlerizes it) of Shakespear,
she is presently perplexed by fresh strokes of comedy—

> He's very knowing.
> I do perceive 't: theres nothing in her yet:
> The fellow has good judgment.

At which what can she do but relapse farcically into the
bourgeoise again, since it is not on the heroic side of her
to feel elegantly self-satisfied whilst she is saying mean and
silly things, as the true Cleopatra does? Miss Achurch's
finest feat in this scene was the terrible look she gave the
messenger when he said, in dispraise of Octavia, "And
I do think she's thirty"—Cleopatra being of course much
more. Only, as Miss Achurch had taken good care not
to look more, the point was a little lost on Manchester.
Later on she is again quite in her heroic element (and
out of Cleopatra's) in making Antony fight by sea. Her
"I have sixty sails, Cæsar none better," and her overbear-
ing of the counsels of Enobarbus and Canidius to fight

by land are effective, but effective in the way of a Boa-
dicea, worth ten guzzling Antonys. There is no suggestion of the petulant folly of the spoiled beauty who has
not imagination enough to know that she will be fright-
ened when the fighting begins. Consequently when the
audience, already puzzled as to how to take Cleopatra,
learns that she has run away from the battle, and afterwards that she has sold Antony to Cæsar, it does not
know what to think. The fact is, Miss Achurch steals
Antony's thunder and Shakespear's thunder and Ibsen's
thunder and her own thunder so that she may ride the
whirlwind for the evening; and though this *Walkürenritt*
is intense and imposing, in spite of the discords, the lapses
into farce, and the failure in comedy and characterization—though once or twice a really memorable effect is
reached—yet there is not a stroke of Cleopatra in it;
and I submit that to bring an ardent Shakespearean like
myself all the way to Manchester to see Antony and
Cleopatra with Cleopatra left out, even with Brynhild-
cum-Nora Helmer substituted, is very different from
bringing down soft-hearted persons like Mr. Clement
Scott and Mr. William Archer, who have allowed Miss
Achurch to make Ibsen-and-Wagner pie of our poor
Bard's historical masterpiece without a word of protest.

And yet all that I have said about Miss Achurch's
Cleopatra cannot convey half the truth to those who
have not seen Mr. Louis Calvert's Antony. It is on
record that Antony's cooks put a fresh boar on the spit
every hour, so that he should never have to wait long
for his dinner. Mr. Calvert looks as if he not only had
the boars put on the spit, but ate them. He is inexcusably
fat: Mr. Bourchier is a sylph by comparison. You will
conclude, perhaps, that his fulness of habit makes him
ridiculous as a lover. But not at all. It is only your
rhetorical tragedian whose effectiveness depends on the
oblatitude of his waistcoat. Mr. Calvert is a comedian—
brimming over with genuine humane comedy. His one
really fine tragic effect is the burst of laughter at the
irony of fate with which, as he lies dying, he learns that
the news of Cleopatra's death, on the receipt of which
he mortally wounded himself, is only one of her theatrical, sympathy-catching lies. As a lover, he leaves his Cleo-

patra far behind. His features are so pleasant, his manner
so easy, his humor so genial and tolerant, and his portli-
ness so frank and unashamed, that no good-natured
woman could resist him; and so the topsiturvitude of
the performance culminates in the plainest evidence that
Antony is the seducer of Cleopatra instead of Cleopatra
of Antony. Only at one moment was Antony's girth awkward. When Eros, who was a slim and rather bony young
man, fell on his sword, the audience applauded sympathetically. But when Antony in turn set about the Happy
Despatch, the consequences suggested to the imagination
were so awful that shrieks of horror arose in the pit; and
it was a relief when Antony was borne off by four stalwart
soldiers, whose sinews cracked audibly as they heaved him
up from the floor.

Here, then, we have Cleopatra tragic in her comedy,
and Antony comedic in his tragedy. We have Cleopatra
heroically incapable of flattery or flirtation, and Antony
with a wealth of blarney in every twinkle of his eye and
every fold of his chin. We have, to boot, certain irrelevant
but striking projections of Miss Achurch's genius, and a
couple of very remarkable stage pictures invented by
the late Charles Calvert. But in so far as we have Antony
and Cleopatra, we have it partly through the genius of
the author, who imposes his conception on us through the
dialogue in spite of everything that can be done to contradict him, and partly through the efforts of the second-
ary performers.

Of these Mr. George F. Black, who plays Octavius
Cæsar, speaks blank verse rightly, if a little roughly, and
can find his way to the feeling of the line by its cadence.
Mr. Mollison—who played Henry IV here to Mr. Tree's
Falstaff—is Enobarbus, and spouts the description of the
barge with all the honors. The minor parts are handled
with the spirit and intelligence that can always be had by
a manager who really wants them. A few of the actors
are certainly very bad; but they suffer rather from an
insane excess of inspiration than from apathy. Charmian
and Iras (Miss Ada Mellon and Miss Maria Fauvet) produce an effect out of all proportion to their scanty lines
by the conviction and loyalty with which they support
Miss Achurch; and I do not see why Cleopatra should

ungratefully take Iras's miraculous death as a matter of course by omitting the lines beginning "Have I the aspic in my lips," nor why Charmian should be robbed of her fine reply to the Roman's "Charmian, is this well done?" "It is well done, and fitted for a princess descended of so many royal kings." No doubt the Cleopatras of the palmy days objected to anyone but themselves dying effectively, and so such cuts became customary; but the objection does not apply to the scene as arranged in Manchester. Modern managers should never forget that if they take care of the minor actors the leading ones will take care of themselves.

May I venture to suggest to Dr. Henry Watson that his incidental music, otherwise irreproachable, is in a few places much too heavily scored to be effectively spoken through? Even in the *entr'actes* the brass might be spared in view of the brevity of the intervals and the almost continuous strain for three hours on the ears of the audience. If the music be revived later as a concert suite, the wind can easily be restored.

Considering that the performance requires an efficient orchestra and chorus, plenty of supernumeraries, ten or eleven distinct scenes, and a cast of twenty-four persons, including two leading parts of the first magnitude; that the highest price charged for admission is three shillings; and that the run is limited to eight weeks, the production must be counted a triumph of management. There is not the slightest reason to suppose that any London manager could have made a revival of Antony and Cleopatra more interesting. Certainly none of them would have planned that unforgettable statue death for Cleopatra, for which, I suppose, all Miss Achurch's sins against Shakespear will be forgiven her. I begin to have hopes of a great metropolitan vogue for that lady now, since she has at last done something that is thoroughly wrong from beginning to end.

Shaw always lamented that Henry Irving, Ellen Terry, and other actors of promise gave themselves to Shakespeare rather than the "new drama" of Ibsen. In The Saturday Review *of May 29, 1897, he bemoaned the fact that The Independent Theatre once dedicated to new plays produced Antony and Cleopatra. In the review he scolded Janet Achurch for playing Cleopatra and giving in to rhetorical acting in the process.*

. . . Let Miss Achurch once learn to make the rhetorical drama plausible, and thenceforth she will never do anything else. Her interest in life and character will be supplanted by an interest in plastique and execution; and she will come to regard emotion simply as the best of lubricants and stimulants, caring nothing for its specific character so long as it is of a sufficiently obvious and facile sort to ensure a copious flow without the fatigue of thought. She will take to the one-part plays of Shakespear, Schiller, Giacometti, and Sardou, and be regarded as a classic person by the Corporation of Stratford-on-Avon. In short, she will become an English Sarah Bernhardt. The process is already far advanced. On Monday last she was sweeping about, clothed with red Rosettian hair and beauty to match; revelling in the power of her voice and the steam pressure of her energy; curving her wrists elegantly above Antony's head as if she were going to extract a globe of gold fish and two rabbits from behind his ear; and generally celebrating her choice between the rare and costly art of being beautifully natural in lifelike human acting, like Duse, and the comparatively common and cheap one of being theatrically beautiful in heroic stage exhibition. Alas for our lost leaders! Shakespear and success capture them all.

As You Like It

In The Saturday Review *of October 9, 1897, Shaw took Augustin Daly to task for his handling of* As You Like It.

I NEVER SEE Miss Ada Rehan act without burning to present Mr. Augustin Daly with a delightful villa in St. Helena, and a commission from an influential committee of his admirers to produce at his leisure a complete set of Shakespear's plays, entirely rewritten, reformed, rearranged, and brought up to the most advanced requirements of the year 1850. He was in full force at the Islington Theatre on Monday evening last with his version of As You Like It just as I dont like it. There I saw Amiens under the greenwood tree, braving winter and rough weather in a pair of crimson plush breeches, a spectacle to benumb the mind and obscure the passions. There was Orlando with the harmony of his brown boots and tunic torn asunder by a piercing discord of dark volcanic green, a walking tribute to Mr. Daly's taste in tights. There did I hear slow music stealing up from the band at all the well-known recitations of Adam, Jaques, and Rosalind, lest we should for a moment forget that we were in a theatre and not in the forest of Arden. There did I look through practicable doors in the walls of sunny orchards into an abyss of pitchy darkness. There saw I in the attitudes, grace, and deportment of the forest dwellers the plastique of an Arcadian past. And the music synchronized with it all to perfection, from La Grande Duchesse and Dichter und Bauer, conducted by the leader of the band, to the inevitable old English airs conducted by the haughty musician who is Mr. Daly's special property. And to think that Mr. Daly will die in his bed, whilst innocent presidents of republics, who never harmed an immortal bard, are falling on all sides under the knives of well-intentioned reformers whose only crime is that they assassinate the wrong people! And yet let me be magnanimous. I confess I would not like to see Mr. Daly assassinated: St. Helena would satisfy me. For Mr. Daly was in his prime an advanced man relatively to his own time and place, and was a real manager, with definite artistic aims which he trained his company to accomplish. His Irish-American Yanko-German comedies, as played under his management by Ada Rehan and Mrs. Gilbert, John Drew, Otis Skinner and the late John Lewis, turned a page in theatrical history here, and secured him a position in London which was never questioned until it became apparent that he was throwing away Miss Rehan's genius. When, after the complete discovery of her gifts by the London public, Mr. Daly could find no better employment for her than in a revival of Dollars and Cents, his annihilation and Miss Rehan's rescue became the critic's first duty. Shakespear saved the situation for a time, and got severely damaged in the process; but The Countess Gucki convinced me that in Mr. Daly's hands Miss Rehan's talent was likely to be lost not only to the modern drama, but to the modern Shakespearean stage: that is to say, to the indispensable conditions of its own fullest development. No doubt starring in Daly Shakespear is as lucrative and secure as the greatest of Duse's achievements are thankless and precarious; but surely it must be better fun making money enough by La Dame aux Camélias to pay for Heimat and La Femme de Claude, and win the position of the greatest actress in the world with all three, than to astonish provincials with verisons of Shakespear which are no longer up even to metropolitan literary and dramatic standards.

However, since I cannot convert Miss Rehan to my view of the position, I must live in hope that some day she will come to the West End of London for a week or two, just as Réjane and Sarah Bernhardt do, with some work of sufficient novelty and importance to make good the provincial wear and tear of her artistic prestige. Just now she is at the height of her powers. The plumpness that threatened the Countess Gucki has vanished: Rosalind is as slim as a girl. The third and fourth acts are as wonderful as ever—miracles of vocal expression. If As You Like It were a typical Shakespearean play, I should unhesitatingly declare Miss Rehan the most perfect

Shakespearean executant in the world. But when I
think of those plays in which our William anticipated
modern dramatic art by making serious attempts to hold
the mirror up to nature—All's Well, Measure for
Measure, Troilus and Cressida, and so on—I must limit
the tribute to Shakespear's popular style. Rosalind is not
a complete human being: she is simply an extension into
five acts of the most affectionate, fortunate, delightful
five minutes in the life of a charming woman. And all
the other figures in the play are cognate impostures.
Orlando, Adam, Jaques, Touchstone, the banished
Duke, and the rest play each the same tune all through.
This is not human nature or dramatic character; it is
juvenile lead, first old man, heavy lead, heavy father,
principal comedian, and leading lady, transfigured by
magical word-music. The Shakespearolators who are
taken in by it do not know drama in the classical sense
from "drama" in the technical Adelphi sense. You have
only to compare Orlando and Rosalind with Bertram
and Helena, the Duke and Touchstone with Leontes
and Autolycus, to learn the difference from Shakespear
himself. Therefore I cannot judge from Miss Rehan's
enchanting Rosalind whether she is a great Shakespearean actress or not: there is even a sense in which I cannot
tell whether she can act at all or not. So far, I have never
seen her create a character: she has always practised the
same adorable arts on me, by whatever name the playbill
has called her—Nancy Brasher (ugh!), Viola, or Rosalind. I have never complained: the drama with all its
heroines levelled up to a universal Ada Rehan has
seemed no such dreary prospect to me; and her voice,
compared to Sarah Bernhardt's *voix d'or,* has been as all
the sounds of the woodland to the chinking of twenty-
franc pieces. In Shakespear (what Mr. Daly leaves of
him) she was and is irresistible: at Islington on Monday
she made me cry faster than Mr. Daly could make me
swear. But the critic in me is bound to insist that Ada
Rehan has as yet created nothing but Ada Rehan. She
will probably never excel that masterpiece; but why
should she not superimpose a character study or two on
it! Duse's greatest work is Duse; but that does not
prevent Césarine, Santuzza, and Camille from being three

totally different women, none of them Duses, though
Duse is all of them. Miss Rehan would charm everybody as Mirandolina as effectually as Duse does. But
how about Magda? It is because nobody in England
knows the answer to that question that nobody in England as yet knows whether Ada Rehan is a creative artist
or a mere virtuosa.

*In the season prior to the Daly production there had been
another version more to Shaw's liking. His comments
appeared on December 5, 1896, in* The Saturday Review.

THE IRONY OF FATE prevails at the St. James's Theatre.
For years we have been urging the managers to give us
Shakespear's plays as he wrote them, playing them intelligently and enjoyingly as pleasant stories, instead of mutilating them, altering them, and celebrating them as superstitious rites. After three hundred years Mr. George Alexander has taken us at our words, as far as the clock
permits, and gives us As You Like It at full four hours'
length. And, alas! it is just too late: the Bard gets his
chance at the moment when his obsolescence has become
unendurable. Nevertheless, we were right; for this production of Mr. Alexander's, though the longest, is infinitely the least tedious, and, in those parts which depend
on the management, the most delightful I have seen. But
yet, what a play! It was in As You Like It that the sententious William first began to openly exploit the fond-
ness of the British Public for sham moralizing and stage
"philosophy." It contains one passage that specially ex-
asperates me. Jaques, who spends his time, like Hamlet,
in vainly emulating the wisdom of Sancho Panza, comes
in laughing in a superior manner because he has met a
fool in the forest, who

> Says very wisely, It is ten o'clock.
> Thus we may see [quoth he] how the world wags.
> Tis but an hour ago since it was nine;
> And after one hour more twill be eleven.
> And so, from hour to hour, we ripe and ripe;
> And then, from hour to hour, we rot and rot;
> And thereby hangs a tale.

Now, considering that this fool's platitude is precisely the "philosophy" of Hamlet, Macbeth ("Tomorrow and tomorrow and tomorrow," etc.), Prospero, and the rest of them, there is something unendurably aggravating in Shakespear giving himself airs with Touchstone, as if he, the immortal, ever, even at his sublimest, had anything different or better to say himself. Later on he misses a great chance. Nothing is more significant than the statement that "all the world's a stage." The whole world *is* ruled by theatrical illusion. Between the Cæsars, the emperors, the Christian heroes, the Grand Old Men, the kings, prophets, saints, judges, and heroes of the newspapers and the popular imagination, and the actual Juliuses, Napoleons, Gordons, Gladstones, and so on, there is the same difference as between Hamlet and Sir Henry Irving. The case is not one of fanciful similitude but of identity. The great critics are those who penetrate and understand the illusion: the great men are those who, as dramatists planning the development of nations, or as actors carrying out the drama, are behind the scenes of the world instead of gaping and gushing in the auditorium after paying their taxes at the doors. And yet Shakespear, with the rarest opportunities of observing this, lets his pregnant metaphor slip, and, with his usual incapacity for pursuing any idea, wanders off into a grandmotherly Elizabethan edition of the advertisement of Cassell's Popular Educator. How anybody over the age of seven can take interest in a literary toy so silly in its conceit and common in its ideas as the Seven Ages of Man passes my understanding. Even the great metaphor itself is inaccurately expressed; for the world is a playhouse, not merely a stage; and Shakespear might have said so without making his blank verse scan any worse than Richard's exclamation, "All the world to nothing!"

And then Touchstone, with his rare jests about the knight that swore by his honor they were good pancakes! Who would endure such humor from anyone but Shakespear?—an Eskimo would demand his money back if a modern author offered him such fare. And the comfortable old Duke, symbolical of the British villa dweller, who likes to find "sermons in stones and good in everything," and then to have a good dinner! This unvenerable impostor, expanding on his mixed diet of pious twaddle and venison, rouses my worst passions. Even when Shakespear, in his efforts to be a social philosopher, does rise for an instant to the level of a sixth-rate Kingsley, his solemn self-complacency infuriates me. And yet, so wonderful is his art, that it is not easy to disentangle what is unbearable from what is irresistible. Orlando one moment says:

> Whate'er you are
> That in this desert inaccessible
> Under the shade of melancholy boughs
> Lose and neglect the creeping hours of time,

which, though it indicates a thoroughly unhealthy imagination, and would have been impossible to, for instance, Chaucer, is yet magically fine of its kind. The next moment he tacks on lines which would have revolted Mr. Pecksniff:

> If ever you have looked on better days,
> If ever been where bells have knolled to church,
> > [*How perfectly the atmosphere of the rented
> > pew is caught in this incredible line!*]
> If ever sat at any good man's feast,
> If ever from your eyelids wiped—

I really shall get sick if I quote any more of it. Was ever such canting, snivelling, hypocritical unctuousness exuded by an actor anxious to shew that he was above his profession, and was a thoroughly respectable man in private life? Why cannot all this putrescence be cut out of the play, and only the vital parts—the genuine storytelling, the fun, the poetry, the drama, be retained? Simply because, if nothing were left of Shakespear but his genius, our Shakespearolaters would miss all that they admire in him.

Notwithstanding these drawbacks, the fascination of As You Like It is still very great. It has the overwhelming advantage of being writen for the most part in prose instead of in blank verse, which any fool can write. And such prose! The first scene alone, with its energy of exposition, each phrase driving its meaning and feeling in up

to the head at one brief, sure stroke, is worth ten acts of
the ordinary Elizabethan sing-song. It cannot be said
that the blank verse is reserved for those passages which
demand a loftier expression, since Le Beau and Corin
drop into it, like Mr. Silas Wegg, on the most inadequate
provocation; but at least there is not much of it. The
popularity of Rosalind is due to three main causes. First,
she only speaks blank verse for a few minutes. Second,
she only wears a skirt for a few minutes (and the dismal
effect of the change at the end to the wedding dress ought
to convert the stupidest champion of petticoats to rational
dress). Third, she makes love to the man instead of waiting for the man to make love to her—a piece of natural
history which has kept Shakespear's heroines alive, whilst
generations of properly governessed young ladies, taught
to say "No" three times at least, have miserably perished.

The performance at the St. James's is in some respects
very good and in no respect very bad or even indifferent.
Miss Neilson's Rosalind will not bear criticism for a
moment; and yet the total effect is pardonable, and even
pleasant. She bungles speech after speech; and her attacks of Miss Ellen Terry and Mrs. Patrick Campbell are
acute, sudden, and numerous; but her personal charm
carries her through; and her song is a great success: besides, who ever failed, or could fail, as Rosalind? Miss
Fay Davis is the best Celia I ever saw, and Miss Dorothea
Baird the prettiest Phœbe, though her part is too much
cut to give her any chance of acting. Miss Kate Phillips
is an appallingly artificial Audrey; for, her style being
either smart or nothing, her conscientious efforts to be
lumpish land her in the impossible. And then, what is
that artistically metropolitan complexion doing in the
Forest of Arden?

Ass as Jaques is, Mr. W. H. Vernon made him more
tolerable than I can remember. Every successive production at the St. James's leaves one with a greater admiration
than before for Mr. Vernon's talent. That servile apostle
of working-class Thrift and Teetotalism (O William
Shakespear, Esquire, you who died drunk, WHAT a
moral chap you were!) hight Adam, was made about
twenty years too old by Mr. Loraine, who, on the other
hand, made a charming point by bidding farewell to the

old home with a smile instead of the conventional tear. Mr. Fernandez impersonated the banished Duke as well as it is in the nature of Jaques's Boswell to be impersonated; Mr. H. B. Irving plays Oliver very much as anybody else would play Iago, yet with his faults on the right side; Mr. Vincent retains his lawful speeches (usually purloined by Jaques) as the First Lord; and Mr. Esmond tries the picturesque, attitudinizing, galvanic, Bedford Park style on Touchstone, worrying all effect out of the good lines, but worrying some into the bad ones. Mr. Wheeler, as Charles, catches the professional manner very happily; and the wrestling bout is far and away the best I have seen on the stage. To me, the wrestling is always the main attraction of an As You Like It performance, since it is so much easier to find a man who knows how to wrestle than one who knows how to act. Mr. Alexander's Orlando I should like to see again later on. The qualities he shewed in it were those which go without saying in his case; and now that he has disposed of the really big achievement of producing the play with an artistic intelligence and practical ability never, as far as my experience goes, applied to it before, he will have time to elaborate a part lying easily within his powers, and already very attractively played by him. There are ten other gentlemen in the cast; but I can only mention Mr. Aubrey Smith, whose appearance as "the humorous Duke" (which Mr. Vincent Sternroyd, as Le Beau, seemed to understand as a duke with a sense of humor, like Mr. Gilbert's Mikado) was so magnificent that it taxed all his powers to live up to his own aspect.

The scene where the two boys come in and sing It was a lover and his lass to Touchstone has been restored by Mr. Alexander with such success that I am inclined to declare it the most delightful moment in the whole representation. Mr. Edward German has rearranged his Henry VIII music for the masque of Hymen at the end. Hymen, beauteous to gorgeousness, is impersonated by Miss Opp.

The production at this Christmas season could not be more timely. The children will find the virtue of Adam and the philosophy of Jaques just the thing for them; whilst their elders will be delighted by the pageantry and the wrestling.

While writing as a music critic, under the pseudonym of
Corno di Bassetto, Shaw saw a presentation of As You
Like It *which provoked some interesting thoughts on*
Shakespearean production. They appeared in his review
in The Star *on April 18, 1890.*

I have been for some time waiting for an opportunity of
saying a word about Mrs. Langtry's revival of As You
Like It at the St. James's Theatre. I submit that the play
is spoiled by the ruthless cutting to bits of the last half
of it. This has been forced on the management by want
of skill and want of thought on the part of the actors.
The problem is to get through a play of so many lines
between eight o'clock and eleven. Any fool can solve
this in the fashion of Alexander (I allude to the man
who stopped a hole to keep the wind away, and not to the
lessee of the Avenue Theatre) by cutting out a chunk here
and a scrap there until the lines are few enough to fit.
But, somehow, the shorter you make your play in this
fashion, the more tedious it becomes. The proper way is
to divide your play into movements like those of a
symphony. You will find that there are several sections
which can be safely taken at a brisk *allegro,* and a few
that may be taken *prestissimo*: those, for instance, which
serve only to explain the mere mechanism of the plot.
Each *allegro* will improve the representation if it is
judiciously chosen and managed. Mr. Benson has introduced one or two in Hamlet with the happiest effect. Of
course the thing must be honestly done: the familiar
star system trick of making the minor characters slur
their work in order to leave plenty of time for the mock
pregnant pauses, head waggings, and elaborate business of
the leading actor, is vile, and shows a pitiful ambition
in the fool that uses it. The star must not take a minute
more than his lines are worth, or put off the third murderer with a minute less. Under these conditions, I believe it would be quite feasible to play As You Like It
right through in a little over three hours without sacrificing a point.
However, it would be necessary to get another Jaques
than Mr. Bourchier, or else to rudely shake his con-

viction that the secret of effective elocution is to pause
at every third word and look significantly out of the
corners of his eyes at anybody who happens to be in that
direction before letting out the fourth. Mr. Bourchier
can easily make himself a competent Jaques; but he
may take it from me that he is at present as bad a one as
London has seen for some years. Mrs. Langtry makes a
very womanly Rosalind, and succeeds better than any
other actress within my recollection in making her love
for Orlando the keynote of the part. I may remark that
in spite of the beauty of the verse and the deep feeling
for sylvan and pastoral scenery which pervades the play,
the human part of it is excessively conventional, and
might almost have been planned by Tom Taylor. Like
Henry V, it belongs to that moment of sympathy with
the common morality and thought of his time which
came between the romanticism of Shakespear's early plays
and the independent thought of his later one; and this is
why it is so easily played by any company with a fair share
of sense and skill. There is no confounded insight required in the business.

On May 2, 1896, in The Saturday Review *Shaw com-
mented on an actress in the part of Rosalind at a Shakespeare celebration.*

. . . Just at present I am more anxious about Miss Dorothea Baird, whom I did see, as Rosalind. Rosalind is to
the actress what Hamlet is to the actor—a part in which,
reasonable presentability being granted, failure is hardly
possible. It is easier than Trilby up to a certain point,
though it will of course hold much more acting. Miss
Baird plays it intelligently and nicely; and this, to such
a very pretty Ganymede, is enough to secure success. How
far the niceness and intelligence of the pretty young lady
will develop into the passion and intuition of the artist,
or whether the prettiness will develop into the "handsome is as handsome does" fascination which holds the
stage for many years against Time, remains to be seen.
All that can be said at present is that Miss Baird's Rosalind is bright and pleasant, with sufficient natural charm

to secure indulgence for all its shortcomings. Of these the most serious is Miss Baird's delivery of the lines. Everybody by this time knows how a modern high-school-mistress talks—how she repudiates the precision, the stateliness, the awe-inspiring oracularity of the old-fashioned schoolmistress who knew nothing, and cloaks her mathematics with a pretty little voice, a pretty little manner, and all sorts of self-conscious calineries and unassumingnesses. "Poor little me! what do *I* know about conic sections?" is the effect she aims at. Miss Baird's Rosalind has clearly been to the high school and modelled herself upon her pet mistress, if not actually taught there herself. But that dainty, pleading, narrow-lipped little torrent of gabble will not do for Shakespear. It is so unintelligible across the footlights that even I, who knows As You Like It almost as well as I know Beethoven's Pastoral Symphony, could not always catch what she was saying. This being so, it may safely be taken that Camberwell did not catch more than a very small conic section of it. For even an expert cannot make sense of Elizabethan blank verse at a first hearing when it is delivered at the rate of 200 words a minute and upwards. Besides, its lyrical flow, if such a tiny ladylike patter can be credited with so broad a quality, is not that of Shakespear's verse. The effect is like a canary trying to sing Handel.

In the same review Shaw discussed other performances.

. . . The scenes from As You Like It included nothing of Jaques except the few scraps of dialogue between the pessimist and Orlando; and no exception can be taken to the way in which these were handled by Mr. Irving. He dressed and looked the part well.

The best bit of work was Mr. Bernard Gould's Orlando; the worst, Mr. Ben Greet's Touchstone. Mr. Greet put himself out of the question before he had been two minutes on the stage by the profound stroke of picking one of Orlando's sonnets from a tree, and reading from it the impromptu burlesque:

> If a hart do lack a hind,
> Let him seek out Rosalind, etc.

This was a new reading with a vengeance. He was not much more successful as executant than as Shakespearean student. He completely missed the piled-up climax of the speech to William, and was, in short, as bad a Touchstone as a critic could desire to see. It is no disgrace to an actor to be unable to play Touchstone; but why, under these circumstances, and being a manager, he should cast himself for it, passes my understanding. Mr. Rawson Buckley played Oliver very well, but persisted, as usual, in dressing himself smartly, and then describing himself as "a wretched ragged man, o'ergrown with hair." Mr. Gould managed his part, especially the difficulties of the sham courtship with Ganymede, better than I can remember having seen it managed before; and some of his lines were finely spoken; but he was not Orlando. Orlando's intelligence is the intelligence of the heart: he always comes out best as an amiable, strong, manly, handsome, shrewd-enough-to-take-care-of-himself, but safely stupid and totally unobservant young man. Now, Mr. Gould plays with his head; his intelligence is always on the alert; and he is so observant that in spite of his many valuable stage qualities he almost disqualifies himself as an actor by his draughtsman's habit of watching himself and everyone else so keenly and interestedly that he is more apt to forget his part than to forget himself in it. The born actor looks in: Mr. Gould looks on. He acts like a good critic, and probably represses his tendencies— if he has any—to the maudlin self-sympathy, the insane egotism, the bottomless folly, the hysterical imaginative mendacity which—with the help of alcohol—make acting easy to some men who are for all other purposes the most hopeless wastrels. However, I do not object: I recognize the fact that the ascendency of the sentimental amorphous actor means the ascendency of the sentimental amorphous drama, and that the critical actor, like Mr. Gould, is indispensable to a drama with any brains in it. Still, the critical actor need not be also a draughtsman actor. I once elaborately explained to Mr. Gould a part of which I was myself the author. He paid me the closest attention; retired to ponder my utterances; and presently returned with a perfectly accurate and highly characteristic drawing of me, which I shall probably never live down. And if I had been Shakespear explaining Orlando, it would have been just the same.

The Comedy of Errors

On December 14, 1895, in The Saturday Review *Shaw reviewed a semi-professional production, praising it as being truer to the spirit of Shakespeare than most contemporary efforts and discussing in some detail the contrast between Henry Irving and Barry Sullivan as interpreters of Shakespeare.*

FOR A DELIGHTFUL, as distinguished from a commercially promising first night, the palm must be given this season to the Elizabethan Stage Society's performance of The Comedy of Errors in Gray's Inn Hall this day week. Usually I enjoy a first night as a surgeon enjoys an operation: this time I enjoyed it as a playgoer enjoys a pleasant performance. I have never, I hope, underrated the importance of the amateur; but I am now beginning to cling to him as the savior of theatrical art. He alone among the younger generation seems to have any experience of acting. Nothing is more appalling to the dramatic author than the discovery that professional actors of ten years standing have acquired nothing but a habit of brazening out their own incompetence. What is an actor nowadays, or an actress? In nine cases out of ten, simply a person who has been "on tour" with half a dozen "London successes," playing parts that involve nothing but a little business thoughtlessly copied from the performances of their London "creators," with long intervals spent between each tour in the ranks of the unemployed. At the end of a lifetime so spent, the "actor" will no doubt be a genuine expert at railway travelling, at taking lodgings, and at cajoling and bullying landladies; but a decent amateur of two years standing, and of the true irrepressible sort, will beat him hopelessly at his art. What a fate is that of these unhappy young professionals, sick to desperation of a provincial routine compared to which that of a commercial traveller is a dream of romance, longing for a chance which they have not skill enough to turn to account even if some accident thrust it upon them, and becoming less interesting and attractive year by year at a profession in which the steady increase of personal fascination should have no limit but positive senility and decrepitude! I remember, years ago, when the Playgoers' Club was in its infancy, hearing Mr. Pinero, in the course of an address to that body, break into an enthusiastic eulogium on the actor of the past, produced by the old stock-company system, versatile, a singer, a dancer, a fencer, an elocutionist, ready to play any part at a day's notice, and equally expert in comedy, drama, melodrama, Christmas pantomime, and the "legitimate." There is some German novel in which a crowd of medieval warriors, fired by the eloquence of Peter the Hermit, burns with a Christian longing to rush to the Holy Land and charge in serried ranks on the Paynim hosts—all except one man, who is obviously not impressed. Indignant at his coldness, they demand what he means by it. "Ive been there," is his sufficient explanation. That is how I felt when I was listening to Mr. Pinero. Having been brought up on the old stock-company actor, I knew that he was the least versatile of beings—that he was nailed helplessly to his own line of heavy or light, young or old, and played all the parts that fell to him as the representative of that line in exactly the same way. I knew that his power of hastily "swallowing" the words of a part and disgorging them at short notice more or less inaccurately and quite unimprovably (three months rehearsal would have left him more at sea than three hours) was incompatible with his ever knowing his part in any serious sense at all. I remembered his one absurd "combat" that passed for fencing, the paltry step-dance between the verses of his song in the pantomime that constituted him a dancer, the obnoxiousness of utterance which he called elocution and would impart to pupils for a consideration, the universal readiness which only meant that in his incorrigible remoteness from nature and art it mattered nothing what he did. Mr. Pinero madly cited Sir Henry Irving as an example of the product of the stock-company training; but the fact is, when Sir Henry first attempted classical acting at the Lyceum, he did not know the A B C of it, and only succeeded by his original and sympathetic notions of the X Y Z. Nobody who is familiar with the best technical work of the Irving of today, its finish, dignity, and grace, and the exactitude of its expression of his thought and feeling, can (unless he remembers) form any idea of what our chief actor had to teach himself before he could carry veteran playgoers with him in his breach with the tradition of superhuman acting of which Barry Sullivan was, as far as I know, the last English exponent (need I say that the great Irish actor was born in Birmingham?). Barry Sullivan was a splendidly monstrous performer in his prime: there was hardly any part sufficiently heroic for him to be natural in it. He had deficiencies in his nature, or rather blanks, but no weaknesses, because he had what people call no heart. Being a fine man, as proud as Lucifer, and gifted with an intense energy which had enabled him to cultivate himself physically to a superb degree, he was the very incarnation of the old individualistic, tyrannical conception of a great actor. By magnifying that conception to sublimity, he reduced it to absurdity. There were just two serious parts which he could play—Hamlet and Richelieu—the two loveless parts in the grand repertory. I know that some people do not like to think of Hamlet as loveless, and that the Irving Hamlet has his heart in the right place, and almost breaks it in the scene with Ophelia; but this I take to be the actor's rebuke to Shakespear rather than an attempt to fulfil his intentions. Sir Henry Irving has never thought much of the immortal William, and has given him more than one notable lesson—for instance, in The Merchant of Venice, where he gave us, not "the Jew that Shakespear drew," but the one he ought to have drawn if he had been up to the Lyceum mark. Barry Sullivan, with his gift of lovelessness, *was* Hamlet, and consequently used to put his Ophelias out of countenance more than it is easy to describe. In Hamlet, as in Richelieu, it was right to create a figure whose utter aloofness from his fellows gave him an almost supernatural distinction, and cut him off from all such trifling intimacy with them as love implies. And it was his success in producing this very curious and very imposing effect that made for Barry Sullivan, in his best days (I am not now speaking of the period after 1870 or thereabout), a unique provincial and Australian reputation which carried him over parts he could not play at all, such as Othello, through which he walked as if the only line in the play that conveyed any idea to him was the description of Othello as "perplexed in the extreme," or Macbeth, who was simply Cibber's Richard (a favorite part of his) in mutton-chop whiskers. No doubt his temperament, with its exceptional combination of imaginative energy with coldness and proud timidity of the sympathetic passions, accentuated the superhuman pretension in the style of acting which he practised; but his predecessor, Macready (if I may judge from that extremely depressing document, his diary), must have been much more like him than like Sir Henry Irving. At all events, both Macready and Sullivan had abominable tempers, and relied for their stage climaxes on effects of violence and impetuosity, and for their ordinary impressiveness on grandiose assumption of style. Once, when my father mentioned to me that he had seen Macready play Coriolanus, and I asked him what it was like, he replied that it was like a mad bull. I do not offer this as evidence that my critical faculty is an inherited one—clearly there must have been some artistic method in the bull's madness to have gained such a reputation—but I feel quite sure that when Sir Henry Irving fulfils his promise to appear as Coriolanus, no father will describe him to his son as my father described Macready to me. Barry Sullivan, then, represented the grandiose and the violent on its last legs, and could do nothing for the young Irving but mislead him. Irving's mission was to re-establish on the stage the touching, appealing nobility of sentiment and affection— the dignity which only asserts itself when it is wounded; and his early attempts to express these by the traditional methods of the old domineering, self-assertive, ambitious, thundering, superb school led him for a time into a grotesque confusion of style. In playing villains, too, his vein of callous, humorous impishness, with its occasional glimpses of a latent bestial dangerousness, utterly defied the methods of expression proper to the heaven-defying, man-quelling tyrant, usurper, and murderer, who was the typical villain of the old school, and whose flavorless

quintessence will be found by the curious distilled into
that instructive Shakespearean forgery, Ireland's Vortigern. In short, Irving had to find the right expression for
a perfectly new dignity and a perfectly new indignity;
and it was not until he had done this that he really accomplished his destiny, broke the old tradition, and left
Barry Sullivan and Macready half a century behind. I
will not say that he also left Shakespear behind: there is
too much of the "not for an age but for all time" about
our bard for that; but it is a pity that the new acting was
not applied to a new author. For though Sir Henry Irving's acting is no longer a falsification of the old style,
his acting versions are falsifications of the old plays. His
Hamlet, his Shylock, his Lear, though interesting in their
own way, are spurious as representations of Shakespear.
His Othello I have never seen: his Macbeth I thought
fine and genuine, indicating that his business is with
Shakespear's later plays and not with his earlier ones.
But he owes it to literature to connect his name with
some greater modern dramatist than the late Wills, or
Tennyson, who was not really a dramatist at all. There
is a nice bishop's part in Ibsen's—— but I digress.

My point is that Sir Henry Irving's so-called training
under the old stock-company system not only did not
give him the individuality of his style—for to that it did
not pretend—but that it failed to give him even those
generalities of stage deportment which are common to all
styles. The stock actor, when the first travelling com-
panies came along, vanished before them, unwept, un-
honored, and unsung, because the only sentiment he had
inspired in the public was an intense desire for some
means of doing without him. He was such an unpresentable impostor that the smart London person, well
dressed and well spoken, figuring in plays ingeniously contrived so as to dispense with any greater powers of acting
than every adroit man of the world picks up, came as an
inexpressible relief. Dare I now confess that I am beginning to have moments of regret for him. The smart
nullity of the London person is becoming intolerably
tedious; and the exhaustion of the novelty of the plays
constructed for him has stripped them of their illusion and left their jingling, rickety mechanism patent to a

disgusted public. The latest generation of "leading ladies" and their heroes simply terrify me: Mr. Bourchier, who had the good fortune to learn his business as an amateur, towers above them as an actor. And the latest crop of plays has been for the most part deliberately selected for production because of the very abjectness and venality which withered them, harvestless, almost as soon as they were above ground.

And yet there is more talent than ever—more skill now than ever—more artistic culture—better taste, better acting, better theatres, better dramatic literature. Mr. Tree, Mr. Alexander, Mr. Hare, have made honorable experiments; Mr. Forbes Robertson's enterprise at the Lyceum is not a sordid one; Mr. Henry Arthur Jones and Mr. Pinero are doing better work than ever before, and doing it without any craven concession to the follies of "the British public." But it is still necessary, if you want to feel quite reassured, to turn your back on the ordinary commercial west end theatre, with its ignoble gambling for "a catch-on," and its eagerly envious whisperings of how much Mr. Penley has made by Charley's Aunt, to watch the forlorn hopes that are led from time to time by artists and amateurs driven into action by the starvation of their artistic instincts. The latest of these is the Elizabethan Stage Society; and I am delighted to be able to taunt those who missed the performance in Gray's Inn Hall with being most pitiably out of the movement. The Lyceum itself could not have drawn a more distinguished audience; and the pleasant effect of the play, as performed on the floor of the hall without proscenium or fittings of any kind, and played straight through in less than an hour and a half without any division into acts, cannot be as much as imagined by any frequenter of our ordinary theatres. The illusion, which generally lapses during performances in our style whenever the principal performers are off the stage, was maintained throughout: neither the torchbearers on the stage nor the very effective oddity of the Dromio costumes interfering with it in the least. Only, the modern dresses of the audience, the gasaliers, and the portrait of Manisty next that of Bacon, were anachronisms which one had to ignore. The stage management was good as regards the exits, entrances, and groupings—not so good in the business of the speeches, which might have been made more helpful to the actors, especially to Adriana, whose best speeches were under-done. On the whole the acting was fair—much better than it would have been at an average professional per-formance. Egeon, one of the Dromios, and the courtezan distinguished themselves most. The evening wound up with a Dolmetsch concert of lute and viol, virginal and voice, a delectable entertainment which defies all descrip-tion by the pen.

CYMBELINE

In August of 1896 Ellen Terry began preparing the role of Imogen which she was to play in Henry Irving's production of Cymbeline *at the Lyceum Theatre. Her letters to Shaw on the part elicited several extensive and provocative replies from him. The full exchange may be found in* Ellen Terry and Bernard Shaw: A Correspondence. *In a letter of August 28, 1896, Shaw discussed the memorization of her part.*

. . . It is downright maddening to think of your slaving over Imogen. Of course you cant remember it: who could? Unless you really want to say the things a character in a play says, your soul is not interested, and without that sort of interest memory is *impossible.* To learn Imogen requires a Bishop's wife, not *you.* Great heavens, doesnt it make you fear that your faculties are decaying and your memory failing when you find that the lines wont come to you *eagerly,* but must be fixed into your head with hairpins, without any security for their sticking? Well, that is because Shakespear is as dead *dramatically* as a doornail. Your only chance of learning him without intolerable effort is to learn him by ear; for his music is unfailing. Never read your part; get somebody to speak it to you over and over again—to urge it on you, hurl it at you, until your mere imitative echo faculty forces you to jabber it as a street piano forces you to hum a tune that you positively dislike. And when you have finished with Imogen, finish with Shakespear. As Carlyle said to the emigrant "Here and now, or nowhere and never, is thy America" so I say to you "Here (at Fitzroy Square) and now, is thy Shakespear." Time flies; and you must act *something* before you die.

On September 6, 1896, Shaw wrote in great detail on the role of Imogen and the play in general.

I really dont know what to say about this silly old Cymbeline, except that it can be done delightfully in a village schoolroom, and cant be done at the Lyceum at all, on any terms. I wish you would tell me something about Imogen for my own instruction. All I can extract from the artificialities of the play is a double image—a real woman *divined* by Shakespear without his knowing it clearly, a natural aristocrat, with a high temper and perfect courage, with two moods—a childlike affection and wounded rage; and an idiotic paragon of virtue produced by Shakespear's *views* of what a woman ought to be, a person who sews and cooks, and reads improving books until midnight, and "always reserves her holy duty," and is anxious to assure people that they may trust her implicitly with their spoons and forks, and is in a chronic state of suspicion of improper behavior on the part of other people (especially her husband) with abandoned females. If I were you I should cut the part so as to leave the paragon out and the woman in; and I should write to The Times explaining the lines of the operation. It would be a magnificent advertisement.

There are four good lines in the part. First

"—how far it is
To this same blessed Milford."

which, like that whole scene, you will do beautifully.

Second, the exit speech, with its touch of vernacular nature:—

"Such a foe! Good heavens!"

Third, to leave the comedy lines for the more painful ones:—

"I'll hide my master from the flies."

Fourth, the only good line of pure rhetoric in Mrs. Siddon's style:—

"Fear not: I'm empty of all things but grief."

Only, Shakespear, like an ass, spoils that line by adding, in words, all that the delivery of the line itself ought to convey. The words "Thy master is not there, who was, indeed, the riches of it" should not be spoken. If anyone says you left them out you can retort "I did not speak them; but I did not leave them out."

If you utter all that rubbish about false Æneas and Dido's weeping, I will rise, snatch the nearest family Shakespear, solemnly throw it at your head, and leave the theatre. The moment Pisanio says "Good Madam, hear me," cut him short with "Come, fellow, be thou honest"; and say it with something of the deep admonition which makes me remember your "Shylock: there's thrice thy money offered thee" since years and years ago. And when you have fairly started cutting the miserable attorney's rhetoric out of the scene, do it with a bold hand. Dont trouble about the Paragonese "Some jay of Italy" stuff, or the wretched impossible logic chopping. And oh, my God, dont read the letter. You *cant* read it: no woman could read it out to a servant. (Oh what a DAMNED fool Shakespear was!) You must manage it in this way. In the second scene of the third act, let Pisanio begin by reading the letter, from "Thy mistress, Pisanio, hath played the strumpet, etc." down to "lie bleeding in me." Then let him break off and exclaim "How! of adultery!" etc. down to "O my master, thy mind to her is now as low as were thy fortunes!" Then let him resume the reading of the letter to the end, when he will find himself with just the right cue for "How! That I should murder her . . . *I! her!* . . ." and so on. The audience will not forget what is in the letter after that; and when Pisanio hands it to you in the fourth scene, you can *play* the reading of it with the certainty that the audience will have the clue in their imaginations burning hot. The pantomime will be easy for you—it goes this way—the horrible shock of the first sentence—"*I* false!"—then the slow, significant look at Pisanio, the man who is to kill you (it is the majesty of death that raises you for a moment from your horror)— then the return to the subject of the accusation and the slipping away of consciousness. Then cut all the rubbish out of the scene which follows, thus:—

P. What shall I need to draw my sword? The paper
   Hath cut her throat already. What cheer, madam?
I. False to his bed, etc. (the whole speech uncut)

P. Alas, good lady (Imogen has nothing to do with this
speech and should go straight on without hearing it)
I. *I* false! Thy conscience witness, Iachimo. (Every-
thing can be conveyed in these 4 words)
P. Good madam, hear me—
I. (Turning on him with solemn sternness)
Come, fellow, be thou honest.
Do thou thy master's bidding, etc. etc. (the whole
speech uncut)
P.   Hence, vile instrument
Thou shalt not damn my hand.
I. (Sharply, not much impressed by his rhetoric at such
a pass)
                              Why, I must die;
And if I do not by thy hand, thou art
No servant of thy master's. Prythee despatch.
The lamb entreats the butcher: where's thy knife,
etc. etc.

All this will mean an intolerable load off your memory
and off the real side of Imogen. Archer will complain in
The World of the violation of the Bard's integrity; and
I will declare in The Saturday Review that your dramatic
instinct and delicacy of feeling have never guided you
more unerringly than in rescuing the live bits of Imogen
from the bombazine trappings of the Bishop's wife.

There is another point which puzzles me—in that other
big scene—that nice Elizabethan morsel of the woman
waking up in the arms of a headless corpse. I cannot for
the life of me follow the business of that long speech
without getting the words "A headless man" in the wrong
place. For instance, you wake up, you sit up, half awake,
and think you are asking the way to Milford Haven—*the
blessed Milford,* since for the moment you have forgotten
your unhappiness. You lie down to sleep again, and in
doing so touch the body of Cloten, whose head (or no
head) is presumably muffled in a cloak. In your dim, half
asleep funny state of consciousness, you still have the idea
that you mustnt go to bed with anybody else but Posthumus, and you say "But soft, no bedfellow." Then in rous-
ing yourself sufficiently to get away from this vaguely apprehended person, you awaken a little more at this very

odd, dreamlike thing, that the bedfellow is covered with flowers. You take up a flower, still puzzly-dreamy, and look curiously at it. It is *bloody*, and then in an instant you are broad awake— "Oh gods and goddesses!" etc. But it is quite clear that you must not know that "this bloody man" is headless, as that would utterly spoil the point later on. He looks simply as if he had swathed his head in his cloak to sleep in. It is the blood under the flowers that makes him so horrible to be alone with. When you utter the prayer "If there be yet left in heaven as small a drop of pity as a wren's eye, feared gods, give me a part of it," I suppose you kneel and cover your eyes with your hands in the hope that when you remove them your prayer will be answered and the nightmare gone. You take down your hands and dare to look again. "The dream's here still. Even when I wake it is without me and within me, not imagined—felt." Now in the text, what follows is "A headless man!" That is what I cannot understand; and I believe it is an overlooked relic of some earlier arrangement of the business. For see how it plays if you omit it. Your attention is caught by the garment of Posthumus; you go on with the recognition step by step (confound those classical allusions; but they cant be helped); at last you lift the cloak to see the face, and then—"Murder in Heaven!" you go tearing, screaming, raging mad and rave your way to the swoon as best you can (a nice thing to play every night for 100 nights). But if you leave in the words "A headless man" the sequel is spoiled, and you are represented as being surprised at finding no face on a man, who, as you have already observed, has lost his whole head. Therefore, I submit that the "headless man" sentence must be left out.

These, dear madam, are the only ideas I have on the subject of Imogen. I daresay you know your own business better than I do; but no matter; your consciousness of your own view will only become more definite and determined if it contradicts everybody else's.

So you see I have no objection whatever to an intelligent cutting out of the dead and false bits of Shakespear. But when you propose to cut me, I am paralyzed at your sacrilegious audacity. I always cut myself to the bone,

reading the thing over and over until I have discovered
the bits that cant be made to play-act anyhow.

*Ellen Terry wrote Shaw further thoughts on Imogen and
sent him a copy of Irving's acting version of the play. In
a letter of September 8, 1896, Shaw praised Miss Terry's
ideas but expressed strong disapproval of Irving's cuts.*

I have read carefully through that copy, but, worse
luck, I must either write hurriedly or miss the post, as
some people have arrived here and I have had to spend a
lot of time mending punctures in female bicycle tyres.
Therefore brief and blunt must I be, O Ellen. Fortunately there is not much to say. Our brains evidently
work in the same way. At the same time I begin to doubt
whether you can really be an actress. Most of 'em have
no brains at all.

You have only once slipped out of the character in your
plan, and that is in the scene between Imogen and
Iachimo in the 2nd Act. Imogen is an impulsive person,
with quick transitions, absolutely frank self-expression,
and no half affections or half forgivenesses. The moment
you abuse anyone she loves, she is in a rage: the moment
you praise them she is delighted. It is quite easy for
Iachimo to put her out of countenance by telling her that
Posthumus has forgotten her; but the instant he makes
the mistake of trying to gratify her by abusing him—"that
runagate"—he brings down the avalanche. It is just the
same with Cloten: she is forbearing with him until he
makes the same mistake. And Iachimo has nothing to do
but praise Posthumus, and lay the butter on thick, and
she is instantly as pleased as Punch, and void of all resent-
ment. It is this that makes her pay him the extra special
compliment of offering to take the chest into her own bed-
room, *a thing she would never have done if she had not
forgiven him* quite thoroughly—honest Injun. Therefore there is no subsiding storm, no "wary of him," no
"polite—words, words, words." The words:—

> "—such a holy witch
> That he enchants societies to him:
> Half all men's hearts are his."

humbug her completely. The sun should come right out through the clouds when she says "You make amends."

You are unerring everywhere else.

On p. 4 the speech "O the gods! When shall we see again?" is really two separate speeches. When Posthumus puts the bracelet on your arm, look for a moment with delight at the present if you like, but that doesnt matter: the great thing is that you shiver with love at his touch on your arm, and say "O the gods!" as a sign of rapture. It is when that subsides that you ask the question a woman always does ask—it being the nature of her sex never to be satisfied—"When will you come again?"

On the same page (4) comes the first quick transition. "I beseech you, sir, harm not yourself with your vexation" is thoroughly petulant and full of temper, Cymbeline having not only sent Posthumus away, but called him "thou basest thing." What she really means is "You may save your breath to cool your porridge, you old wretch."

On page 33—the last line—throw up your engagement and bid H. I. farewell for ever sooner than allow Pisanio to make "and too much too" a comic aside. It is a perfectly serious, tender, *nurselike* thing to say. Any Irish peasant would say "and too much too, darlint," quite naturally. I hasten on, lest I should use bad language.

I still think you should let Tyars read the letter. My reasons are that if you read it so as to convey your own feelings on seeing it you cannot also read it with the decision and point needed to enable the audience to take in the force of Posthumus's instructions to Pisanio. Further, I have a particular liking for the absolute truth of effect produced by the *acting* of the reading only, without the clumsiness of an aside, not to mention the force of effect derived from the audience's foreknowledge of what is happening to you; so that they can watch you without listening to the verbal instructions. However, I dont press that. Shakespear preferred to convey the foreknowledge by Pisanio's speech in the former scene, and the fact that his knowledge of his business was always a clever half-knowledge (the result of a hurry to get things done anyhow) is known to me only. So read the letter by all means; but just take another look at my way of cutting the following scene. At all events you must cut out "to pieces with me!" (p. 38) as it is not only unintelligible as it stands, but actually suggests a quite wrong idea. In the original it means "Now that there is another woman, to pieces with poor me!" As you have it, it represents Imogen as inviting Pisanio to carve her up like a chicken, which is ridiculous and spitefully out of character. And "Come: be honest—look" is nothing like so beautiful or expressive as "Come, fellow, be thou honest: do thou thy master's bidding etc." To cut out such fine bits and leave in such tawdry trash as "slander whose tongue outvenoms all the worms of Nile" is idiotic. The tearing of Posthumus's letters from her bosom seems to me very poor business—at least for you. Cut out the Roman courtesan on page 39: she belongs to the Bishopess side of the part, as you have noted.

But do *not* cut out the "clouted brogues" on p. 52; but rather "put thy shoes from off thy feet, for the place on which thou standest is holy ground." And I adjure you, do not cut out the prayer to heaven for "as small a drop of pity as a wren's eye" (54). You will find it a blessed relief (prayer is better than crying for that purpose) and to kneel and pray with your eyes covered will be beautiful. On p. 63 do not let them cut the speech of Lucius, "I do not bid thee beg my life, good lad, and yet I know thou wilt." It belongs to *your* part, your reply being important as a bit of play.

Generally speaking, the cutting of the play is stupid to the last extremity. Even from the broadest popular point of view, the omission of the grandiose scene about England and Cæsar for the queen, Cloten and the Roman, is a mistake. Cloten's part is spoiled. Every part is spoiled except "the governor's"; and he has actually damaged his own by wantonly cutting off your white and azure eyelids laced with blue of heaven's own tinct. Posthumus's exit on p. 32 is utterly spoiled by a fragment of another scene stuck in in the wrong place, lest Posthumus should complain that Iachimo was jealous of him and would not let him have that scene. The prudery of the cutting is silly: Pisanio says "disloyal" instead of adultery; Iachimo discreetly omits the lines "where, I profess, I slept not etc.," and Cloten's irresistibly turned remark that if Imogen doesnt like his serenade "it is a vice in her ears which horsehairs and calves' guts, nor the voice of unpaved eunuch to boot [a quite delightful bit of writing] can never amend"—is sacrificed to please the curates for whom the Lyceum seems chiefly to exist.

Forgive these splenetic remarks; but really H. I.'s acting versions of Shakespear are past all bearing. The man has no artistic sense outside his own person: he is an ogre who has carried you off to his cave; and now Childe Roland is coming to the dark tower to rescue you.

As the performance drew near Miss Terry wrote Shaw of her confusion about Imogen and her fears that she would not be able to play the part well. Shaw wrote her several letters of encouragement prior to the opening. After the première Shaw wrote Miss Terry, on September 23, 1896, mentioning his forthcoming review and giving some of his initial reactions.

Yes, that is all very well, but the real event is yet to come—the event that London is waiting for, to which the Lyceum business is the merest insignificant preliminary—that is G. B. S.'s article in the Saturday. I have to do that unaided and alone: nobody writes *me* sixteen or seventeen nice letters a day to encourage me, but no matter. If there is a thing I hate, it is ingratitude. Some people think of nobody but themselves. But I say no more.

My article is half written, and oh! isnt it nasty! All the natural malignity which I have been suppressing for weeks on your account is now simply boiling over. So it is to be "Madame Sans Gêne" after all. Oh VERY well, Sir Henry Irving. A homemade Napoleon isnt good enough for you, isnt it? Very good: we shall see. And you are going to play Richard III, are you? Then I think I know who is going to play Richmond: that's all.

I shall begin that article over again to-morrow: it's not half nasty enough.

I was greatly shocked by your entrance last night. You must have spent hours before the glass, getting up that success of personal beauty, merely to écraser Mrs. Pat. Do you think, at your age, it is right?

I consider the way you went on with Posthumus positively indecent. Who is he, pray, that he should be made love to in that fashion? I consider myself to the full as good-looking a man.

Look here: I shall go again in a week or two. I am not satisfied: there is a crumple in the roseleaf here and there. You made one AWFUL mistake. You actually bawled out the words "a headless man!" before you had half seen him. Good heavens! you mustnt do that: it's ridiculous. You must simply start in horror, give the audience time to see in your face what is the matter, and then say "a headless man" in a frozen whisper. If you must make a noise, screech like mad when you start. Then it will be all right.

In playing Shakespear, play *to* the lines, *through* the lines, *on* the lines, but never between the lines. There simply isnt time for it. You would not stick five bars rest into a Beethoven symphony to pick up your drumsticks; and similarly you must not stop the Shakespear orchestra for business. Nothing short of a procession or a fight should make anything so extraordinary as a silence during a Shakespearean performance. All that cave business wants pulling together: from the line about " 'tis some savage hold" to "Such a foe! Good heavens!" you ought to get all the business of peeping and hesitating and so on packed into the duration of the speech, spoken without a single interval except a pause after the call. Otherwise it drags. Mind, I dont propose that you should omit or slur anything, but only that you should do it with the utmost economy of time.

The scene of the waking up should be moonlit: full bank holiday sunlight is too prosaic to make Imogen's dreamy condition and the uncanny effect of the mysterious body covered with flowers credible. On the other hand the low light in the scene where you read the fatal letter is not good. Somehow, at the Lyceum, the scenery is always imagined pictorially instead of dramatically.

How extra-OR-dinarily young and charming you have made yourself by that American trip! Or is it all tricks? Hurst put me five rows further back than usual. Heavens! am I the victim of a conspiracy!

Oh my article, my article, how am I to keep my style

fresh if I sit up all night writing to you now that it is all over and I can be of no further use.

On September 25, 1896, Shaw wrote his final letter on the subject.

Now this is positively my last letter. The thing is getting ridiculous. The article is finished and gone irrevocably to press. A mass of pounded, smashed, lacerated fragments, with here and there a button or a splinter of bone, is all that is left of your unhappy son, of H. I., of Shakespear, of Webster, and of the Lyceum stage management. On the latter point I want you to consider the article carefully with reference to that headless business. I am furious with myself for having omitted to urge upon you the importance of the scenic setting—I ought to have known that without a vigorous protest you would be put off with something between Bellinzona and Tintern, and two nice young men out of a studio, instead of a land of lions murderers and hobgoblins, with dreadful lonely distances and threatening darknesses. Why should you ask for a drop of pity on a nice pretty warm comfortable reassuring lovely day in the country, with "tea for tourists" obviously just round the corner? Great Lord, if I were a scene painter I'd have painted such an endless valley of desolation for you that at your appearance in its awful solitudes, lost and encompassed by terrors, everybody would have caught their breath with a sob before you opened your mouth. I should like to see Hawes Craven offering that cosy little hill and millstream to Mrs. Siddons. The idiot! You would rank as the greatest actress in the world if only you were not surrounded by fools, duffers, blockheads, people with heads like croquet balls, solid all through. How would Iachimo like to play his scene in one of the bedrooms in Maple's shop window, with a nice new portmaneau to hide in?

Ellen: art is one and indivisible. If ever you play Shakespear again, dictate the scene plot before you think of anything else—even of your dresses.

Shaw's review of this production of Cymbeline *is one of his most famous. It appeared on September 26, 1896, in* The Saturday Review *and he entitled it "Blaming the Bard."*

I CONFESS to a difficulty in feeling civilized just at present. Flying from the country, where the gentlemen of England are in an ecstasy of chicken-butchering, I return to town to find the higher wits assembled at a play three hundred years old, in which the sensation scene exhibits a woman waking up to find her husband reposing gorily in her arms with his head cut off.

Pray understand, therefore, that I do not defend Cymbeline. It is for the most part stagey trash of the lowest melodramatic order, in parts abominably written, throughout intellectually vulgar, and judged in point of thought by modern intellectual standards, vulgar, foolish, offensive, indecent, and exasperating beyond all tolerance. There are moments when one asks despairingly why our stage should ever have been cursed with this "immortal" pilferer of other men's stories and ideas, with his monstrous rhetorical fustian, his unbearable platitudes, his pretentious reduction of the subtlest problems of life to commonplaces against which a Polytechnic debating club would revolt, his incredible unsuggestiveness, his sententious combination of ready reflection with complete intellectual sterility, and his consequent incapacity for getting out of the depth of even the most ignorant audience, except when he solemnly says something so transcendently platitudinous that his more humble-minded hearers cannot bring themselves to believe that so great a man really meant to talk like their grand-mothers. With the single exception of Homer, there is no eminent writer, not even Sir Walter Scott, whom I can despise so entirely as I despise Shakespear when I measure my mind against his. The intensity of my impatience with him occasionally reaches such a pitch, that it would positively be a relief to me to dig him up and throw stones at him, knowing as I do how incapable he and his worshippers are of understanding any less obvious form of indignity. To read Cymbeline and to think of Goethe, of Wagner, of Ibsen, is, for me, to imperil the habit of studied moderation of statement which years of public responsibility as a journalist have made almost second nature in me.

But I am bound to add that I pity the man who cannot enjoy Shakespear. He has outlasted thousands of abler thinkers, and will outlast a thousand more. His gift of telling a story (provided some one else told it to him first); his enormous power over language, as conspicuous in his senseless and silly abuse of it as in his miracles of expression; his humor; his sense of idiosyncratic character; and his prodigious fund of that vital energy which is, it seems, the true differentiating property behind the faculties, good, bad, or indifferent, of the man of genius, enable him to entertain us so effectively that the imaginary scenes and people he has created become more real to us than our actual life—at least, until our knowledge and grip of actual life begins to deepen and glow beyond the common. When I was twenty I knew everybody in Shakespear, from Hamlet to Abhorson, much more intimately than I knew my living contemporaries; and to this day, if the name of Pistol or Polonius catches my eye in a newspaper, I turn to the passage with more curiosity than if the name were that of—but perhaps I had better not mention any one in particular.

How many new acquaintances, then, do you make in reading Cymbeline, provided you have the patience to break your way into it through all the fustian, and are old enough to be free from the modern idea that Cymbeline must be the name of a cosmetic and Imogen of the latest scientific discovery in the nature of a hitherto unknown gas? Cymbeline is nothing; his queen nothing, though some attempt is made to justify her description as "a woman that bears all down with her brain"; Posthumus, nothing—most fortunately, as otherwise he would be an unendurably contemptible hound; Belarius, nothing—at least, not after Kent in King Lear (just as the Queen is nothing after Lady Macbeth); Iachimo, not much—only a *diabolus ex machina* made plausible; and Pisanio, less than Iachimo. On the other hand, we have Cloten, the prince of numbsculls, whose part, indecencies and all, is a literary masterpiece from the first line to the last; the two princes—fine presentments of that impressive and

generous myth, the noble savage; Caius Lucius, the
Roman general, urbane among the barbarians; and,
above all, Imogen. But do, please, remember that there
are two Imogens. One is a solemn and elaborate example
of what, in Shakespear's opinion, a real lady ought to be.
With this unspeakable person virtuous indignation is
chronic. Her object in life is to vindicate her own propriety and to suspect everybody else's, especially her husband's. Like Lothaw in the jeweller's shop in Bret
Harte's burlesque novel, she cannot be left alone with
unconsidered trifles of portable silver without officiously
assuring the proprietors that she has stolen naught, nor
would not, though she had found gold strewed i' the floor.
Her fertility and spontaneity in nasty ideas is not to be
described: there is hardly a speech in her part that you
can read without wincing. But this Imogen has another
one tied to her with ropes of blank verse (which can fortunately be cut)—the Imogen of Shakespear's genius, an
enchanting person of the most delicate sensitiveness, full
of sudden transitions from ecstasies of tenderness to transports of childish rage, and reckless of consequences in
both, instantly hurt and instantly appeased, and of the
highest breeding and courage. But for this Imogen, Cymbeline would stand about as much chance of being revived now as Titus Andronicus.

The instinctive Imogen, like the real live part of the
rest of the play, has to be disentangled from a mass of
stuff which, though it might be recited with effect and
appropriateness by young amateurs at a performance by
the Elizabethan Stage Society, is absolutely unactable and
unutterable in the modern theatre, where a direct illusion
of reality is aimed at, and where the repugnance of the
best actors to play false passages is practically insuperable.
For the purposes of the Lyceum, therefore, Cymbeline
had to be cut, and cut liberally. Not that there was any
reason to apprehend that the manager would flinch from
the operation: quite the contrary. In a true republic of
art Sir Henry Irving would ere this have expiated his
acting versions on the scaffold. He does not merely cut
plays: he disembowels them. In Cymbeline he has quite
surpassed himself by extirpating the antiphonal third
verse of the famous dirge. A man who would do that

would do anything—cut the coda out of the first movement of Beethoven's Ninth Symphony, or shorten one of
Velasquez's Philips into a kitcat to make it fit over his
drawing room mantelpiece. The grotesque character trac-
ery of Cloten's lines, which is surely not beyond the appreciation of an age educated by Stevenson, is defaced
with Cromwellian ruthlessness; and the patriotic scene,
with the Queen's great speech about the natural bravery
of our isle, magnificent in its Walkürenritt swing, is shorn
away, though it might easily have been introduced in the
Garden scene. And yet, long screeds of rubbish about
"slander, whose edge is sharper than the sword," and so
on, are preserved with superstitious veneration.

This curious want of connoisseurship in literature
would disable Sir Henry Irving seriously if he were an
interpretative actor. But it is, happily, the fault of a great
quality—the creative quality. A prodigious deal of nonsense has been written about Sir Henry Irving's conception of this, that, and the other Shakespearean character.
The truth is that he has never in his life conceived or
interpreted the characters of any author except himself.
He is really as incapable of acting another man's play as
Wagner was of setting another man's libretto; and he
should, like Wagner, have written his plays for himself.
But as he did not find himself out until it was too late for
him to learn that supplementary trade, he was compelled
to use other men's plays as the framework for his own
creations. His first great success in this sort of adaptation
was with the Merchant of Venice. There was no question
then of a bad Shylock or a good Shylock: he was simply
not Shylock at all; and when his own creation came into
conflict with Shakespear's, as it did quite openly in the
Trial scene, he simply played in flat contradiction of the
lines, and positively acted Shakespear off the stage. This
was an original policy, and an intensely interesting one
from the critical point of view; but it was obvious that its
difficulty must increase with the vividness and force of
the dramatist's creation. Shakespear at his highest pitch
cannot be set aside by any mortal actor, however gifted;
and when Sir Henry Irving tried to interpolate a most
singular and fantastic notion of an old man between the
lines of a fearfully mutilated acting version of King Lear,

he was smashed. On the other hand, in plays by persons of no importance, where the dramatist's part of the business is the merest trash, his creative activity is unhampered and uncontradicted; and the author's futility is the opportunity for the actor's masterpiece. Now I have already described Shakespear's Iachimo as little better than any of the lay figures in Cymbeline—a mere *diabolus ex machina*. But Irving's Iachimo is a very different affair. It is a new and independent creation. I knew Shakespear's play inside and out before last Tuesday; but this Iachimo was quite fresh and novel to me. I witnessed it with unqualified delight: it was no vulgar bagful of "points," but a true impersonation, unbroken in its life-current from end to end, varied on the surface with the finest comedy, and without a single lapse in the sustained beauty of its execution. It is only after such work that an artist can with perfect naturalness and dignity address himself to his audience as "their faithful and loving servant"; and I wish I could add that the audience had an equal right to offer him their applause as a worthy acknowledgment of his merit. But when a house distributes its officious first-night plaudits impartially between the fine artist and the blunderer who roars a few lines violently and rushes off the stage after compressing the entire art of How Not to Act into five intolerable minutes, it had better be told to reserve its impertinent and obstreperous demonstrations until it has learnt to bestow them with some sort of discrimination. Our first-night people mean well, and will, no doubt, accept my assurance that they are donkeys with all possible good humor; but they should remember that to applaud for the sake of applauding, as schoolboys will cheer for the sake of cheering, is to destroy our own power of complimenting those who, as the greatest among us, are the servants of all the rest.

Over the performances of the other gentlemen in the cast let me skate as lightly as possible. Mr. Norman Forbes's Cloten, though a fatuous idiot rather than the brawny "beef-witted" fool whom Shakespear took from his own Ajax in Troilus and Cressida, is effective and amusing, so that one feels acutely the mangling of his part, especially the cutting of that immortal musical criti-

cism of his upon the serenade. Mr. Gordon Craig and
Mr. Webster are desperate failures as the two noble sav-
ages. They are as spirited and picturesque as possible;
but every pose, every flirt of their elfin locks, proclaims
the wild freedom of Bedford Park. They recite the poor
maimed dirge admirably, Mr. Craig being the more musical of the twain; and Mr. Webster's sword-and-cudgel
fight with Cloten is very lively; but their utter deficiency
in the grave, rather sombre, uncivilized primeval strength
and Mohican dignity so finely suggested by Shakespear,
takes all the ballast out of the fourth act, and combines
with the inappropriate prettiness and sunniness of the
landscape scenery to handicap Miss Ellen Terry most
cruelly in the trying scene of her awakening by the side
of the flower-decked corpse: a scene which, without every
accessory to heighten its mystery, terror, and pathos, is
utterly and heart-breakingly impossible for any actress,
even if she were Duse, Ristori, Mrs. Siddons, and Miss
Terry rolled into one. When I saw this gross and pal-
pable oversight, and heard people talking about the
Lyceum stage management as superb, I with difficulty
restrained myself from tearing out my hair in handfuls
and scattering it with imprecations to the four winds.
That cave of the three mountaineers wants nothing but
a trellised porch, a bamboo bicycle, and a nice little bed
of standard roses, to complete its absurdity.

With Mr. Frederic Robinson as Belarius, and Mr.
Tyars as Pisanio, there is no reasonable fault to find, except that they might, perhaps, be a little brighter with
advantage; and of the rest of their male colleagues I
think I shall ask to be allowed to say nothing at all, even
at the cost of omitting a tribute to Mr. Fuller Mellish's
discreet impersonation of the harmless necessary Philario.
There remains Miss Geneviève Ward, whose part, with
the Neptune's park speech lopped off, was not worth
her playing, and Miss Ellen Terry, who invariably fasci-
nates me so much that I have not the smallest confidence
in my own judgment respecting her. There was no Bedford Park about the effect she made as she stepped into
the King's garden; still less any of the atmosphere of
ancient Britain. At the first glance, we were in the
Italian fifteenth century; and the house, unversed in the

cinquecento, but dazzled all the same, proceeded to roar until it stopped from exhaustion. There is one scene in Cymbeline, the one in which Imogen receives the summons to "that same blessed Milford," which might have been written for Miss Terry, so perfectly does its innocent rapture and frank gladness fit into her hand. Her repulse of Iachimo brought down the house as a matter of course, though I am convinced that the older Shakespeareans present had a vague impression that it could not be properly done except by a stout, turnip-headed matron, with her black hair folded smoothly over her ears and secured in a classic bun. Miss Terry had evidently cut her own part; at all events the odious Mrs. Grundyish Imogen had been dissected out of it so skilfully that it went without a single jar. The circumstances under which she was asked to play the fourth act were, as I have explained, impossible. To wake up in the gloom amid the wolf and robber-haunted mountain gorges which formed the Welsh mountains of Shakespear's imagination in the days before the Great Western existed is one thing: to wake up at about three on a nice Bank-holiday afternoon in a charming spot near the valley of the Wye is quite another. With all her force, Miss Terry gave us faithfully the whole process which Shakespear has presented with such dramatic cunning—Imogen's bewilderment, between dreaming and waking, as to where she is; the vague discerning of some strange bed-fellow there; the wondering examination of the flowers with which he is so oddly covered; the frightful discovery of blood on the flowers, with the hideous climax that the man is headless and that his clothes are her husband's; and it was all ruined by that blazing, idiotic, prosaic sunlight in which everything leapt to the eye at once, rendering the mystery and the slowly growing clearness of perception incredible and unintelligible, and spoiling a scene which, properly stage-managed, would have been a triumph of histrionic intelligence. Cannot somebody be hanged for this?—men perish every week for lesser crimes. What consolation is it to me that Miss Terry, playing with infinite charm and delicacy of appeal, made up her lost ground in other directions, and had more than as much success as the roaring gallery could feel the want of?

A musical accompaniment to the drama has been specially composed; and its numbers are set forth in the bill of the play, with the words "LOST PROPERTY" in conspicuous red capitals in the margin. Perhaps I can be of some use in restoring at least some of the articles to their rightful owner. The prelude to the fourth act belongs to Beethoven—first movement of the Seventh Symphony. The theme played by "the ingenious instrument" in the cave is Handel's, and is familiar to lovers of Judas Maccabeus as O never bow we down to the rude stock or sculptured stone. J. F. R. will, I feel sure, be happy to carry the work of identification further if necessary.

Sir Henry Irving's next appearance will be on Bosworth Field. He was obviously astonished by the startling shout of approbation with which the announcement was received. We all have an old weakness for Richard.

In 1945, almost fifty years after "Blaming the Bard," Shaw had mellowed in his opinion of Cymbeline, but this did not prevent him from rewriting, in a spirit of devilment and daring, the last act of the play. Shaw's version is written in blank verse, all his except for a few lines taken from Shakespeare. He called it Cymbeline Refinished and explained his reasons for writing it in a foreword.

THE PRACTICE of improving Shakespear's plays, more especially in the matter of supplying them with what are called happy endings, is an old established one which has always been accepted without protest by British audiences. When Mr. Harley Granville-Barker, following up some desperate experiments by the late William Poel, introduced the startling innovation of performing the plays in the West End of London exactly as Shakespear wrote them, there was indeed some demur; but it was expressed outside the theatre and led to no rioting. And it set on foot a new theory of Shakespearean representation. Up to that time it had been assumed as a matter of course that everyone behind the scenes in a theatre must know

much better than Shakespear how plays should be written, exactly as it is believed in the Hollywood studios
today that everyone in a film studio knows better than
any professional playwright how a play should be filmed.
But the pleasure given by Mr. Granville-Barker's productions shook that conviction in the theatre; and the superstition that Shakespear's plays as written by him are impossible on the stage, which had produced a happy ending
to King Lear, Cibber's Richard III, a love scene in the
tomb of the Capulets between Romeo and Juliet before
the poison takes effect, and had culminated in the crude
literary butcheries successfully imposed on the public
and the critics as Shakespear's plays by Henry Irving and
Augustin Daly at the end of the last century, is for the
moment heavily discredited. It may be asked then why
I, who always fought fiercely against that superstition
in the days when I was a journalist-critic, should perpe-
trate a spurious fifth act to Cymbeline, and do it too, not
wholly as a literary *jeu d'esprit,* but in response to an
actual emergency in the theatre when it was proposed to
revive Cymbeline at no less sacred a place than the Shakespear Memorial Theatre at Stratford-upon-Avon.

Cymbeline, though one of the finest of Shakespear's
later plays now on the stage, goes to pieces in the last
act. In fact I mooted the point myself by thoughtlessly
saying that the revival would be all right if I wrote a last
act for it. To my surprise this blasphemy was received
with acclamation; and as the applause, like the proposal,
was not wholly jocular, the fancy began to haunt me,
and persisted until I exorcised it by writing the pages
which ensue.

I had a second surprise when I began by reading the
authentic last act carefully through. I had not done so
for many years, and had the common impression about it
that it was a cobbled-up affair by several hands, including
a vision in prison accompanied by scraps of quite ridiculous doggerel.

For this estimate I found absolutely no justification nor
excuse. I must have got it from the last revival of the
play at the old Lyceum theatre, when Irving, as Iachimo,
a statue of romantic melancholy, stood dumb on the stage
for hours (as it seemed) whilst the others toiled through

a series of *dénouements* of crushing tedium, in which the characters lost all their vitality and individuality, and had nothing to do but identify themselves by moles on their necks, or explain why they were not dead. The vision and the verses were cut out as a matter of course; and I ignorantly thanked Heaven for it.

When I read the act as aforesaid I found that my notion that it is a cobbled-up *pasticcio* by other hands was an unpardonable stupidity. The act is genuine Shakespear to the last full stop, and late phase Shakespear in point of verbal workmanship.

The doggerel is not doggerel: it is a versified masque, in Shakespear's careless woodnotes wild, complete with Jupiter as *deus ex machina*, eagle and all, introduced, like the Ceres scene in The Tempest, to please King Jamie, or else because an irresistible fashion had set in, just as at all the great continental opera houses a ballet used to be *de rigueur*. Gounod had to introduce one into his Faust, and Wagner into his Tannhäuser, before they could be staged at the Grand Opera in Paris. So, I take it, had Shakespear to stick a masque into Cymbeline. Performed as such, with suitable music and enough pictorial splendor, it is not only entertaining on the stage, but, with the very Shakespearean feature of a comic jailor which precedes it, just the thing to save the last act.

Without it the act is a tedious string of unsurprising *dénouements* sugared with insincere sentimentality after a ludicrous stage battle. With one exception the characters have vanished and left nothing but dolls being moved about like the glass balls in the game of solitaire until they are all got rid of but one. The exception is the hero, or rather the husband of the heroine, Leonatus Posthumus. The late Charles Charrington, who with his wife Janet Achurch broke the ice for Ibsen in England, used to cite Posthumus as Shakespear's anticipation of his Norwegian rival. Certainly, after being theatrically conventional to the extent of ordering his wife to be murdered, he begins to criticize, quite on the lines of Mrs. Alving in Ghosts, the slavery to an inhuman ideal of marital fidelity which led him to this villainous extremity. One may say that he is the only character left really alive in the last act; and as I cannot change him

for the better I have left most of his part untouched.
I make no apology for my attempt to bring the others
back to dramatic activity and individuality.

I should like to have retained Cornelius as the exponent of Shakespear's sensible and scientific detestation
of vivisection. But as he has nothing to say except that
the Queen is dead, and nobody can possibly care a rap
whether she is alive or dead, I have left him with her in
the box of puppets that are done with.

I have ruthlessly cut out the surprises that no longer
surprise anybody. I really could not keep my countenance over the identification of Guiderius by the mole on
his neck. That device was killed by Maddison Morton,
once a famous farce writer, now forgotten by everyone
save Mr. Gordon Craig and myself. In Morton's masterpiece, Box and Cox, Box asks Cox whether he has a
strawberry mark on his left arm. "No" says Cox. "Then
you are my long lost brother" says Box as they fall into
one another's arms and end the farce happily. One could
wish that Guiderius had anticipated Cox.

Plot has always been the curse of serious drama, and
indeed of serious literature of any kind. It is so out-of-
place there that Shakespear never could invent one. Unfortunately, instead of taking Nature's hint and discarding plots, he borrowed them all over the place and got
into trouble through having to unravel them in the last
act, especially in The Two Gentlemen of Verona and
Cymbeline. The more childish spectators may find some
delight in the revelation that Polydore and Cadwal are
Imogen's long lost brothers and Cymbeline's long lost
sons; that Iachimo is now an occupant of the penitent
form and very unlike his old self; and that Imogen is so
dutiful that she accepts her husband's attempt to have
her murdered with affectionate docility. I cannot share
these infantile joys. Having become interested in Iachimo, in Imogen, and even in the two long lost princes,
I wanted to know how their characters would react to
the éclaircissement which follows the battle. The only
way to satisfy this curiosity was to rewrite the act as
Shakespear might have written it if he had been post-
Ibsen and post-Shaw instead of post-Marlowe.

In doing so I had to follow the Shakespearean verse

pattern to match the 89 lines of Shakespear's text which I retained. This came very easily to me. It happened when I was a child that one of the books I delighted in was an illustrated Shakespear, with a picture and two or three lines of text underneath it on every third or fourth page. Ever since, Shakespearean blank verse has been to me as natural a form of literary expression as the Augustan English to which I was brought up in Dublin, or the latest London fashion in dialogue. It is so easy that if it were possible to kill it it would have been burlesqued to death by Tom Thumb, Chrononhotonthologos, and Bombastes Furioso. But Shakespear will survive any possible extremity of caricature.

I shall not deprecate the most violent discussion as to the propriety of meddling with masterpieces. All I can say is that the temptation to do it, and sometimes the circumstances which demand it, are irresistible. The results are very various. When a mediocre artist tries to improve on a great artist's work the effect is ridiculous or merely contemptible. When the alteration damages the original, as when a bad painter repaints a Velasquez or a Rembrandt, he commits a crime. When the changed work is sold or exhibited as the original, the fraud is indictable. But when it comes to complete forgery, as in the case of Ireland's Vortigern, which was much admired and at last actually performed as a play by Shakespear, the affair passes beyond the sphere of crime and becomes an instructive joke.

But what of the many successful and avowed variations? What about the additions made by Mozart to the score of Handel's Messiah? Elgar, who adored Handel, and had an unbounded contempt for all the lesser meddlers, loved Mozart's variations, and dismissed all purist criticism of them by maintaining that Handel must have extemporized equivalents to them on the organ at his concerts. When Spontini found on his visit to Dresden that Wagner had added trombone parts to his choruses, he appropriated them very gratefully. Volumes of variations on the tunes of other composers were published as such by Mozart and Beethoven, to say nothing of Bach and Handel, who played Old Harry with any air that amused them. Would anyone now remember Diabelli's vulgar waltz but for Beethoven's amazing variations, one of which is also a variation on an air from Don Giovanni?

And now consider the practice of Shakespear himself. Tolstoy declared that the original Lear is superior to Shakespear's rehandling, which he abhorred as immoral. Nobody has ever agreed with him. Will it be contended that Shakespear had no right to refashion Hamlet? If he had spoiled both plays, that would be a reason for reviving them without Shakespear's transfigurations, but not for challenging Shakespear's right to remake them.

Accordingly, I feel no qualm of conscience and have no apology to make for indulging in a variation on the last act of Cymbeline. I stand in the same time relation to Shakespear as Mozart to Handel, or Wagner to Beethoven. Like Mozart, I have not confined myself to the journeyman's job of writing "additional accompaniments": I have luxuriated in variations. Like Wagner dealing with Gluck's overture to *Iphigenia in Aulis* I have made a new ending for its own sake. Beethoven's Ninth Symphony towers among the classic masterpieces; but if Wagner had been old enough in his Dresden days not only to rescore the first and greatest movement as he did, but to supply the whole work with a more singable ending I should not have discouraged him; for I must agree with Verdi that the present ending, from the change to six-four onward, though intensely Beethovenish, is in performance usually a screaming voice destroying orgy.

I may be asked why all my instances are musical instead of literary. Is it a plot to take the literary critics out of their depth? Well, it may have that good effect; but I am not aiming at it. It is, I suppose, because music has succeeded to the heroic rank taken by literature in the sixteenth century. I cannot pretend to care much about what Nat Lee did in his attempts to impart Restoration gentility to Shakespear, or about Thomas Corneille's bowdlerization of Molière's *Festin de Pierre,* or any of the other literary precedents, though I am a little ashamed of being found in the company of their perpetrators. But I do care a good deal about what Mozart did to Handel, and Wagner to Gluck; and it seems to me that to discuss the artistic morality of my alternative ending without reference to them would be waste of time.

Anyhow, what I have done I have done; and at that I must leave it.

I shall not press my version on managers producing Cymbeline if they have the courage and good sense to present the original word-for-word as Shakespear left it, and the means to do justice to the masque. But if they are halfhearted about it, and inclined to compromise by leaving out the masque and the comic jailor and mutilating the rest, as their manner is, I unhesitatingly recommend my version. The audience will not know the difference; and the few critics who have read Cymbeline will be too grateful for my shortening of the last act to complain.

G. B. S.

Ayot Saint Lawrence
December 1945

ACT V

A rocky defile. A wild evening. Philario, in armor, stands on a tall rock, straining his eyes to see into the distance. In the foreground a Roman captain, sword in hand, his helmet badly battered, rushes in panting. Looking round before he sits down on a rock to recover his breath, he catches sight of Philario.

CAPTAIN. Ho there, signor! You are in danger there.
You can be seen a mile off.
PHILARIO [*hastening down*] Whats your news?
I am sent by Lucius to find out how fares
Our right wing led by General Iachimo.
CAPTAIN. He is outgeneralled. There's no right wing
now.
Broken and routed, utterly defeated,
Our eagles taken and the few survivors
In full flight like myself. And you?
PHILARIO.   My news
Is even worse. Lucius, I fear, is taken.
Our centre could not stand the rain of arrows.
CAPTAIN. Someone has disciplined these savage
archers.
They shoot together and advance in step:
Their horsemen trot in order to the charge
And then let loose th' entire mass full speed.
No single cavaliers but thirty score
As from a catapult four hundred tons
Of horse and man in one enormous shock
Hurled on our shaken legions. Then their chariots
With every axle furnished with a scythe
Do bloody work. They made us skip, I promise you.
    Their slingers! [*He points to his helmet*]
—Well: see their work! Two inches further down

68

I had been blind or dead. The crackbrained Welshmen
Raged like incarnate devils.
  PHILARIO.   Yes: they thought
We were the Britons. So our prisoners tell us.
  CAPTAIN. Where did these bumpkins get their disci-
   pline?
  PHILARIO. Ay: thats the marvel. Where?
  CAPTAIN.   Our victors say
Cassivelaunus is alive again.
But thats impossible.
  PHILARIO.   Not so impossible
As that this witless savage Cymbeline,
Whose brains were ever in his consort's head,
Could thus defeat Roman-trained infantry.
  CAPTAIN. 'Tis my belief that old Belarius,
Banned as a traitor, must have been recalled.
That fellow knew his job. These fat civilians
When we're at peace, rob us of our rewards
By falsely charging us with this or that;
But when the trumpet sounds theyre on their knees to
  us.
  PHILARIO. Well, Captain, I must hasten back to
   Lucius
To blast his hopes of any help from you.
Where, think you, is Iachimo?
  CAPTAIN.   I know not.
And yet I think he cannot be far off.
  PHILARIO. He lives then?
  CAPTAIN.   Perhaps. When all was lost he fought
Like any legionary, sword in hand.
His last reported word was "Save yourselves:
Bid all make for the rocks; for there
Their horsemen cannot come." I took his counsel;
And here I am.
  PHILARIO. You were best come with me.
Failing Iachimo, Lucius will require
Your tale at first hand.
  CAPTAIN.   Good. But we shall get
No laurel crowns for what we've done today.
*Exeunt together. Enter Posthumus dressed like a
peasant, but wearing a Roman sword and a soldier's iron
cap. He has in his hand a bloodstained handkerchief.*

POSTHUMUS. Yea, bloody cloth, I'll keep thee; for I
     wish'd
Thou shouldst be colour'd thus. You married ones,
If each of you should take this course, how many
Must murder wives much better than themselves
For wrying but a little? O Pisanio!
Every good servant does not all commands:
No bond, but to do just ones. Gods, if you
Should have ta'en vengeance on my faults, I ne'er
Had liv'd to put on this: so had you sav'd
The noble Imogen to repent, and struck
Me (wretch) more worth your vengeance. But, alack,
You snatch some hence for little faults: that's love,
To have them fall no more. You some permit
To second ills with ills, each elder worse,
And make them dread it, to the doers' thrift;
But Imogen is your own: do your best wills,
And make me blest to obey! I am brought hither
Among the Italian gentry, and to fight
Against my lady's kingdom: 'tis enough
That, Britain, I have kill'd thy mistress. Peace!
I'll give no wound to thee. I have disrobed me
Of my Italian weeds, and drest myself
As does a Briton peasant; so I've fought
Against the part I came with; so I'll die
For thee, O Imogen, even for whom my life
Is every breath a death; and thus unknown,
Pitied nor hated, to the face of peril
Myself I'll dedicate. Let me make men know
More valour in me than my habits shew.
Gods, put the strength o' the Leonati in me!
To shame the guise o' the world, I'll begin
The fashion, less without and more within.
He is hurrying off when he is confronted with Iachimo,
battle stained, hurrying in the opposite direction. Seeing
a British enemy he draws his sword.
     POSTHUMUS. Iachimo! Peace, man: 'tis I, Posthumus.
     IACHIMO. Peace if you will. The battle's lost and
          won.
Pass on.
     POSTHUMUS. Do you not know me?
     IACHIMO.   No.

POSTHUMUS.   Look closer.
You have some reason to remember me
And I to hate you. Yet we're sworn friends.
   IACHIMO. By all the gods, Leonatus!
   POSTHUMUS.   At your service,
Seducer of my wife.
   IACHIMO.   No more of that.
Your wife, Posthumus, is a noble creature.
I'll set your mind at rest upon that score.
   POSTHUMUS. At rest! Can you then raise her from the
      grave?
Where she lies dead to expiate our crime?
   IACHIMO. Dead! How? Why? When? And expiate!
      What mean you?
   POSTHUMUS. This only: I have had her murdered, I.
And at my best am worser than her worst.
   IACHIMO. We are damned for this. [On guard] Let's
cut each other's throats.
   POSTHUMUS [drawing] Ay, let us.
   They fight furiously. Enter Cymbeline, Belarius,
Guiderius, Arviragus, Pisanio, with Lucius and Imogen
as Fidele: both of them prisoners guarded by British
soldiers.
   BELARIUS [taking command instinctively] Part them
there. Make fast the Roman.
   Guiderius pounces on Iachimo and disarms him. Ar-
viragus pulls Posthumus back.
   ARVIRAGUS. In the King's presence sheath your
sword, you lout.
   IACHIMO. In the King's presence I must yield per-
force;
But as a person of some quality
By rank a gentleman, I claim to be
Your royal highness's prisoner, not this lad's.
   LUCIUS. His claim is valid, sir. His blood is princely.
   POSTHUMUS. 'Tis so: he's noble.
   CYMBELINE.   What art thou?
   POSTHUMUS.   A murderer.
   IMOGEN. His voice! His voice! Oh, let me see his
face. [She rushes to Posthumus and puts her hand on
his face].
   POSTHUMUS. Shall's have a play with this? There lies

thy part [*he knocks her down with a blow of his fist*].
GUIDERIUS. Accursed churl: take that. [*He strikes
Posthumus and brings him down on one knee*].
ARVIRAGUS. You dog, how dare you [*threatening
him*].
POSTHUMUS. Soft, soft, young sirs. One at a time, an
't please you. [*He springs up and stands on the
defensive*].
PISANIO [*interposing*] Hands off my master! He is kin
to the king.
POSTHUMUS [*to Cymbeline*] Call off your bulldogs, sir.
Why all this coil
About a serving boy?
CYMBELINE.   My son-in-law!
PISANIO. Oh, gentlemen, your help. My Lord Post-
humus:
You ne'er killed Imogen till now. Help! help!
IMOGEN. Oh, let me die. I heard my husband's voice
Whom I thought dead; and in my ecstasy,
The wildest I shall ever feel again,
He met me with a blow.
POSTHUMUS.   Her voice. 'Tis Imogen.
Oh, dearest heart, thou livest. Oh, you gods,
What sacrifice can pay you for this joy?
IMOGEN. You dare pretend you love me.
POSTHUMUS.   Sweet, I dare
Anything, everything. Mountains of mortal guilt
That crushed me are now lifted from my breast.
I am in heaven that was but now in hell.
You may betray me twenty times again.
IMOGEN. Again! And pray, when have I e'er betrayed
you?
POSTHUMUS. I had the proofs. There stands your
paramour.
Shall's have him home? I care not, since thou liv'st.
IMOGEN. My paramour! [*To Iachimo*] Oh, as you
are a gentleman,
Give him the lie.
IACHIMO.   He knows no better, madam.
We made a wager, he and I, in Italy
That I should spend a night in your bedchamber.

IMOGEN [*to Posthumus*] You made this wager! And
I'm married to you!

POSTHUMUS. I did. He won it.

IMOGEN.   How? He never came
Within my bedchamber.

IACHIMO.   I spent a night there.
It was the most uncomfortable night
I ever passed.

IMOGEN.   You must be mad, signor.
Or else the most audacious of all liars
That ever swore away a woman's honor.

IACHIMO. I think, madam, you do forget that chest.

IMOGEN. I forget nothing. At your earnest suit
Your chest was safely houséd in my chamber;
But where were you?

IACHIMO. I? I was in the chest [*Hilarious sensation*].
And on one point I do confess a fault.
I stole your bracelet while you were asleep.

POSTHUMUS. And cheated me out of my diamond
ring!

IACHIMO. Both ring and bracelet had some magic in
them
That would not let me rest until I laid them
On Mercury's altar. He's the god of thieves.
But I can make amends. I'll pay for both
At your own price, and add one bracelet more
For the other arm.

POSTHUMUS.   With ten thousand ducats
Due to me for the wager you have lost.

IMOGEN. And this, you think, signors, makes good to
me
All you have done, you and my husband there!

IACHIMO. It remedies what can be remedied.
As for the rest, it cannot be undone.
We are a pitiable pair. For all that
You may go further and fare worse; for men
Will do such things to women.

IMOGEN.   You at least
Have grace to know yourself for what you are.
My husband thinks that all is settled now
And this a happy ending!

POSTHUMUS.   Well, my dearest,
What could I think? The fellow did describe
The mole upon your breast.
    IMOGEN.   And thereupon
You bade your servant kill me.
    POSTHUMUS.   It seemed natural.
    IMOGEN. Strike me again; but do not say such things.
    GUIDERIUS. An if you do, by Thor's great hammer
        stroke
I'll kill you, were you fifty sons-in-law.
    BELARIUS. Peace, boy: we're in the presence of the
        king.
    IMOGEN. Oh, Cadwal, Cadwal, you and Polydore,
My newfound brothers, are my truest friends.
Would either of you, were I ten times faithless,
Have sent a slave to kill me?
    GUIDERIUS [shuddering]   All the world
Should die first.
    ARVIRAGUS.   Whiles we live, Fidele,
Nothing shall harm you.
    POSTHUMUS.   Child: hear me out.
Have I not told you that my guilty conscience
Had almost driven me mad when heaven opened
And you appeared? But prithee, dearest wife,
How did you come to think that I was dead?
    IMOGEN. I cannot speak of it: it is too dreadful.
I saw a headless man drest in your clothes.
    GUIDERIUS. Pshaw! That was Cloten: son, he said,
        to the king.
I cut his head off.
    CYMBELINE.   Marry, the gods forefend!
I would not thy good deeds should from my lips
Pluck a hard sentence: prithee, valiant youth,
Deny 't again.
    GUIDERIUS. I have spoke it, and I did it.
    CYMBELINE. He was a prince.
    GUIDERIUS. A most incivil one: the wrongs he did me
Were nothing prince-like; for he did provoke me
With language that would make me spurn the sea
If it could so roar to me. I cut off 's head;
And am right glad he is not standing here
To tell this tale of mine.

CYMBELINE. I am sorry for thee:
By thine own tongue thou art condemn'd, and must
Endure our law: thou 'rt dead. Bind the offender,
And take him from our presence.
BELARIUS. Stay, sir king:
This man is better than the man he slew,
As well descended as thyself, and hath
More of thee merited than a band of Clotens
Had ever scar for. [To the Guard] Let his arms alone,
They were not born for bondage.
CYMBELINE. Why, old soldier,
Wilt thou undo the worth thou art unpaid for,
By tasting of our wrath? How of descent
As good as we?
GUIDERIUS. In that he spake too far.
CYMBELINE. And thou shalt die for 't.
BELARIUS. We will die all three:
But I will prove that two on 's are as good
As I have given out him.
CYMBELINE. Take him away.
The whole world shall not save him.
BELARIUS. Not so hot.
First pay me for the nursing of thy sons;
And let it be confiscate all so soon
As I've received it.
CYMBELINE. Nursing of my sons!
BELARIUS. I am too blunt and saucy: here's my knee.
Ere I arise I will prefer my sons.
Then spare not the old father. Mighty sir:
These two young gentlemen that call me father,
And think they are my sons, are none of mine.
They are the issue of your loins, my liege,
And blood of your begetting.
CYMBELINE. How? my issue?
BELARIUS. So sure as you your father's. These your
    princes
(For such and so they are) these twenty years
Have I train'd up: those arts they have as I
Could put into them; my breeding was, sir, as
Your highness knows. Come hither, boys, and pay
Your loves and duties to your royal sire.

GUIDERIUS. We three are fullgrown men and perfect
strangers.
Can I change fathers as I'd change my shirt?
CYMBELINE.   Unnatural whelp! What doth thy
brother say?
ARVIRAGUS. I, royal sir? Well, we have reached an
age
When fathers' helps are felt as hindrances.
I am tired of being preached at.
CYMBELINE [to Belarius]   So, sir, this
Is how you have bred my puppies.
GUIDERIUS.   He has bred us
To tell the truth and face it.
BELARIUS.   Royal sir:
I know not what to say: not you nor I
Can tell our children's minds. But pardon him.
If he be overbold the fault is mine.
GUIDERIUS. The fault, if fault there be, is in my
Maker.
I am of no man's making. I am I:
Take me or leave me.
IACHIMO [to Lucius] Mark well, Lucius, mark.
There spake the future king of this rude island.
GUIDERIUS. With you, Sir Thief, to tutor me? No, no:
This kingly business has no charm for me.
When I lived in a cave methought a palace
Must be a glorious place, peopled with men
Renowned as councillors, mighty as soldiers,
As saints a pattern of holy living,
And all at my command were I a prince.
This was my dream. I am awake today.
I am to be, forsooth, another Cloten,
Plagued by the chatter of his train of flatterers,
Compelled to worship priest invented gods,
Not free to wed the woman of my choice,
Being stopped at every turn by some old fool
Crying "You must not," or, still worse, "You must."
Oh no, sir: give me back the dear old cave
And my unflattering four footed friends.
I abdicate, and pass the throne to Polydore.
ARVIRAGUS. Do you, by heavens? Thank you for
nothing, brother.

CYMBELINE. I'm glad you're not ambitious. Seated monarchs
Do rarely love their heirs. Wisely, it seems.

ARVIRAGUS. Fear not, great sir: we two have never learnt
To wait for dead men's shoes, much less their crowns.

GUIDERIUS. Enough of this. Fidele: is it true
Thou art a woman, and this man thy husband?

IMOGEN. I am a woman, and this man my husband.
He would have slain me.

POSTHUMUS. Do not harp on that.

CYMBELINE. God's patience, man, take your wife home to bed.
You're man and wife: nothing can alter that.
Are there more plots to unravel? Each one here,
It seems, is someone else. [To Imogen] Go change your dress
For one becoming to your sex and rank.
Have you no shame?

IMOGEN. None.

CYMBELINE. How? None!

IMOGEN. All is lost.
Shame, husband, happiness, and faith in Man.
He is not even sorry.

POSTHUMUS. I'm too happy.

IACHIMO. Lady: a word. When you arrived just now
I, as you saw, was hot on killing him.
Let him bear witness that I drew on him
To avenge your death.

IMOGEN. Oh, do not make me laugh.
Laughter dissolves too many just resentments,
Pardons too many sins.

IACHIMO. And saves the world
A many thousand murders. Let me plead for him.
He has his faults; but he must suffer yours.
You are, I swear, a very worthy lady;
But still, not quite an angel.

IMOGEN. No, not quite,
Nor yet a worm. Subtle Italian villain!
I would that chest had smothered you.

IACHIMO. Dear lady
It very nearly did.

IMOGEN.　　　I will not laugh.
I must go home and make the best of it
As other women must.
　　POSTHUMUS.　　　That's all I ask. [*He clasps her.*]
　　BELARIUS. The fingers of the powers above do tune
The harmony of this peace.
　　LUCIUS.　　　　　　Peace be it then.
For by this gentleman's report and mine
I hope imperial Cæsar will reknit
His favour with the radiant Cymbeline,
Which shines here in the west.
　　CYMBELINE.　　　　　　Laud we the gods,
And let our crooked smokes climb to their nostrils
From our blest altars. Publish we this peace
To all our subjects. Set we forward: let
A Roman and a British ensign wave
Friendly together: so through Lud's town march,
And in the temple of great Jupiter
Our peace we'll ratify; seal it with feasts.
Set on there! Never was a war did cease,
Ere bloody hands were wash'd, with such a peace.

CURTAIN

HAMLET

As a Shakespeare critic Shaw was an exception in many respects but not in the fascination which Hamlet *held for him. During his life he wrote extensively about both the play and the way it should be played. He gave a short summary of his ideas in a postscript to the Oxford World's Classics' 1947 edition of* Back to Methuselah. *Shaw suggested that if Shakespeare had been asked to choose one of his plays for a World's Classics series he would have chosen* Hamlet.

. . . As a playwright I must not pass over my predecessor Shakespear. If he could be consulted as to the inclusion of one of his plays in the present series he would probably choose his Hamlet, because in writing it he definitely threw over his breadwinning trade of producing potboilers which he frankly called As You Like It, Much Ado About Nothing, and What You Will. After a few almost Ibsenish essays in As You Dont Like It, he took up an old play about the ghost of a murdered king who haunted his son crying for revenge, with comic relief provided by the son pretending to be that popular curiosity and laughingstock, a village idiot. Shakespear, transfiguring this into a tragedy on the ancient Athenian level, could not have been quite unconscious of the evolutionary stride he was taking. But he did not see his way clearly enough to save the tons of ink and paper and years of 'man's time' that have been wasted, and are still being wasted, on innumerable volumes of nonsense about the meaning of Hamlet, though it is now as clear as daylight. Hamlet as a prehistoric Dane is morally bound to kill his uncle, politically as rightful heir to the usurped throne, and filially as 'the son of a dear father murdered' and a mother seduced by an incestuous adulterer. He has no doubt as to his duty in the matter. If he can convince himself that the ghost who has told him all this is really his father's

spirit and not a lying devil tempting him to perdition,
then, he says, 'I know my course.'

But when fully convinced he finds to his bewilderment
that he cannot kill his uncle deliberately. In a sudden
flash of rage he can and does stab at him through the
arras, only to find that he has killed poor old Polonius by
mistake. In a later transport, when the unlucky uncle
poisons not only Hamlet's mother, but his own accomplice and Hamlet himself, Hamlet actually does at last
kill his enemy on the spur of the moment; but this is no
solution of his problem: it cuts the Gordian knot instead
of untying it, and makes the egg stand on end only by
breaking it. In the soliloquy beginning 'Oh what a rogue
and peasant slave am I' Shakespear described this moral
bewilderment as a fact (he must have learnt it from his
own personal development); but he did not explain it,
though the explanation was staring him in the face as it
stares in mine. What happened to Hamlet was what had
happened fifteen hundred years before to Jesus. Born
into the vindictive morality of Moses he has evolved into
the Christian perception of the futility and wickedness of
revenge and punishment, founded on the simple fact that
two blacks do not make a white. But he is not philosopher enough to comprehend this as well as apprehend it.
When he finds he cannot kill in cold blood he can only
ask 'Am I a coward?' When he cannot nerve himself to
recover his throne he can account for it only by saying 'I
lack ambition.' Had Shakespear plumbed his play to the
bottom he would hardly have allowed Hamlet to send
Rosencrantz and Guildenstern to their death by a forged
death warrant without a moment's scruple.

Shaw refers to the matter of madness in Hamlet *in his
preface to* Major Barbara.

. . . Formerly, the contrast between madness and sanity was deemed comic: Hogarth shews us how fashionable
people went in parties to Bedlam to laugh at the lunatics.
I myself have had a village idiot exhibited to me as something irresistibly funny. On the stage the madman was
once a regular comic figure: that was how Hamlet got his

opportunity before Shakespear touched him. The originality of Shakespear's version lay in his taking the lunatic
sympathetically and seriously, and thereby making an advance towards the eastern consciousness of the fact that
lunacy may be inspiration in disguise, since a man who
has more brains than his fellows necessarily appears as
mad to them as one who has less. But Shakespear did not
do for Pistol and Parolles what he did for Hamlet. The
particular sort of madman they represented, the romantic
make-believer, lay outside the pale of sympathy in literature: he was pitilessly despised and ridiculed here as he
was in the east under the name of Alnaschar, and was
doomed to be, centuries later, under the name of Simon
Tappertit. When Cervantes relented over Don Quixote,
and Dickens relented over Pickwick, they did not become
impartial: they simply changed sides, and became friends
and apologists where they had formerly been mockers.

*Many managers in Shaw's day omitted Fortinbras in their
productions of* Hamlet, *a practice which Shaw deplored.
Shaw held up Fortinbras as the perfect hero type in a
review of Henry Arthur Jones's* Michael and His Lost
Angel *in* The Saturday Review *on January 18, 1896.*

. . . In Hamlet one cannot approve unreservedly of the
views of Fortinbras; but, generations of foolish actor-
managers to the contrary notwithstanding, what true
Shakespearean ever thinks of Hamlet without seeing Fortinbras, in his winged helmet, swoop down at the end,
and take, by the divine right of a born "captain of his
soul," the crown that slips through the dead fingers of the
philosopher who went, at the bidding of his father's
ghost, in search of a revenge which he did not feel and a
throne which he did not want? Fortinbras can, of course,
never be anything more than an Adelphi hero, because
his bellicose instincts and imperial ambitions are comfortably vulgar; but both the Adelphi hero and the tragic
hero have fundamentally the same heroic qualification—
fearless pursuit of their own ends and championship of
their own faiths *contra mundum.*

Mr. Alfred Cruikshank wrote a monograph, "The True Character of Hamlet," which he sent to Shaw. In a letter of reply on October 4, 1918, Shaw amplified his own ideas. (The letter is reprinted in Archibald Henderson's Bernard Shaw: Playboy and Prophet.)

I am much obliged to you for sending me your book about the character of Hamlet. You are entirely right as to the proper way to play Hamlet: the most successful Hamlet of my day was Barry Sullivan, an actor of superb physical vigour, who excelled in the impersonation of proud, noble and violent characters. All the sentimental Hamlets have been bores. Forbes Robertson's gallant, alert Hamlet, thoughtful but not in the least sentimental, is *the* Hamlet of to-day. I have always myself contended for your view, and used the same illustrations, the ghost scene, the killing of Polonius, above all, perhaps, the disposal of poor Rosencrantz and Guildenstern as if they were mice in the king's pantry rather than men.

But you must not push your view to the complete exclusion of all the others, muddle-headed as most of them are. Hamlet was not a single consistent character: like most men he was half a dozen characters rolled into one. There can be no question, in the face of the text and the action of the play, that Hamlet was greatly puzzled by the fact that he wanted neither the crown nor his revenge badly enough to kill the king, or even to shove him out of his way. He can kill him in a moment of excitement (his killing of Polonius is in intention a killing of the king); but when he is in his normal state, he simply reflects and criticizes. He is amazed at his own futility from the point of view of Fortinbras, the man of action. He watches Fortinbras' men "going to their graves like beds" about a scrap of land "that is not tomb enough and continent to hide the slain"; and yet, though he has ten times as much cause for action, he finds somehow that a crown, for which his uncle committed fratricide, does not interest him as much as the players, and that revenge is not worth the mess the king's blood would make on the floor. He asks himself whether he is a coward, pigeon livered and lacking gall to make oppression bitter.

All this is quite natural. Men who are superior to vul-

gar cupidities and ambitions, and to vulgar rancours,
always do seem weak and cowardly to men who act on
them. Sometimes they seem so to themselves. There is
no contradiction or inconsistency in Hamlet to anyone
who understands this.

Your interpretation of "we'll teach you to drink deep
ere you depart" is a sporting one; but it is irreconcilable
with Hamlet's little temperance lecture on the battlements when he is waiting for the ghost. He loathes the
king's drunkenness as he loathes his general sensuality: it
is part of his fastidious refinement. He hates women
painting themselves; hates his mother for being as sensual
as the king; and hates Ophelia for having reduced him to
concupiscence. All that is quite in character.

Salvini's Hamlet was a very fine performance; but
somehow he did not create a Hamlet. I have never seen
a more wonderful piece of acting than the agony of
shame with which he saturated the scene with the queen.
The art of the performance was beyond all praise; I
learnt a great deal technically from it. But there was a
certain physical stoutness and mature self-possession
about him that one could not associate with Hamlet. He
was a middle aged man of the world, not a young and
perplexed poet-philosopher. To return for a moment to
Barry Sullivan. He played the first scene in the traditional "inky cloak" manner; and it was the only ineffective and heavy part of his performance, which began
really with "the Nemean lion's nerve." This confirms
your view exactly. But you are too kind to Shakespear in
trying to explain away the inky cloak scene. Shakespear,
like Dickens, like Cervantes, like most geniuses of their
type, made the acquaintance of their characters as they
went along. Dick Swiveller on his first appearance is a
quite loathsome stage villain from whom the heroine is
to be rescued at the last moment. Pickwick and Don
Quixote begin as mere contemptible butts, to be made
ridiculous and beaten and discomfited at every turn. Falstaff is a mere supernumerary butt for the prince and for
his philosopher friend Poins (who was to have been the
Jaques or Hamlet of the play). But these puppets suddenly spring to life after the first two or three pulls of
the strings and become leading and very alive and real

characters. I see no reason to doubt that the same thing happened during the writing of Hamlet. Shakespear began with nothing more definite in his mind than the old zany Hamlet, crazy with grief for the death of his father and horror at the incest of his mother. But when Shakespear got him going, he ran right away with his creator. This does not happen to uninspired writers, who plan everything laboriously beforehand. If it did, they, taking themselves and their art very portentously, would carefully revise their opening scenes to suit the subsequent development. Not so your Shakespear. He leaves the thing as it grew. I do not defend this carelessness; but there are innumerable instances of it in dramatic literature. I have been guilty of it myself.

In a letter of July 27, 1897, to Ellen Terry Shaw hinted at what he would do with a Hamlet *production as opposed to what Henry Irving had done and what he assumed Forbes Robertson would do in his forthcoming production.*

. . . I am certain I could make Hamlet a success by having it played as Shakespear meant it. H. I. makes it a sentimental affair of his own; and this generation has consequently never seen the real thing. However, I am afraid F. R. will do the usual dreary business in the old way, and play the bass clarinet for four hours on end, with disastrous results. Lord! how I could make that play jump along at the Lyceum if I were manager. I'd make short work of that everlasting "room in the castle." You should have the most beautiful old English garden to go mad in, with the flowers to pluck fresh from the bushes, and a trout stream of the streamiest and ripplingest to drown yourself in. I'd make such a scene of "How all occasions do inform against me!"—Hamlet in his traveling furs on a heath like a polar desert, and Fortinbras and his men "going to their graves like beds"—as should never be forgotten. I'd make lightning and thunder (comedy and tragedy) of the second and third acts: the people should say they had never seen such a play before. I'd—but no matter.

*Contrary to Shaw's expectations the Forbes Robertson
production turned out to be much to his liking. Shaw's
review appeared on October 2, 1897, in* The Saturday
Review.

THE FORBES ROBERTSON Hamlet at the Lyceum is, very
unexpectedly at that address, really not at all unlike
Shakespear's play of the same time. I am quite certain I
saw Reynaldo in it for a moment; and possibly I may
have seen Voltimand and Cornelius; but just as the time
for their scene arrived, my eye fell on the word "Fortinbras" in the program, which so amazed me that I hardly
know what I saw for the next ten minutes. Ophelia, instead of being a strenuously earnest and self-possessed
young lady giving a concert and recitation for all she was
worth, was mad—actually mad. The story of the play was
perfectly intelligible, and quite took the attention of the
audience off the principal actor at moments. What is the
Lyceum coming to? Is it for this that Sir Henry Irving
has invented a whole series of original romantic dramas,
and given the credit of them without a murmur to the
immortal bard whose profundity (as exemplified in the
remark that good and evil are mingled in our natures) he
has just been pointing out to the inhabitants of Cardiff,
and whose works have been no more to him than the
word-quarry from which he has hewn and blasted the
lines and titles of masterpieces which are really all his
own? And now, when he has created by these means a
reputation for Shakespear, he no sooner turns his back
for a moment on London than Mr. Forbes Robertson
competes with him on the boards of his own theatre by
actually playing off against him the authentic Swan of
Avon. Now if the result had been the utter exposure and
collapse of that impostor, poetic justice must have proclaimed that it served Mr. Forbes Robertson right. But
alas! the wily William, by literary tricks which our simple
Sir Henry has never quite understood, has played into
Mr. Forbes Robertson's hands so artfully that the scheme
is a prodigious success. The effect of this success, coming
after that of Mr. Alexander's experiment with a Shakespearean version of As You Like It, makes it almost prob-
able that we shall presently find managers vying with

each other in offering the public as much of the original
Shakespearean stuff as possible, instead of, as heretofore,
doing their utmost to reassure us that everything that the
most modern resources can do to relieve the irreducible
minimum of tedium inseparable from even the most
heavily cut acting version will be lavished on their revivals. It is true that Mr. Beerbohm Tree still holds to
the old scepticism, and calmly proposes to insult us by
offering us Garrick's puerile and horribly caddish knock-
about farce of Katharine and Petruchio for Shakespear's
Taming of the Shrew; but Mr. Tree, like all romantic
actors, is incorrigible on the subject of Shakespear.

Mr. Forbes Robertson is essentially a classical actor, the
only one, with the exception of Mr. Alexander, now established in London management. What I mean by classical
is that he can present a dramatic hero as a man whose
passions are those which have produced the philosophy,
the poetry, the art, and the statecraft of the world, and
not merely those which have produced its weddings, coro-
ners' inquests, and executions. And that is just the sort
of actor that Hamlet requires. A Hamlet who only understands his love for Ophelia, his grief for his father, his
vindictive hatred of his uncle, his fear of ghosts, his impulse to snub Rosencrantz and Guildenstern, and the
sportsman's excitement with which he lays the "mouse-
trap" for Claudius, can, with sufficient force or virtuosity
of execution, get a great reputation in the part, even
though the very intensity of his obsession by these senti-
ments (which are common not only to all men but to
many animals) shews that the characteristic side of Hamlet, the side that differentiates him from Fortinbras, is
absolutely outside the actor's consciousness. Such a reputation is the actor's, not Hamlet's. Hamlet is not a man
in whom "common humanity" is raised by great vital
energy to a heroic pitch, like Coriolanus or Othello. On
the contrary, he is a man in whom the common personal
passions are so superseded by wider and rarer interests,
and so discouraged by a degree of critical self-consciousness which makes the practical efficiency of the instinctive
man on the lower plane impossible to him, that he finds
the duties dictated by conventional revenge and ambition as disagreeable a burden as commerce is to a poet.

Even his instinctive sexual impulses offend his intellect; so that when he meets the woman who excites them he invites her to join him in a bitter and scornful criticism of their joint absurdity, demanding "What should such fellows as I do crawling between heaven and earth?" "Why wouldst thou be a breeder of sinners?" and so forth, all of which is so completely beyond the poor girl that she naturally thinks him mad. And, indeed, there is a sense in which Hamlet is insane; for he trips over the mistake which lies on the threshold of intellectual self-consciousness: that of bringing life to utilitarian or Hedonistic tests, thus treating it as a means instead of an end. Because Polonius is "a foolish prating knave," because Rosencrantz and Guildenstern are snobs, he kills them as remorselessly as he might kill a flea, shewing that he has no real belief in the superstitious reason which he gives for not killing himself, and in fact anticipating exactly the whole course of the intellectual history of Western Europe until Schopenhauer found the clue that Shakespear missed. But to call Hamlet mad because he did not anticipate Schopenhauer is like calling Marcellus mad because he did not refer the Ghost to the Psychical Society. It is in fact not possible for any actor to represent Hamlet as mad. He may (and generally does) combine some notion of his own of a man who is the creature of affectionate sentiment with the figure drawn by the lines of Shakespear; but the result is not a madman, but simply one of those monsters produced by the imaginary combination of two normal species, such as sphinxes, mermaids, or centaurs. And this is the invariable resource of the instinctive, imaginative, romantic actor. You will see him weeping bucketsful of tears over Ophelia, and treating the players, the gravedigger, Horatio, Rosencrantz, and Guildenstern as if they were mutes at his own funeral. But go and watch Mr. Forbes Robertson's Hamlet seizing delightedly on every opportunity for a bit of philosophic discussion or artistic recreation to escape from the "cursed spite" of revenge and love and other common troubles; see how he brightens up when the players come; how he tries to talk philosophy with Rosencrantz and Guildenstern the moment they come into the room; how he stops on his country walk with Horatio to lean over

the churchyard wall and draw out the gravedigger whom
he sees singing at his trade; how even his fits of excitement find expression in declaiming scraps of poetry; how
the shock of Ophelia's death relieves itself in the fiercest
intellectual contempt for Laertes's ranting, whilst an
hour afterwards, when Laertes stabs him, he bears no
malice for that at all, but embraces him gallantly and
comradely; and he dies as we forgive everything to
Charles II for dying, and makes "the rest is silence" a
touchingly humorous apology for not being able to finish
his business. See all that; and you have seen a true classical Hamlet. Nothing half so charming has been seen by
this generation. It will bear seeing again and again.

And please observe that this is not a cold Hamlet. He
is none of your logicians who reason their way through
the world because they cannot feel their way through it:
his intellect is the organ of his passion: his eternal self-
criticism is as alive and thrilling as it can possibly be. The
great soliloquy—no: I do NOT mean "To be or not to
be": I mean the dramatic one, "O what a rogue and peasant slave am I!"—is as passionate in its scorn of brute
passion as the most bull-necked affirmation or sentimental
dilution of it could be. It comes out so without violence:
Mr. Forbes Robertson takes the part quite easily and
spontaneously. There is none of that strange Lyceum intensity which comes from the perpetual struggle between
Sir Henry Irving and Shakespear. The lines help Mr.
Forbes Robertson instead of getting in his way at every
turn, because he wants to play Hamlet, and not to slip
into his inky cloak a changeling of quite another race.
We may miss the craft, the skill double-distilled by constant peril, the subtlety, the dark rays of heat generated
by intense friction, the relentless parental tenacity and
cunning with which Sir Henry nurses his own pet creations on Shakespearean food like a fox rearing its litter
in the den of a lioness; but we get light, freedom, naturalness, credibility, and Shakespear. It is wonderful how
easily everything comes right when you have the right
man with the right mind for it—how the story tells itself,
how the characters come to life, how even the failures in
the cast cannot confuse you, though they may disappoint
you. And Mr. Forbes Robertson has certainly not escaped

such failures, even in his own family. I strongly urge him
to take a hint from Claudius and make a real ghost of
Mr. Ian Robertson at once; for there is no sort of use in
going through that scene night after night with a Ghost
so solidly, comfortably, and dogmatically alive as his
brother. The voice is not a bad voice; but it is the voice
of a man who does not believe in ghosts. Moreover, it is
a hungry voice, not that of one who is past eating. There
is an indescribable little complacent drop at the end of
every line which no sooner calls up the image of purgatory by its words than by its smug elocution it convinces
us that this particular penitent is cosily warming his shins
and toasting his muffin at the flames instead of expiating
his bad acting in the midst of them. His aspect and bearing are worse than his recitations. He beckons Hamlet
away like a beadle summoning a timid candidate for the
post of junior footman to the presence of the Lord Mayor.
If I were Mr. Forbes Robertson I would not stand that
from my brother: I would cleave the general ear with
horrid speech at him first. It is a pity; for the Ghost's
part is one of the wonders of the play. And yet, until Mr.
Courtenay Thorpe divined it the other day, nobody
seems to have had a glimpse of the reason why Shakespear
would not trust anyone else with it, and played it himself. The weird music of that long speech which should
be the spectral wail of a soul's bitter wrong crying from
one world to another in the extremity of its torment, is
invariably handed over to the most squaretoed member
of the company, who makes it sound, not like Rossetti's
Sister Helen, or even, to suggest a possible heavy treatment, like Mozart's statue-ghost, but like Chambers's In-
formation for the People.

Still, I can understand Mr. Ian Robertson, by sheer
force of a certain quality of sententiousness in him, over-
bearing the management into casting him for the Ghost.
What I cannot understand is why Miss Granville was cast
for the Queen. It is like setting a fashionable modern
mandolinist to play Haydn's sonatas. She does her best
under the circumstances; but she would have been more
fortunate had she been in a position to refuse the part.

On the other hand, several of the impersonations are
conspicuously successful. Mrs. Patrick Campbell's Ophe-

lia is a surprise. The part is one which has hitherto
seemed incapable of progress. From generation to generation actresses have, in the mad scene, exhausted their
musical skill, their ingenuity in devising fantasies in the
language of flowers, and their intensest powers of portray-
ing anxiously earnest sanity. Mrs. Patrick Campbell, with
that complacent audacity of hers which is so exasperating
when she is doing the wrong thing, this time does the
right thing by making Ophelia really mad. The resent-
ment of the audience at this outrage is hardly to be described. They long for the strenuous mental grasp and
attentive coherence of Miss Lily Hanbury's conception of
maiden lunacy; and this wandering, silly, vague Ophelia,
who no sooner catches an emotional impulse than it
drifts away from her again, emptying her voice of its tone
in a way that makes one shiver, makes them horribly
uncomfortable. But the effect on the play is conclusive.
The shrinking discomfort of the King and Queen, the
ranking grief of Laertes, are created by it at once; and
the scene, instead of being a pretty interlude coming in
just when a little relief from the inky cloak is welcome,
touches us with a chill of the blood that gives it its right
tragic power and dramatic significance. Playgoers naturally murmur when something that has always been pretty
becomes painful; but the pain is good for them, good for
the theatre, and good for the play. I doubt whether Mrs.
Patrick Campbell fully appreciates the dramatic value of
her quite simple and original sketch—it is only a sketch
—of the part; but in spite of the occasional triviality of
its execution and the petulance with which it has been
received, it seems to me to settle finally in her favor the
question of her right to the very important place which
Mr. Forbes Robertson has assigned to her in his enter-
prises.

I did not see Mr. Bernard Gould play Laertes: he was
indisposed when I returned to town and hastened to the
Lyceum; but he was replaced very creditably by Mr.
Frank Dyall. Mr. Martin Harvey is the best Osric I have
seen: he plays Osric from Osric's own point of view,
which is, that Osric is a gallant and distinguished courtier, and not, as usual, from Hamlet's, which is that Osric
is "a waterfly." Mr. Harrison Hunter hits off the modest,

honest Horatio capitally; and Mr. Willes is so good a
Gravedigger that I venture to suggest to him that he
should carry his work a little further, and not virtually
cease to concern himself with the play when he has
spoken his last line and handed Hamlet the skull. Mr.
Cooper Cliffe is not exactly a subtle Claudius; but he
looks as if he had stepped out of a picture by Madox
Brown, and plays straightforwardly on his very successful
appearance. Mr. Barnes makes Polonius robust and elderly instead of aged and garrulous. He is good in the
scenes where Polonius appears as a man of character and
experience; but the senile exhibitions of courtierly tact
do not match these, and so seem forced and farcical.

Mr. Forbes Robertson's own performance has a continuous charm, interest, and variety which are the result
not only of his well-known grace and accomplishment as
an actor, but of a genuine delight—the rarest thing on
our stage—in Shakespear's art, and a natural familiarity
with the plane of his imagination. He does not superstitiously worship William: he enjoys him and understands his methods of expression. Instead of cutting
every line that can possibly be spared, he retains every
gem, in his own part or anyone else's, that he can make
time for in a spiritedly brisk performance lasting three
hours and a half with very short intervals. He does not
utter half a line; then stop to act; then go on with another half line; and then stop to act again, with the clock
running away with Shakespear's chances all the time. He
plays as Shakespear should be played, on the line and to
the line, with the utterance and acting simultaneous, inseparable and in fact identical. Not for a moment is he
solemnly conscious of Shakespear's reputation or of Hamlet's momentousness in literary history: on the contrary,
he delivers us from all these boredoms instead of heaping
them on us. We forgive him the platitudes, so engagingly
are they delivered. His novel and astonishingly effective
and touching treatment of the final scene is an inspiration, from the fencing match onward. If only Fortinbras
could also be inspired with sufficient force and brilliancy
to rise to the warlike splendor of his helmet, and make
straight for that throne like a man who intended to keep
it against all comers, he would leave nothing to be de-

sired. How many generations of Hamlets, all thirsting to outshine their competitors in effect and originality, have regarded Fortinbras, and the clue he gives to this kingly death for Hamlet, as a wildly unpresentable blunder of the poor foolish old Swan, than whom they all knew so much better! How sweetly they have died in that faith to slow music, like Little Nell in The Old Curiosity Shop! And now how completely Mr. Forbes Robertson has bowled them all out by being clever enough to be simple.

By the way, talking of slow music, the sooner Mr. Hamilton Clark's romantic Irving music is stopped, the better. Its effect in this Shakespearean version of the play is absurd. The four Offenbachian young women in tights should also be abolished, and the part of the player-queen given to a man. The courtiers should be taught how flatteringly courtiers listen when a king shews off his wisdom in wise speeches to his nephew. And that nice wooden beach on which the ghost walks would be the better for a seaweedy looking cloth on it, with a handful of shrimps and a pennorth of silver sand.

Shaw went back to see the Forbes Robertson presentation after it had been running for several weeks. He expressed his disappointment at what had happened to it in The Saturday Review *of December 18, 1897.*

PUBLIC FEELING has been much harrowed this week by the accounts from America of the 144 hours' bicycle race; but what are the horrors of such an exhibition compared to those of the hundred-nights run of Hamlet! On Monday last I went, in my private capacity, to witness the last lap but five of the Lyceum trial of endurance. The performers had passed through the stage of acute mania, and were for the most part sleep-walking in a sort of dazed blank-verse dream. Mr. Barnes raved of some New England maiden named Affection Poo; the subtle distinctions made by Mrs. Patrick Campbell between madness and sanity had blurred off into a placid idiocy turned to favor and to prettiness: Mr. Forbes Robertson, his lightness of heart all gone, wandered into another play at the words

"Sleep? No more!" which he delivered as, "Sleep no more." Fortunately, before he could add "Macbeth does murder sleep," he relapsed into Hamlet and saved the situation. And yet some of the company seemed all the better for their unnatural exercise. The King was in uproarious spirits; and the Ghost, always comfortable, was now positively pampered, his indifference to the inconveniences of purgatory having developed into a bean-fed enjoyment of them. Fortinbras, as I judged, had sought consolation in religion: he was anxious concerning Hamlet's eternal welfare; but his general health seemed excellent. As Mr. Gould did not play on the occasion of my first visit, I could not compare him with his former self; but his condition was sufficiently grave. His attitude was that of a castaway mariner who has no longer hope enough to scan the horizon for a sail; yet even in this extremity his unconquerable generosity of temperament had not deserted him. When his cue came, he would jump up and lend a hand with all his old alacrity and resolution. Naturally the players of the shorter parts had suffered least: Rosencrantz and Guildenstern were only beginning to enjoy themselves; and Bernardo (or was it Marcellus?) was still eagerly working up his part to concert pitch. But there could be no mistake as to the general effect. Mr. Forbes Robertson's exhausting part had been growing longer and heavier on his hands; whilst the support of the others had been falling off; so that he was keeping up the charm of the representation almost single-handed just when the torturing fatigue and monotony of nightly repetition had made the task most difficult. To the public, no doubt, the justification of the effort is its success. There was no act which did not contain at least one scene finely and movingly played; indeed some of the troubled passages gained in verisimilitude by the tormented condition of the actor. But Hamlet is a very long play; and it only seems a short one when the high-mettled comedy with which it is interpenetrated from beginning to end leaps out with all the lightness and spring of its wonderful loftiness of temper. This was the secret of the delighted surprise with which the public, when the run began, found that Hamlet, far from being a funereally classical bore, was full of a celestial gaiety and fascination. It is this rare vein that gives out first when the exigencies of theatrical commerce force an actor to abuse it. A sentimental Hamlet can go on for two years, or ten for the matter of that, without much essential depreciation of the performance; but the actor who sounds Hamlet from the lowest note to the top of his compass very soon finds that compass contracting at the top. On Monday night the first act, the third act, and the fifth act from the entrance of Laertes onward, had lost little more than they had gained as far as Mr. Forbes Robertson was concerned; but the second act, and the colloquy with the grave-digger, which were the triumphs of the representation in its fresher stages, were pathetically dulled, with the result that it could no longer be said that the length of the play was forgotten.

The worst of the application of the long-run system to heroic plays is that, instead of killing the actor, it drives him to limit himself to such effects as he can repeat to infinity without committing suicide. The opposite system, in its extreme form of the old stock company playing two or three different pieces every night, led to the same evasion in a more offensive form. The recent correspondence in the Morning Post on The Stage as a Profession, to which I have myself luminously contributed, has produced the usual fallacious eulogies of the old stock company as a school of acting. You can no more prevent contributors to public correspondences falling into this twenty-times-exploded error than from declaring that duelling was a school of good manners, that the lash suppressed garotting, or any other of the gratuitous ignorances of the amateur sociologist. The truth is, it is just as impossible for a human being to study and perform a new part of any magnitude every day as to play Hamlet for a hundred consecutive nights. Nevertheless, if an actor is required to do these things, he will find some way out of the difficulty without refusing. The stock actor solved the problem by adopting a "line": for example, if his "line" was old age, he acquired a trick of doddering and speaking in a cracked voice: if juvenility, he swaggered and effervesced. With these accomplishments, eked out by a few rules of thumb as to wigs and face-painting,

one deplorable step dance, and one still more deplorable
"combat," he "swallowed" every part given to him in a
couple of hours, and regurgitated it in the evening over
the footlights, always in the same manner, however finely
the dramatist might have individualized it. His infamous
incompetence at last swept him from the reputable theatres into the barns and booths; and it was then that he
became canonized, in the imagination of a posterity that
had never suffered from him, as the incarnation of the
one quality in which he was quite damnably deficient:
to wit, versatility. His great contribution to dramatic art
was the knack of earning a living for fifty years on the
stage without ever really acting, or either knowing or
caring for the difference between the Comedy of Errors
and Box and Cox.

A moment's consideration will shew that the results of
the long-run system at its worst are more bearable than
the horrors of the past. Also, that even in point of giving
the actor some chance of varying his work, the long-run
system is superior, since the modern actor may at all
events exhaust the possibilities of his part before it exhausts him, whereas the stock actor, having barely time to
apply his bag of tricks to his daily task, never varies his
treatment by a hair's breadth from one half century to
another. The best system, of course, lies between these
extremes.

When John Barrymore played Hamlet *in London he invited Shaw to see the performance. On February 22,
1925, Shaw wrote Barrymore a letter giving his reactions.
(The letter is reprinted in John Barrymore's* Confessions
of an Actor.)

My dear Mr. Barrymore:
I have to thank you for inviting me—and in such kind
terms too—to your first performance of Hamlet in London; and I am glad you had no reason to complain of
your reception, or, on the whole, of your press. Everyone
felt that the occasion was one of extraordinary interest;

and so far as your personality was concerned they were not disappointed.

I doubt, however, whether you have been able to follow the course of Shakespearean production in England during the last fifteen years or so enough to realize the audacity of your handling of the play. When I last saw it performed at Stratford-on-Avon, practically the entire play was given in three hours and three quarters, with one interval of ten minutes; and it made the time pass without the least tedium, though the cast was not in any way remarkable. On Thursday last you played five minutes longer with the play cut to ribbons, even to the breath-bereaving extremity of cutting out the recorders, which is rather like playing King John without little Arthur.

You saved, say, an hour and a half on Shakespear by the cutting, and filled it up with an interpolated drama of your own in dumb show. This was a pretty daring thing to do. In modern shop plays, without characters or anything but the commonest dialogue, the actor has to supply everything but the mere story, getting in the psychology between the lines, and presenting in his own person the fascinating hero whom the author has been unable to create. He is not substituting something of his own for something of the author's: he is filling up a void and doing the author's work for him. And the author ought to be extremely obliged to him.

But to try this method on Shakespear is to take on an appalling responsibility and put up a staggering pretension. Shakespear, with all his shortcomings, was a very great playwright; and the actor who undertakes to improve his plays undertakes thereby to excel to an extraordinary degree in two professions in both of which the highest success is extremely rare. Shakespear himself, though by no means a modest man, did not pretend to be able to play Hamlet as well as write it; he was content to do a recitation in the dark as the ghost. But you have ventured not only to act Hamlet, but to discard about a third of Shakespear's script and substitute stuff of your own, and that, too, without the help of dialogue. Instead of giving what is called a reading of Hamlet, you say, in effect, "I am not going to read Hamlet at all: I am going to leave it out. But see what I give you in exchange!"

Such an enterprise must justify itself by its effect on the public. You discard the recorders as hackneyed back chat, and the scene with the king after the death of Polonius, with such speeches as "How all occasions do inform against me!" as obsolete junk, and offer instead a demonstration of that very modern discovery called the Œdipus complex, thereby adding a really incestuous motive on Hamlet's part to the merely conventional incest of a marriage (now legal in England) with a deceased husband's brother. You change Hamlet and Ophelia into Romeo and Juliet. As producer, you allow Laertes and Ophelia to hug each other as lovers instead of lecturing and squabbling like hectoring big brother and little sister: another complex!

Now your success in this must depend on whether the play invented by Barrymore on the Shakespear foundation is as gripping as the Shakespear play, and whether your dumb show can hold an audience as a straightforward reading of Shakespear's rhetoric can. I await the decision with interest.

My own opinion is, of course, that of an author. I write plays that play for three hours and a half even with instantaneous changes and only one short interval. There is no time for silences or pauses: the actor must play on the line and not between the lines, and must do nine-tenths of his acting with his voice. Hamlet—Shakespear's Hamlet—can be done from end to end in four hours in that way; and it never flags nor bores. Done in any other way Shakespear is the worst of bores, because he has to be chopped into a mere cold stew. I prefer my way. I wish you would try it, and concentrate on acting rather than on authorship, at which, believe me, Shakespear can write your head off. But that may be vicarious professional jealousy on my part.

I did not dare to say all this to Mrs. Barrymore on the night. It was chilly enough for her without a coat in the stalls without any cold water from

Yours perhaps too candidly,

G. Bernard Shaw.

Henry Irving played the closet scene from Hamlet *in a
Shakespeare Festival and Shaw discussed the performance
in* The Saturday Review *of May 2, 1896.*

Mr. H. B. Irving is in the full flood of that Shakespearean enthusiasm which exalts the Bard so far above
common sense that any prosaic suiting of the action to
the word and the word to the action seems to be a deg-
radation of his genius to what Nicholas Rowe called
"a mere light of reason." Mr. Irving gave us the closet
scene from Hamlet. He entered, surcharged with Fate,
and instead of Hamlet's sharp, dry, "Now, mother: whats
the matter?" followed by his reply to her affected "Thou
hast thy father much offended," with the purposely blunt
"Mother: *you* have my father much offended," gave us
a most tragic edition of the conversation, with the yous
altered to thous, and an agitated slip or two to enhance
the effect. When he lifted the arras and found that he
had killed Polonius instead of the King, he betrayed
not the smallest surprise, but said, in a superior tone,
"Thou wretched, rash, intruding fool, farewell!" much
as if he were dismissing a deservedly and quite intention-
ally flogged schoolboy. He was resolved to make an
effect by seizing the Queen and throwing her down on
the floor; and the moment he selected was in the middle
of the following passage:

> At your age
> The heyday in the blood is tame: it's humble,
> And waits upon the judgment; and what judgment
> Would step from this to this?

The Queen was floored after the phrase "and waits
upon the judgment," shewing that at Mr. Irving's age
the heyday in the blood does not wait upon the judgment, but has its fling (literally) regardless of reason.
The only dramatic profit from this proceeding was the
point given to the Ghost's "But see! amazement on thy
mother sits." Nevertheless, the performance, nonsensical
as it was, was not ridiculous. Mr. Irving is not altogether
unsuccessful in his attempts to be tragic and to make
effects; and if he could only bring his tragedy and his
effects into some intelligent relation to the drama in

hand, he would find himself highly complimented in the Saturday Review. To be abstractly and irrelevantly tragic; to brandish a sword; to discourse in blank verse; to stagger and fall and hurl frail heroines away, is just as absurd in Hamlet, if done at the wrong moment, as it would be in Box and Cox. There are people so unfit for the stage that they could not do these things even at the right moment without making the audience laugh. That is not Mr. Irving's case. When he learns what to do and when to do it, he will not be at a loss as to how to do it. More than that it is impossible to grant him at present.

On May 15, 1897, in The Saturday Review *Shaw mentioned a production of* Hamlet *at the Olympic Theatre.*

I found Hamlet at the Olympic not a bad anodyne after the anguish of the Helmer household. Throwing off the critic, I indulged a silly boyish affection of mine for the play, which I know nearly by heart, thereby having a distinct advantage over Mr. Nutcombe Gould, whose acquaintance with the text is extremely precarious. His aptitude for transposing the adverb "so" in such a way as to spoil the verse, not to mention putting in full stops where there is no stop, and no stop where there is a full stop, is calamitous and appalling. For example:

For in that sleep of death what dreams may come [*full stop*].
When we have shuffled off this mortal coil [*full stop*].
Must give us pause.

And

When the grass grows the proverb is somewhat musty.

The effect of changing " 'tis" into "it is" was also fully exploited. Thus—

Whether it is nobler in the mind to suffer.

Even Mr. Foss, otherwise better than most Laerteses, said:

O Heaven, is it possible a young maid's wits
Should be as mortal as an old man's life?

Mr. Nutcombe Gould gave us all Hamlet's appearance, something of his feeling, and but little of his brains. He died in the full possession of his faculties, and had but just announced with unimpaired vigor that the rest was silence when an elderly gentleman rose in the middle of the front row of the stalls, and addressed the house vehemently on burning political questions of the day. Miss Lily Hanbury went through the familiar ceremony of playing Ophelia with success, thanks to a delicate ear for the music and a goodly person. Mr. Ben Greet was an exasperatingly placid Polonius, and Mr. Kendrick an unwontedly spirited Horatio. The only really noteworthy feature of the performance was, as aforesaid, the Ghost. Mr. Courtenay Thorpe's articulation deserted him towards the end; so that the last half-dozen lines of his long narrative and the whole of his part in the closet scene were a mere wail, in which no man could distinguish any words; but the effect was past spoiling by that time; and a very remarkable effect it was, well imagined and well executed.

HENRY IV, PART I

In The Saturday Review *of May 16, 1896, Shaw reviewed Beerbohm Tree's production of the play. Shaw begins his piece by pointing out how men believe in the professions of medicine, law, and such "as they believe in ghosts, because they want to believe in them." Shaw goes on to say that his own weakness is "neither medicine, nor law, nor tailoring, nor any of the respectable departments of bogusdom." It is, he says, the theatre. The mystery man who takes Shaw in "is not the doctor nor the lawyer, but the actor." Shaw adds that he had always assumed that acting was a "real profession." He then turns to the Tree production.*

. . . However, I am cured now. It is all a delusion: there is no profession, no art, no skill about the business at all. We have no actors: we have only authors, and not many of them. When Mendolssohn composed Son and Stranger for an amateur performance, he found that the bass could only sing one note. So he wrote the bass part all on that one note; and when it came to the fateful night, the bass failed even at that. Our authors do as Mendelssohn did. They find that the actors have only one note, or perhaps, if they are very clever, half a dozen. So their parts are confined to these notes, often with the same result as in Mendelssohn's case. If you doubt me, go and see Henry IV at the Haymarket. It is as good work as our stage can do; but the man who says that it is skilled work has neither eyes nor ears; the man who mistakes it for intelligent work has no brains; the man who finds it even good fun may be capable of Christy Minstrelsy but not of Shakespear. Everything that charm of style, rich humor, and vivid natural characterization can do for a play are badly wanted by Henry IV, which has neither the romantic beauty of Shakespear's earlier plays nor the tragic greatness of the later ones. One can hardly forgive Shakespear quite for the worldly phase in which he tried to thrust such a Jingo hero as his Harry V down our throats. The combination of conventional propriety and brute masterfulness in his public capacity with a low-lived blackguardism in his private tastes is not a pleasant one. No doubt he is true to nature as a picture of what is by no means uncommon in English society, an able young Philistine inheriting high position and authority, which he holds on to and goes through with by keeping a tight grip on his conventional and legal advantages, but who would have been quite in his place if he had been born a gamekeeper or a farmer. We do not in the first part of Henry IV see Harry sending Mrs. Quickly and Doll Tearsheet to the whipping-post, or handing over Falstaff to the Lord Chief Justice with a sanctimonious lecture; but he repeatedly makes it clear that he will turn on them later on, and that his self-indulgent good-fellowship with them is consciously and deliberately treacherous. His popularity, therefore, is like that of a prizefighter: nobody feels for him as for Romeo or Hamlet. Hotspur, too, though he is stimulating as ginger cordial is stimulating, is hardly better than his horse; and King Bolingbroke, preoccupied with his crown exactly as a miser is preoccupied with his money, is equally useless as a refuge for our affections, which are thus thrown back undivided on Falstaff, the most human person in the play, but none the less a besotted and disgusting old wretch. And there is neither any subtlety nor (for Shakespear) much poetry in the presentation of all these characters. They are labelled and described and insisted upon with the roughest directness; and their reality and their humor can alone save them from the unpopularity of their unlovableness and the tedium of their obviousness. Fortunately, they offer capital opportunities for interesting acting. Bolingbroke's long discourse to his son on the means by which he struck the imagination and enlisted the snobbery of the English people gives the actor a chance comparable to the crafty early scenes in Richelieu. Prince Hal's humor is seasoned with sportsmanlike cruelty and the insolence of conscious mastery and contempt to the point of occasionally making one shudder. Hotspur is full of energy;

and Falstaff is, of course, an unrivalled part for the right
sort of comedian. Well acted, then, the play is a good
one in spite of there not being a single tear in it. Ill
acted—O heavens!

Of the four leading parts, the easiest—Hotspur—becomes pre-eminent at the Haymarket, not so much by
Mr. Lewis Waller's superiority to the rest as by their inferiority to him. Some of the things he did were astonishing in an actor of his rank. At the end of each of his
first vehement speeches, he strode right down the stage
and across to the prompt side of the proscenium on
the frankest barnstorming principles, repeating this absurd "cross"—a well-known convention of the booth for
catching applause—three times, step for step, without a
pretence of any dramatic motive. In the camp scene before the battle of Shrewsbury, he did just what I blamed
Miss Violet Vanbrugh for trying to do in Monsieur de
Paris: that is, to carry through a long crescendo of excitement by main force after beginning fortissimo. Would
it be too far-fetched to recommend Mr. Waller to study
how Mozart, in rushing an operatic movement to a
spirited conclusion, knew how to make it, when apparently already at its utmost, seem to bound forward by a
sudden pianissimo and lightsome change of step, the
speed and force of the execution being actually reduced
instead of intensified by the change? Such skilled, re-
sourceful husbandry is the secret of all effects of this
kind; and it is in the entire absence of such husbandry
that Mr. Waller shewed how our miserable theatre has
left him still a novice for the purposes of a part which
he is fully equipped by nature to play with most brilliant
success, and which he did play very strikingly considering
he was not in the least sure how to set about it, and
hardly dared to stop blazing away at full pitch for an
instant lest the part should drop flat on the boards. Mr.
Mollison presented us with an assortment of effects, and
tones, and poses which had no reference, as far as I could
discover, to the part of Bolingbroke at any single point.
I did not catch a glimpse of the character from one end
of his performance to the other, and so must conclude
that Shakespear has failed to convey his intention to him.

Mr. Gillmore's way of playing Hal was as bad as the traditional way of playing Sheridan. He rattled and swaggered and roystered, and followed every sentence with a forced explosion of mirthless laughter, evidently believing that, as Prince Hal was reputed to be a humorous character, it was his business to laugh at him. Like most of his colleagues, he became more tolerable in the plain sailing of the battle scene, where the parts lose their individuality in the general warlike excitement, and an energetic display of the commonest sort of emotion suffices. Mr. Tree only wants one thing to make him an excellent Falstaff, and that is to get born over again as unlike himself as possible. No doubt, in the course of a month or two, when he begins to pick up a few of the lines of the part, he will improve on his first effort; but he will never be even a moderately good Falstaff. The basket-work figure, as expressionless as that of a Jack in the Green; the face, with the pathetic wandering eye of Captain Swift belying such suggestion of character as the lifeless mask of paint and hair can give; the voice, coarsened, vulgarized, and falsified without being enriched or colored; the hopeless efforts of the romantic imaginative actor, touching only in unhappy parts, to play the comedian by dint of mechanical horseplay: all that is hopeless, irremediable. Mr. Tree might as well try to play Juliet; and if he were wise he would hand over his part and his breadbasket to Mr. Lionel Brough, whose Bardolph has the true comic force which Mr. Tree never attains for a moment.

Two ideas have been borrowed from the last London revival of Henry V by Mr. Coleman at the Queen's Theatre in Long Acre. One is the motionless battle tableau, which is only Mr. Coleman's Agincourt over again, and which might just as well be cut out of cardboard. The other is the casting of Miss Kate Phillips for Mrs. Quickly. As Mrs. Quickly is plainly a slovenly, greasy, Gampish old creature, and Miss Phillips is unalterably trim, smart, and bright, a worse choice could not have been made. One would like to have seen Miss Mansfield in the part. Mrs. Tree, as Lady Percy, did what I have never seen her do before: that is, played her part stupidly. The laws of nature seem to be suspended when

Shakespear is in question. A Lady Percy who is sentimentally affectionate, who recites her remonstrance with
Percy in the vein of Clarence's dream in Richard III,
and who comes on the stage to share the applause elicited
by the combats in the battle of Shrewsbury, only makes
me rub my eyes and wonder whether I am dreaming.

Besides Mr. Lionel Brough and Mr. Lewis Waller,
there were three performers who came off with credit.
Mr. Holman Clark played Glendower like a reasonable
man who could read a Shakespearean play and understand it—a most exceptional achievement in his profession, as it appears. Mr. D. J. Williams, who played
William in As You Like It the other day at the Métro-
pole, and played him well, was a Smike-like and effective
Francis; and Miss Marion Evans was a most musical Lady
Mortimer, both in her Welsh song and Welsh speech.

The chief merit of the production is that the play has
been accepted from Shakespear mainly as he wrote it.
There are cuts, of course, the worst of them being the
sacrifice of the nocturnal innyard scene, a mutilation
which takes the reality and country midnight freshness
from the Gadshill robbery, and reduces it to a vapid interlude of horseplay. But the object of these cuts is to
save time: there is no alteration or hotch-potch, and consequently no suspicion of any attempt to demonstrate the
superiority of the manager's taste and judgment to Shakespear's, in the Daly fashion. This ought to pass as a matter of course; but as things are at present it must be
acknowledged as highly honorable to Mr. Tree. However
it is not my cue just now to pay Mr. Tree compliments.
His *tours de force* in the art of make-up do not impose
on me: any man can get into a wicker barrel and pretend to be Falstaff, or put on a false nose and call himself Svengali. Such tricks may very well be left to the
music-halls: they are altogether unworthy of an artist of
Mr. Tree's pretensions. When he returns to the serious
pursuit of his art by playing a part into which he can
sincerely enter without disguise or mechanical denaturali-
zation, may I be there to see! Until then let him guard
the Haymarket doors against me; for I like him best
when he is most himself.

In The Quintessence of Ibsenism *Shaw states that "all very serious revolutionary propositions begin as huge jokes," and he suggests that the same thing happens with literary creations. He points to Falstaff as an example.*

. . . Falstaff is introduced as a subordinate stage figure with no other function than to be robbed by the Prince and Poins, who was originally meant to be the *raisonneur* of the piece, and the chief figure among the prince's dissolute associates. But Poins soon fades into nothing, like several characters in Dickens's early works; whilst Falstaff develops into an enormous joke and an exquisitely mimicked human type. Only in the end the joke withers. The question comes to Shakespear: *Is* this really a laughing matter? Of course there can be only one answer; and Shakespear gives it as best he can by the mouth of the prince become king, who might, one thinks, have the decency to wait until he has redeemed his own character before assuming the right to lecture his boon companion. Falstaff, rebuked and humiliated, dies miserably. His followers are hanged, except Pistol, whose exclamation "Old do I wax; and from my weary limbs honor is cudgelled" is a melancholy exordium to an old age of beggary and imposture.

But suppose Shakespear had begun where he left off! Suppose he had been born at a time when, as the result of a long propaganda of health and temperance, sack had come to be called alcohol, alcohol had come to be called poison, corpulence had come to be regarded as either a disease or a breach of good manners, and a conviction had spread throughout society that the practice of consuming "a half-pennyworth of bread to an intolerable deal of sack" was the cause of so much misery, crime, and racial degeneration that whole States prohibited the sale of potable spirits altogether, and even moderate drinking was more and more regarded as a regrettable weakness! Suppose (to drive the change well home) the women in the great theatrical centres had completely lost that amused indulgence for the drunken man which still exists in some out-of-the-way places, and felt nothing but disgust and anger at the conduct and habits of Falstaff and Sir Toby Belch! Instead of Henry IV and The

Merry Wives of Windsor, we should have had something like Zola's L'Assommoir. Indeed, we actually have Cassio, the last of Shakespear's gentleman-drunkards, talking like a temperance reformer, a fact which suggests that Shakespear had been roundly lectured for the offensive vulgarity of Sir Toby by some woman of refinement who refused to see the smallest fun in giving a knight such a name as Belch, with characteristics to correspond to it. Suppose, again, that the first performance of The Taming of the Shrew had led to a modern Feminist demonstration in the theatre, and forced upon Shakespear's consideration a whole century of agitatresses, from Mary Wollstonecraft to Mrs. Fawcett and Mrs. Pankhurst, is it not likely that the jest of Katharine and Petruchio would have become the earnest of Nora and Torvald Helmer?

Henry V

Shaw did not review a production of Henry V, *but on several occasions he referred to its jingoism. Shaw once classified it as a play belonging to "that moment of sympathy with the common morality and thought of his time which came between the romanticism of Shakespear's early plays and the independent thought of his later one."*

Henry VI, Part 1

In the preface to St. Joan *Shaw takes up Shakespeare's treatment of Joan.*

. . . English readers would probably like to know how these idolizations and reactions have affected the books they are most familiar with about Joan. There is the first part of the Shakespearean, or pseudo-Shakespearean trilogy of Henry VI, in which Joan is one of the leading characters. This portrait of Joan is not more authentic than the descriptions in the London papers of George Washington in 1780, of Napoleon in 1803, of the German Crown Prince in 1915, or of Lenin in 1917. It ends in mere scurrility. The impression left by it is that the playwright, having begun by an attempt to make Joan a beautiful and romantic figure, was told by his scandalized company that English patriotism would never stand a sympathetic representation of a French conqueror of English troops, and that unless he at once introduced all the old charges against Joan of being a sorceress and a harlot, and assumed her to be guilty of all of them, his play could not be produced. As likely as not, this is what actually happened: indeed there is only one other apparent way of accounting for the sympathetic representation of Joan as a heroine culminating in her eloquent appeal to the Duke of Burgundy, followed by the blackguardly scurrility of the concluding scenes. That other way is to assume that the original play was wholly scurrilous, and that Shakespear touched up the earlier scenes. As the work belongs to a period at which he was only beginning his practice as a tinker of old works, before his own style was fully formed and hardened, it is impossible to verify this guess. His finger is not unmistakeably evident in the play, which is poor and base in its moral tone; but he may have tried to redeem it from downright infamy by shedding a momentary glamor on the figure of The Maid.

JULIUS CAESAR

Shaw discusses Julius Caesar *in his introduction to* Caesar and Cleopatra, *entitled "Better than Shakespear?", found in another section. He reviewed Beerbohm Tree's production of the play in* The Saturday Review *on January 29, 1898.*

THE TRUCE with Shakespear is over. It was only possible whilst Hamlet was on the stage. Hamlet is the tragedy of private life—nay, of individual bachelor-poet life. It belongs to a detached residence, a select library, an exclusive circle, to no occupation, to fathomless boredom, to impenitent mugwumpism, to the illusion that the futility of these things is the futility of existence, and its contemplation philosophy: in short, to the dream-fed gentlemanism of the age which Shakespear inaugurated in English literature: the age, that is, of the rising middle class bringing into power the ideas taught it by its servants in the kitchen, and its fathers in the shop—ideas now happily passing away as the onslaught of modern democracy offers to the kitchen-taught and home-bred the alternative of achieving a real superiority or going ignominiously under in the class conflict.

It is when we turn to Julius Cæsar, the most splendidly written political melodrama we possess, that we realize the apparently immortal author of Hamlet as a man, not for all time, but for an age only, and that, too, in all solidly wise and heroic aspects, the most despicable of all the ages in our history. It is impossible for even the most judicially minded critic to look without a revulsion of indignant contempt at this travestying of a great man as a silly braggart, whilst the pitiful gang of mischief-makers who destroyed him are lauded as statesmen and patriots. There is not a single sentence uttered by Shakespear's Julius Cæsar that is, I will not say worthy of him, but even worthy of an average Tammany boss. Brutus is nothing but a familiar type of English suburban preacher: politically he would hardly impress the Thames Conservancy Board. Cassius is a vehemently assertive nonentity. It is only when we come to Antony, unctuous voluptuary and self-seeking sentimental demagogue, that we find Shakespear in his depth; and in his depth, of course, he is superlative. Regarded as a crafty stage job, the play is a triumph: rhetoric, claptrap, effective gushes of emotion, all the devices of the popular playwright, are employed with a profusion of power that almost breaks their backs. No doubt there are slips and slovenliness of the kind that careful revisers eliminate; but they count for so little in the mass of accomplishment that it is safe to say that the dramatist's art can be carried no further on that plane. If Goethe, who understood Cæsar and the significance of his death—"the most senseless of deeds" he called it—had treated the subject, his conception of it would have been as superior to Shakespear's as St. John's Gospel is to the Police News; but his treatment could not have been more magnificently successful. As far as sonority, imagery, wit, humor, energy of imagination, power over language, and a whimsically keen eye for idiosyncrasies can make a dramatist, Shakespear was the king of dramatists. Unfortunately, a man may have them all, and yet conceive high affairs of state exactly as Simon Tappertit did. In one of the scenes in Julius Cæsar a conceited poet bursts into the tent of Brutus and Cassius, and exhorts them not to quarrel with one another. If Shakespear had been able to present his play to the ghost of the great Julius, he would probably have had much the same reception. He certainly would have deserved it.

When it was announced that Mr. Tree had resolved to give special prominence to the character of Cæsar in his acting version, the critics winked, and concluded simply that the actor-manager was going to play Antony and not Brutus. Therefore I had better say that Mr. Tree must stand acquitted of any belittlement of the parts which compete so strongly with his own. Before going to Her Majesty's I was curious enough to block out for myself a division of the play into three acts; and I found that Mr. Tree's division corresponded exactly with mine.

Mr. Waller's opportunities as Brutus, and Mr. McLeay's as Cassius, are limited only by their own ability to take advantage of them; and Mr. Louis Calvert figures as boldly in the public eye as he did in his own production of Antony and Cleopatra last year at Manchester. Indeed, Mr. Calvert is the only member of the company who achieves an unequivocal success. The preference expressed in the play by Cæsar for fat men may, perhaps, excuse Mr. Calvert for having again permitted himself to expand after his triumphant reduction of his girth for his last appearance in London. However, he acted none the worse: in fact, nobody else acted so skilfully or originally. The others, more heavily burdened, did their best, quite in the spirit of the man who had never played the fiddle, but had no doubt he could if he tried. Without oratory, without style, without specialized vocal training, without any practice worth mentioning, they assaulted the play with cheerful self-sufficiency, and gained great glory by the extent to which, as a masterpiece of the playwright's trade, it played itself. Some small successes were not lacking. Cæsar's nose was good: Calpurnia's bust was worthy of her: in such parts Garrick and Siddons could have achieved no more. Miss Evelyn Millard's Roman matron in the style of Richardson—Cato's daughter as Clarissa—was an unlooked-for novelty; but it cost a good deal of valuable time to get in the eighteenth century between the lines of the first B.C. By operatic convention—the least appropriate of all conventions—the boy Lucius was played by Mrs. Tree, who sang Sullivan's ultra-nineteenth-century Orpheus with his Lute, modulations and all, to a pizzicato accompaniment supposed to be played on a lyre with eight open and unstoppable strings, a feat complexly and absurdly impossible. Mr. Waller, as Brutus, failed in the first half of the play. His intention clearly was to represent Brutus as a man superior to fate and circumstance; but the effect he produced was one of insensibility. Nothing could have been more unfortunate; for it is through the sensibility of Brutus that the audience have to learn what they cannot learn from the phlegmatic pluck of Casca or the narrow vindictiveness of Cassius: that is, the terrible momentousness, the harrowing anxiety and dread, of the impending catastrophe. Mr. Waller left that function to the thunderstorm. From the death of Cæsar onward he was better; and his appearance throughout was effective; but at best his sketch was a water-color one. Mr. Franklyn McLeay carried off the honors of the evening by his deliberate staginess and imposing assumptiveness: that is, by as much of the grand style as our playgoers now understand; but in the last act he was monotonously violent, and died the death of an incorrigible poseur, not of a noble Roman. Mr. Tree's memory failed him as usual; and a good deal of the technical part of his work was botched and haphazard, like all Shakespearean work nowadays; nevertheless, like Mr. Calvert, he made the audience believe in the reality of the character before them. But it is impossible to praise his performance in detail. I cannot recall any single passage in the scene after the murder that was well done: in fact, he only secured an effective curtain by bringing Calpurnia on the stage to attitudinize over Cæsar's body. To say that the demagogic oration in the Forum produced its effect is nothing; for its effect is inevitable, and Mr. Tree neither made the most of it nor handled it with any pretence of mastery or certainty. But he was not stupid, nor inane, nor Bard-of-Avon ridden; and he contrived to interest the audience in Antony instead of trading on their ready-made interest in Mr. Beerbohm Tree. And for that many sins may be forgiven him nowadays, when the playgoer, on first nights at all events, goes to see the cast rather than the play.

What is missing in the performance, for want of the specific Shakespearean skill, is the Shakespearean music. When we come to those unrivalled grandiose passages in which Shakespear turns on the full organ, we want to hear the sixteen-foot pipes booming, or, failing them (as we often must, since so few actors are naturally equipped with them), the ennobled tone, and the tempo suddenly steadied with the majesty of deeper purpose. You have, too, those moments when the verse, instead of opening up the depths of sound, rises to its most brilliant clangor, and the lines ring like a thousand trumpets. If we cannot have these effects, or if we can only have genteel drawing room arrangements of them, we cannot have

Shakespear; and that is what is mainly the matter at Her Majesty's: there are neither trumpets nor pedal pipes there. The conversation is metrical and emphatic in an elocutionary sort of way; but it makes no distinction between the arid prairies of blank verse which remind one of Henry VI at its crudest, and the places where the morass suddenly piles itself into a mighty mountain. Cassius in the first act has a twaddling forty-line speech, base in its matter and mean in its measure, followed immediately by the magnificent torrent of rhetoric, the first burst of true Shakespearean music in the play, beginning—

> Why, man, he doth bestride the narrow world
> Like a Colossus, and we petty men
> Walk under his huge legs and peep about
> To find ourselves dishonorable graves.

I failed to catch the slightest change of elevation or reinforcement of feeling when Mr. McLeay passed from one to the other. His tone throughout was dry; and it never varied. By dint of energetic, incisive articulation, he drove his utterances harder home than the others; but the best lines seemed to him no more than the worst: there were no heights and depths, no contrast of black thundercloud and flaming lightning flash, no stirs and surprises. Yet he was not inferior in oratory to the rest. Mr. Waller certainly cannot be reproached with dryness of tone; and his delivery of the speech in the Forum was perhaps the best piece of formal elocution we got; but he also kept at much the same level throughout, and did not at any moment attain to anything that could be called grandeur. Mr. Tree, except for a conscientiously desperate effort to cry havoc and let slip the dogs of war in the robustious manner, with no better result than to all but extinguish his voice, very sensibly left oratory out of the quetsion, and tried conversational sincerity, which answered so well that his delivery of "This was the noblest Roman of them all" came off excellently.

The real hero of the revival is Mr. Alma Tadema. The scenery and stage coloring deserve everything that has been said of them. But the illusion is wasted by want of discipline and want of thought behind the scenes.

Every carpenter seems to make it a point of honor to set the cloths swinging in a way that makes Rome reel and the audience positively seasick. In Brutus's house the door is on the spectators' left: the knocks on it come from the right. The Roman soldiers take the field each man with his two javelins neatly packed up like a fishing-rod. After a battle, in which they are supposed to have made the famous Roman charge, hurling these javelins in and following them up sword in hand, they come back carrying the javelins still undisturbed in their rug-straps, in perfect trim for a walk-out with the nursery-maids of Philippi.

The same want of vigilance appears in the acting version. For example, though the tribunes Flavius and Marullus are replaced by two of the senators, the lines referring to them by name are not altered. But the oddest oversight is the retention in the tent scene of the obvious confusion of the original version of the play, in which the death of Portia was announced to Brutus by Messala, with the second version, into which the quarrel scene was written to strengthen the fourth act. In this version Brutus, already in possession of the news, reveals it to Cassius. The play has come down to us with the two alternative scenes strung together; so that Brutus's reception of Messala's news, following his own revelation of it to Cassius, is turned into a satire on Roman fortitude, the suggestion being that the secret of the calm with which a noble Roman received the most terrible tidings in public was that it had been carefully imparted to him in private beforehand. Mr. Tree has not noticed this; and the two scenes are gravely played one after the other at Her Majesty's. This does not matter much to our playgoers, who never venture to use their common sense when Shakespear is in question; but it wastes time. Mr. Tree may without hesitation cut out Pindarus and Messala, and go straight on from the bowl of wine to Brutus's question about Philippi.

The music, composed for the occasion by Mr. Raymond Roze, made me glad that I had already taken care to acknowledge the value of Mr. Roze's services to Mr. Tree; for this time he has missed the Roman vein rather badly. To be a Frenchman was once no disqualification for the antique, because French musicians used to be brought up on Gluck as English ones were brought up on Handel. But Mr. Roze composes as if Gluck had been supplanted wholly in his curriculum by Gounod and Bizet. If that prelude to the third act were an attempt to emulate the overtures to Alceste or Iphigenia I could have forgiven it. But to give us the soldiers' chorus from Faust, crotchet for crotchet and triplet for triplet, with nothing changed but the notes, was really too bad.

In writing about an endowed National Theatre under consideration at Manchester Shaw refers to Julius Caesar *and his earlier review of it.* This appeared in The *Saturday* Review *on February 12, 1898.*

. . . A fortnight ago I ventured to point out in these columns that Julius Cæsar in Shakespear's play says nothing worthy, or even nearly worthy, of Julius Cæsar. The number of humbugs who have pretended to be shocked by this absolutely incontrovertible remark has lowered my opinion of the human race. There are only two dignified courses open to those who disagree with me. One is to suffer in silence. The other, obviously, is to quote the passage which, in the opinion of the objectors, *is* worthy of Julius Cæsar. The latter course, however, would involve reading the play; and they would almost as soon think of reading the Bible. Besides, it would be waste of time; for since Shakespear is accepted as the standard of first-rate excellence, an adverse criticism of him need only be quoted to be accepted as damning evidence against itself. I do not mention this by way of complaint: if these gentlemen saw eye to eye with me they would all be G. B. S.'s; and a press written entirely in my style would be, like an exclusively Shakespearean municipal theatre, a little too much of a good thing. I merely wish to shew how the difficulty about guaranteeing the future good conduct of an endowed theatre can always be got over by simply mentioning our William's name. Assure the public that you will play Shakespear and that you will not play Ibsen, and your endowment fund will be second in respectability only to the restoration fund of a cathedral.

KING LEAR

Unfortunately Shaw never reviewed a production of King Lear; *moreover, the specific references he did make to the play appear in articles of a more general nature. While these cannot be placed here they can be found elsewhere in the book. Among his observations on the play Shaw noted that* King Lear *could pass for pure tragedy, "for even the fool in Lear is tragic"; Shaw spoke of "the blasphemous despair of Lear"; he also stated that "no man will ever write a better tragedy than Lear."*

LOVE'S LABOUR'S LOST

In what was undoubtedly his first Shakespearean review Shaw wrote on Love's Labour's Lost *in the August 1, 1886, issue of a short-lived magazine called* Our Corner.

A PERFORMANCE of Love's Labor Lost is a sort of entertainment to be valued rather for Shakespear's sake than for its own. The Dramatic Students did not tempt many people into the St. James's Theatre on the sultry afternoon of 2nd July by the experiment; and it is perhaps as well that they did not, for their efforts bore much the same relation to fine acting as the play does to Antony and Cleopatra. They failed not only in skill and finish, but in intelligence. Having gathered from their study of the play that they must all be very amusing and in desperately high spirits, they set to work to produce that effect by being obstreperous in action, and in speech full of the unnatural archness by which people with no sense of humor betray their deficiency when they desire to appear jocund. Though they devoutly believed the play a funny one, they did not see the joke themselves, and so, ill at ease in their merriment, forgot that dignity and grace may be presumed to have tempered the wit of the gentlemen of the Court of Navarre, and the vivacity of the ladies of the Court of France. In some scenes, consequently, the performance was like an Elizabethan version of High Life Below Stairs. I shall say nothing of the feminine parts, except that they were all unfortunately cast. The men were better. Mr. G. R. Foss as Boyet and Mr. Frank Evans as Holofernes were quite efficient; and Mr. Lugg as Costard, though as yet a raw actor and prone to overdo his business, enlivened the performance considerably by his fun and mimetic turn. He sang "When Icicles Hang by the Wall" with commendable spirit, and with the recklessness of a man who has got the tune on his ear and considers that it is the conductor's business to keep the band with the singer, which poor Herr Schoen-

ing tried gallantly to do, with more or less success. Mr.
Bernard Gould and Mr. de Cordova, as Biron and Armado, were next best; but they made very little of their
large share of the best opportunities of the afternoon.
Mr. Gould's gaiety lacked dignity and variety: he swaggered restlessly, and frittered away all the music of his
lines. His colleague looked Armado, but did not act him.
Mr. de Cordova is always picturesque; but his elocution,
correct as far as it goes, is monotonous; and the adapt-
ability and subtlety which go to constitute that imperson-
ative power which is the distinctive faculty of the actor
are not at present apparent in him. His qualifications, so
far, are those of an artist's model: he has yet to make himself an actor.

The play itself showed more vitality than might have
been expected. Three hundred years ago, its would-be
wits, with their forced smartness, their indecent waggeries,
their snobbish sneers at poverty, and their ill-bred and
ill-natured mockery of age and natural infirmity, passed
more easily as ideal compounds of soldier, courtier, and
scholar than they can nowadays. Among people of moderate culture in this century they would be ostracised as
insufferable cads. Something of their taste survives in
the puns and chaff of such plays as those of the late H. J.
Byron, and even in the productions of so able a writer as
Mr. Gilbert, who seems to consider a comic opera incomplete without a middle-aged woman in it to be ridiculed
because she is no longer young and pretty. Most of us, it
is to be hoped, have grace enough to regard Ruth, Lady
Jane, Katisha and the rest as detestable blemishes on Mr.
Gilbert's works. Much of Love's Labor Lost is as objec-
tionable and more tedious. Nothing, it seems to me, but
a perverse hero-worship can see much to admire in the
badinage of Biron and Rosaline. Benedick and Beatrice
are better; and Orlando and Rosalind much better: still,
they repeatedly annoy us by repartees of which the trivial
ingenuity by no means compensates the silliness, coarseness, or malice. It is not until Shakespear's great period
began with the seventeenth century that, in Measure for
Measure, we find this sort of thing shown in its proper
light and put in its proper place in the person of Lucio,
whose embryonic stages may be traced in Mercutio and

Biron. Fortunately for Love's Labor Lost, Biron is not quite so bad as Mercutio: you never absolutely long to kick him off the stage as you long to kick Mercutio when he makes game of the Nurse. And Shakespear, though a very feeble beginner then in comparison to the master he subsequently became, was already too far on the way to his greatness to fail completely when he set himself to write a sunny, joyous, and delightful play. Much of the verse is charming: even when it is rhymed doggrell it is full of that bewitching Shakespearean music which tempts the susceptible critic to sugar his ink and declare that Shakespear can do no wrong. The construction of the play is simple and effective. The only absolutely impossible situation was that of Biron hiding in the tree to overlook the king, who presently hides to watch Longaville, who in turn spies on Dumain; as the result of which we had three out of four gentlemen shouting "asides" through the sylvan stillness, No. 1 being inaudible to 2, 3, and 4; No. 2 audible to No. 1, but not to 3 and 4; No. 3 audible to 1 and 2, but not to No. 4; and No. 4 audible to all the rest, but himself temporarily stone deaf. Shakespear has certainly succeeded in making this arrangement intelligible; but the Dramatic Students' stage manager did not succeed in making it credible. For Shakespear's sake one can make-believe a good deal; but here the illusion was too thin. Matters might have been mended had Biron climbed among the foliage of the tree instead of affixing himself to the trunk in an attitude so precarious and so extraordinarily prominent that Dumain (or perhaps it was Longaville), though supposed to be unconscious of his presence, could not refrain from staring at him as if fascinated for several seconds. On the whole, I am not sure that Love's Labor Lost is worth reviving at this time of day; but I am bound to add that if it were announced to-morrow with an adequate cast, I should make a point of seeing it.

MACBETH

In an article called "A New Lady Macbeth and a New Mrs. Ebbsmith" in The Saturday Review *of May 25, 1885, Shaw discussed an amateur performance of Macbeth. (Lillah McCarthy later became not only a well-known actress, but the wife of Granville-Barker and a great friend of Shaw's as well.)*

. . . Readers who have noticed the heading of this article may possibly want to know what Lady Macbeth has to do with it. Well, I have discovered a new Lady Macbeth. It is one of my eccentricities to be old-fashioned in my artistic tastes. For instance, I am fond—unaffectedly fond— of Shakespear's plays. I do not mean actor-managers' editions and revivals; I mean the plays as Shakespear wrote them, played straight through line by line and scene by scene as nearly as possible under the conditions of representation for which they were designed. I have seen the suburban amateurs of the Shakespear Reading Society, seated like Christy minstrels on the platform of the lecture hall at the London Institution, produce, at a moderate computation, about sixty-six times as much effect by reading straight through Much Ado About Nothing as Mr. Irving with his expensively mounted and superlatively dull Lyceum version. When these same amateurs invited me to a regular stage performance of Macbeth in aid of the Siddons Memorial Fund, I went, not for the sake of Sarah the Respectable, whose great memory can take care of itself (how much fresher it is, by the way, than those of many writers and painters of her day, though no actor ever makes a speech without complaining that he is cheated out of the immortality every other sort of artist enjoys!), but simply because I wanted to see Macbeth. Mind, I am no admirer of the Elizabethan school. When Mr. Henry Arthur Jones, whose collected essays on the English drama I am now engaged in reading, says: "Surely the crowning glory of our nation is our

Shakespear; and remember he was one of a great school,"
I almost burst with the intensity of my repudiation of the
second clause in that utterance. What Shakespear got
from his "school" was the insane and hideous rhetoric
which is all that he has in common with Jonson, Webster,
and the whole crew of insufferable bunglers and dullards
whose work stands out as vile even at the beginning of
the seventeenth century, when every art was corrupted to
the marrow by the orgie called the Renaissance, which
was nothing but the vulgar exploitation in the artistic
professions of the territory won by the Protestant movement. The leaders of that great self-assertion of the growing spirit of man were dead long before the Elizabethan
literary rabble became conscious that "ideas" were in
fashion, and that any author who could gather a cheap
stock of them from murder, lust, and obscenity, and for-
mulate them in rhetorical blank verse, might make the
stage pestiferous with plays that have no ray of noble
feeling, no touch of faith, beauty, or even common kind-
ness in them from beginning to end. I really cannot keep
my temper over the Elizabethan dramatists and the Renaissance; nor would I if I could. The generation which
admired them equally admired the pictures of Guido,
Giulio Romano, Domenichino, and the Carracci; and I
trust it is not nowadays necessary to offer any further
samples of its folly. A masterpiece by Carracci—say the
smirking Susanna in the National Gallery—would not
fetch seven pounds ten at Christie's today; but our literary men, always fifty years behind their time because they
never look at anything nor listen to anything, but go on
working up what they learnt in their boyhood when they
read books instead of writing them, still serve up Charles
Lamb's hobby, and please themselves by observing that
Cyril Tourneur could turn out pretty pairs of lines and
string them monotonously together, or that Greene had a
genuine groatsworth of popular wit, or that Marlowe,
who was perhaps good enough to make it possible to believe that if he had been born thirty years ago he might
now have been a tolerable imitator of Mr. Rudyard Kip-
ling, dealt in a single special quality of "mighty line."
On the strength of these discoveries, they keep up the
tradition that these men were slightly inferior Shake-

spears. Beaumont and Fletcher are, indeed, sometimes cited as hardly inferior; but I will not go into that. I could not do justice to it in moderate language.

As to this performance of Macbeth at St. George's Hall, of course it was, from the ordinary professional standpoint, a very bad one. I say this because I well know what happens to a critic when he incautiously praises an amateur. He gets by the next post a letter in the following terms: "Dear Sir,—I am perhaps transgressing the bounds of etiquette in writing privately to you; but I thought you might like to know that your kind notice of my performance as Guildenstern has encouraged me to take a step which I have long been meditating. I have resigned my position as Governor of the Bank of England with a view to adopting the stage as a profession, and trust that the result may justify your too favorable opinion of my humble powers." Therefore I desire it to be distinctly understood that I do not recommend any members of the Macbeth cast to go on the stage. The three witches, Miss Florence Bourne, Miss Longvil, and Miss Munro, were as good as any three witches I ever saw; but the impersonation of witches, as a profession, is almost as precarious as the provision of smoked glasses for looking at eclipses through. Macduff was bad: I am not sure that with his natural advantages he could very easily have been worse; but still, if he feels himself driven to some artistic career by a radical aversion to earning an honest livelihood, and is prepared for a hard apprenticeship of twenty years in mastering the art of the stage—for that period still holds as good as when Talma prescribed it— he can become an actor if he likes. As to Lady Macbeth, she, too, was bad; but it is clear to me that unless she at once resolutely marries some rich gentleman who disapproves of the theatre on principle, she will not be able to keep herself off the stage. She is as handsome as Miss Neilson; and she can hold an audience whilst she is doing everything wrongly. The murder scene was not very good, because Macbeth belonged to the school of the Irish fiddler who, when Ole Bull asked him whether he played by ear or from notes, replied that he played "by main strength"; and you cannot get the brooding horror of the dagger scene by that method. Besides, Miss Lillah

McCarthy—that is the lady's name as given in my program—is happily too young to conceive ambition and
murder, or the temptation of a husband with a sickly conscience, as realities: they are to her delicious excitements
of the imagination, with a beautiful, splendid terror
about them, to be conveyed by strenuous pose, and flashing eye, and indomitable bearing. She went at them
bravely in this spirit; and they came off more or less happily as her instinct and courage helped her, or her skill
failed her. The banquet scene and the sleep-walking scene,
which are the easiest passages in the part technically to a
lady with the requisite pluck and personal fascination,
were quite successful; and if the earlier scenes were immature, unskilful, and entirely artificial and rhetorical in
their conception, still, they were very nearly thrilling. In
short, I should like to see Miss Lillah McCarthy play
again. I venture on the responsibility of saying that her
Lady Macbeth was a highly promising performance, and
that some years of hard work would make her a valuable
recruit to the London stage. And with that very rash remark I will leave Macbeth, with a fervent wish that Mr.
Pinero, Mr. Grundy, and Monsieur Sardou could be persuaded to learn from it how to write a play without
wasting the first hour of the performance in tediously
explaining its "construction." They really are mistaken
in supposing that Scribe was cleverer than Shakespear.

Mr. Frank Harris, the editor of The Saturday Review
*when Shaw wrote for it, had a theory that Macbeth was
basically a contemplative, literary man and that the violence and action of the play was incongruous with his
basic nature. Shaw agreed with this and took the matter
up in a review of April 23, 1898, in* The Saturday Review.

. . . I went off to see Macbeth, and found that Mr. Ben
Greet had collected as much as he could get of the company of the recent Manchester revival. He had failed to
capture Miss Janet Achurch, whose place was taken by
Miss Eleanor Calhoun. The editor of this journal has so
completely and convincingly knocked the bottom out of

Macbeth as a character-study, that the incongruity of the ferocious murders and treacheries and brutalities of the legendary Thane of Fife with the humane and reflective temperament of the nervous literary gentleman whom Shakespear thrust into his galligaskins, was more than usually glaring. Mr. William Mollison did his best under the circumstances, and occasionally recited a passage with a fair degree of impressiveness. Both he and Miss Calhoun were much bothered by a few unlucky accidents and hitches which occurred, and they were a very ill-matched pair artistically, Miss Calhoun being modern, brilliant, mettlesome, and striking in appearance, and Mr. Mollison heavy, parental, and almost boastfully abstinent in the matter of ideas. He was so disdainful of modern realism and so Shakespearean that, like Cassio or Tybalt, he fought Macduff "by the book of arithmetic," and counted the prearranged strokes aloud—One, Two, Three, Four, Five, Six. His scenes with Lady Macbeth, on the other hand, were obviously unrehearsed and unconcerted. After his long Manchester engagement he had no doubt become completely dependent on Miss Achurch's "business"; and Miss Calhoun, dragged one way by the necessity for giving him this business, and the other by her own view of the part, could do little more than keep up appearances, except in the scenes where she had the stage to herself, when she displayed all that exceptional training and professional competence which is, I suppose, the reason why one sees so little of her nowadays in that Duffer's Paradise, the West End stage. On the whole, the most successful scenes were those of Macduff (Mr. Black), Malcolm (Mr. Penny), and Lennox (Mr. Pearce), where there were no stage difficulties, and the actors had their work at their fingers' end.

In November, 1920, the American actor James K. Hackett produced Macbeth *in London with Mrs. Patrick Campbell playing Lady Macbeth. Mrs. Campbell wrote Shaw asking his opinion of the production. He replied in a letter dated December 22, 1920. (The letter is reprinted in* Bernard Shaw and Mrs. Patrick Campbell: **Their Correspondence.**)

. . . Macbeth, as a production, was an ancient Victorian absurdity. Hackett is still in the XVIII century. He would have done just as well with Rhoda Symons; and you would have done just as well with Aubrey Smith: the intervals, with the *entracte* music played sixteen times over, killed the play; and the people know now that it is not Shakespear who is the bore, and that Barker or Bridges Adams could have made a success of it with principals at fifteen pounds a week. Hackett's game is as dead as Victorian croquet and archery.

As it happened, when I saw it you played Hackett off the stage, and made only a few blunders. Blunder 1. You should not have played the dagger scene in that best evening dress of Lady M's, but in a black wrap like a thundercloud, with a white face. 2. You should not have repeated the exit business by which Macbeth conveyed that he was going to see a ghost on every step of the stairs up to Duncan; you should have gone straight off like a woman of iron. 3. You should not have forgotten that there was blood on your hands and on his, and that you dared not touch one another for fear of messing your clothes with gore. 4. In the sleepwalking scene you should not have scrubbed your hands *realistically* (Drat the blood! it wont come off) nor worn an idiotic Handley-Seymour confection that wound your feet up more and more at every step, and finally pitched you off the stage on your head. That scene needs the whole cavernous depth of the stage, and the draperies of a ghost. If you are determined to be a Paffick Lidy all the time (Mrs. P. C's dresses by HS & co) you cannot be Lady Macbeth or Mrs. Siddons. It was maddening to hear you deliver the lines splendidly, and be in a different class to all the others, and then throw it all away by half a dozen stupidities that the call boy could have corrected. I persuaded Massingham to go; but he came back chuckling and said you had sleepwalked all through the play. I could not understand this. I *did* understand when Archer told me that on the first night you twittered through the part and pecked at it like a canary trying to eat a cocoa nut. I knew that game: you were trying to make Lady Macbeth a lady just as you made Higgins a gentleman. But I couldnt understand the sleepwalking until D.D. told me

someone had told you that Lady M. should be seen
through a sheet of glass. I wish I had been there with a
few bricks: there would not have been much left of your
glass. Why do you believe every ASS who talks nonsense to you—no: why should I insult the asses?—every
NOODLE who talks nonsense to you, and bite everyone
who talks skilled common sense?

You might at least have made the scenepainter put in
a martin's nest or two over the castle windows. You can
bully effectively enough when you really want anything.
Why dont you want the right things and bully to some
useful purpose?

*Shaw wrote Mrs. Campbell again on January 13, 1921,
suggesting that she wished to make Lady Macbeth too
ladylike. (The suggestion in the letter that Lady Macbeth
is an inconsistent character is found also in "A Dressing
Room Secret" in another section of the book. The Mackail referred to was an English classical scholar and
writer.)*

. . . Mackail thinks that acting is unladylike, and that,
like the celebrated decayed gentlewoman who had to cry
laces in the street for a living but hoped that nobody
heard her, Lady Macbeth should be unobtrusive and inaudible. Perhaps he thinks, too, that Macbeth was a
strong silent man, and that Hackett should have cut out
all his lines. That is, he doesnt think at all about it: no
man ever really does think about a thing until it is his
job, though he may play with it intellectually in a very
pretty manner. When you play Shakespear, dont worry
about the character, but go for the music. It was by word
music that he expressed what he wanted to express; and
if you get the music right, the whole thing will come
right. And neither he nor any other musician ever wrote
music without *fortissimi* and thundering ones too. It is
only your second rate people who write whole movements
for muted strings and never let the trombones and the
big drum go. It is not by tootling to him *con sordino* that
Lady Macbeth makes Macbeth say "Bring forth men children only." She lashes him into murder.

And then you must modulate. Unless you can produce
in speaking exactly the same effect that Mozart produces
when he stops in C and then begins again in A flat, you
cant play Shakespear. Ask Thoughtless Jack how he
would say to the servant with the air of gratified hostess
and gracious fine lady "He brings GREAT news," and
then, when the man is gone "the raven himself is hoarse
that croaks the fatal entrance of Duncan beneath *my*
battlements." Unless you lift that to utter abandonment,
how can you drop to the terrible invocation "Come, you
spirits." Imagine an actress, instead of studying that until
she had got it as safe as a pianola reflecting on what a
perfect wife Lady Macbeth was and trying to imagine herself a sheet of glass!

If you want to know the truth about Lady Macbeth's
character, she hasnt one. There never was no such person. She says things that will set people's imagination to
work if she says them in the right way: that is all. *I*
know: I do it myself. You ought to know: *you* set people's imaginations to work, don't you? though you know
very well that what they imagine is not there, and that
when they believe you are thinking ineffable things you
are only wondering whether it would be considered vulgar to have shrimps for tea, or whether you could seduce
me into ruining my next play by giving you a part in it.

MEASURE FOR MEASURE

Shaw did not review a production of Measure for Measure, *but, along with* All's Well That Ends Well *and* Troilus and Cressida, *he referred to it often as a play ahead of its time and a play that holds "the mirror up to nature." He classified it as one of the "new species of Tragi-Comedy." He praised the character drawing in the play, particularly that of Isabella and Lucio. In a review of* Much Ado About Nothing *of February 26, 1898, he explained his admiration for Shakespeare's handling of Lucio. (This may be found in the section on* Much Ado.) *Shaw did make a brief statement on* Measure for Measure *in a note to Felix Grendon quoted in Grendon's article, "Some Misconceptions Concerning Shakespeare," which appeared in* Poet Lore *for September-October, 1909.*

. . . I read Measure for Measure through carefully some time ago with some intention of saying something positive myself; but its flashes of observation were so utterly uncoordinated and so stuck together with commonplaces and reach-me-downs that I felt that the whole thing would come to pieces in my hand if I touched it; so I though it best to leave it as he left it, and let the stories and the characters hide the holes in the philosophic fabric.

THE MERRY WIVES OF WINDSOR

In writing about Verdi's Falstaff *in* The Anglo-Saxon Review *for March, 1901, Shaw referred to the* Merry Wives of Windsor.

. . . Unfortunately, very few people know The Merry Wives of Windsor as it was when Falstaff was capably played according to the old tradition, and the playgoer went to hear the actor pile up a mighty climax, culminating in "Think of that, Master Brook." In those palmy days it was the vision of the man-mountain baked in the buck-basket and suddenly plunged hissing hot into the cool stream of the Thames at Datchet that focused the excitement of the pit; and if the two conversations between Ford and Falstaff were played for all they were worth, Shakespear was justified of his creation, and the rest was taken cheerfully as mere filling up. Now, it cannot be supposed that either Boito or Verdi had ever seen such a performance; and the criticisms of modern quite futile productions of The Merry Wives have shown that a mere literary acquaintance with the text will not yield up the secret to the ordinary unShakespearean man; yet it is just here, on Ford and Falstaff, that Verdi has concentrated his attack and trained his heaviest artillery. His Ford carries Shakespear's a step higher: it exhausts what Shakespear's resources could only suggest. And this seems to me to dispose of the matter in Verdi's favor.

A Midsummer Night's Dream

In The Saturday Review *of July 13, 1895, Shaw criticized
Augustin Daly's production of the play.*

THE TWO GENTLEMEN of Verona has been succeeded at
Daly's Theatre by A Midsummer Night's Dream. Mr.
Daly is in great form. In my last article I was rash enough
to hint that he had not quite realized what could be done
with electric lighting on the stage. He triumphantly an-
swers me by fitting up all his fairies with portable bat-
teries and incandescent lights, which they switch on and
off from time to time, like children with a new toy. He
has trained Miss Lillian Swain in the part of Puck until
it is safe to say that she does not take one step, strike one
attitude, or modify her voice by a single inflexion that is
not violently, wantonly, and ridiculously wrong and absurd. Instead of being merciurial, she poses academically,
like a cheap Italian statuette; instead of being impish and
childish, she is elegant and affected; she laughs a solemn,
measured laugh, like a heavy German Zamiel; she announces her ability to girdle the earth in forty minutes in
the attitude of a professional skater, and then begins the
journey awkwardly in a swing, which takes her in the
opposite direction to that in which she indicated her
intention of going: in short, she illustrates every folly and
superstition that still clings round what Mr. Daly no
doubt calls "the legitimate." Another stroke of his is to
make Oberon a woman. It must not be supposed that he
does this solely because it is wrong, though there is no
other reason apparent. He does it partly because he was
brought up to do such things, and partly because they
seem to him to be a tribute to Shakespear's greatness,
which, being uncommon, ought not to be interpreted according to the dictates of common sense. A female
Oberon and a Puck who behaves like a page-boy earnestly
training himself for the post of footman recommend
themselves to him because they totally destroy the natu-

ralness of the representation, and so accord with his conception of the Shakespearean dramas as the most artificial
of all forms of stage entertainment. That is how you find
out the man who is not an artist. Verse, music, the beauties
of dress, gesture, and movement are to him interesting
aberrations instead of being the natural expression which
human feeling seeks at a certain degree of delicacy and
intensity. He regards art as a quaint and costly ring in
the nose of Nature. I am loth to say that Mr. Daly is such
a man; but after studying all his Shakespearean revivals
with the thirstiest desire to find as much art as possible in
them, I must mournfully confess that the only idea I can
see in them is the idea of titivation. As to his slaughter-
ings of the text, how can one help feeling them acutely
in a play like A Midsummer Night's Dream, in which
Shakespear, having to bring Nature in its most enchanting aspect before an audience without the help of theatrical scenery, used all his power of description and
expression in verse with such effect that the utmost any
scene-painter can hope for is to produce a picture that
shall not bitterly disappoint the spectator who has read
the play beforehand? Mr. Daly is, I should say, one of
those people who are unable to conceive that there could
have been any illusion at all about the play before scenery
was introduced. He certainly has no suspicion of the fact
that every accessory he employs is brought in at the dead-
liest risk of destroying the magic spell woven by the poet.
He swings Puck away on a clumsy trapeze with a ridiculous clash of the cymbals in the orchestra, in the fullest
belief that he is thereby completing instead of destroying
the effect of Puck's lines. His "panoramic illusion of the
passage of Theseus's barge to Athens" is more absurd
than anything that occurs in the tragedy of Pyramus and
Thisbe in the last act. The stage management blunders
again and again through feeble imaginative realization of
the circumstances of the drama. In the first act it should
be clear to any stage manager that Lysander's speech, beginning, "I am, my lord, as well derived as he," should
be spoken privately and not publicly to Theseus. In the
rehearsal scene in the wood, Titania should not be conspicuously exhibited under a limelight in the very centre
of the stage, where the clowns have, in defiance of all

common sanity, to pretend not to see her. We are expected, no doubt, to assume that she is invisible because
she is a fairy, though Bottom's conversation with her
when she wakes and addresses him flatly contradicts that
hypothesis. In the fourth act, Theseus has to enter from
his barge down a bank, picking his way through the sleep-
ing Lysander and Hermia, Demetrius and Helena. The
four lions in Trafalgar Square are not more conspicuous
and unoverlookable than these four figures are. Yet
Theseus has to make all his hunting speeches in an impossible unconsciousness of them, and then to look at
them amazedly and exclaim, "But soft, what nymphs are
these?" as if he could in any extremity of absence of mind
have missed seeing them all along. Most of these absurdities are part of a systematic policy of sacrificing the credibility of the play to the chance of exhibiting an effective
"living picture."

> I swear to thee by Cupid's strongest bow,
> By his best arrow with the golden head,
> By the simplicity of Venus' doves,
> By that which knitteth souls and prospers loves, etc.

Mr. Daly's powerful mind perceived at a glance that the
second and third lines are superfluous, as their omission
does not destroy the sense of the passage. He accordingly
omitted them. In the same sense, Shakespear makes the
two star-crossed lovers speak in alternate lines with an
effect which sets the whole scene throbbing with their
absorption in one another:

LYSANDER. The course of true love never did run smooth.
   But either it was different in blood—
HERMIA. O cross! too high to be enthralled to low!
LYSANDER. Or else misgraffed in respect of years,
HERMIA. O spite! too old to be engaged to young!
LYSANDER. Or else it stood upon the choice of friends,
HERMIA. O hell! to choose love by another's eye!
LYSANDER. Or if there were a sympathy in choice,
   War, death, or sickness did lay siege to it, etc.

With a Hermia who knew how to breathe out these
parentheses, the duet would be an exquisite one; but Mr.
Daly, shocked, as an American and an Irishman, at a

young lady using such an expression as "Oh hell!" cuts
out the whole antiphony, and leaves Lysander to deliver
a long lecture without interruption from the lady. At
such moments, the episode of the ass's head rises to the
dignity of allegory. From any other manager I should
accept the excuse that the effects of verse for which I am
pleading require a virtuosity of delivery on the part of
the actor which is practically not to be had at present.
But Mr. Daly has Miss Rehan, who is specially famous
for just this virtuosity of speech; and yet her lines are
treated just as the others are. The fact is, beautiful elocution is rare because the managers have no ears.

The play, though of course very poorly spoken in comparison with how it ought to be spoken, is tolerably acted.
Mr. George Clarke, clad in the armor of Alcibiades and
the red silk gown of Charley's Aunt, articulates most in-
dustriously, and waves his arms and flexes his wrists in
strict accordance, not for a moment with the poetry, but
with those laws of dramatic elocution and gesture which
veteran actors are always willing to impart to novices at a
reasonable price per dozen lessons. Mr. Lewis as Bottom
is not as funny as his part, whereas in modern plays he is
always funnier than his part. He seemed to me to miss
the stolid, obstinate, self-sufficient temperament of Bottom altogether. There is a definite conception of some
particular sort of man at the back of all Shakespear's
characters. The quantity of fun to be got out of Bottom
and Autolycus, for instance, is about the same; but underneath the fun there are two widely different persons, of
types still extant and familiar. Mr. Lewis would be as
funny in Autolycus as he is in Bottom; but he would be
exactly the same man in both parts.

As to Miss Rehan, her scenes in the wood with Demetrius were very fine, although, in the passage where
Hermia frightens her, she condescends to arrant clowning.
Her treatment of Shakespearean verse is delightful after
the mechanical intoning of Sarah Benrhardt. She gives
us beauty of tone, grace of measure, delicacy of articulation: in short, all the technical qualities of verse music,
along with the rich feeling and fine intelligence without
which those technical qualities would soon become monotonous. When she is at her best, the music melts in

the caress of the emotion it expresses, and thus completes
the conditions necessary for obtaining Shakespear's effects
in Shakespear's way. When she is on the stage, the play
asserts its full charm; and when she is gone, and the stage
carpenters and the orchestra are doing their best to pull
the entertainment through in Mr. Daly's way, down drops
the whole affair into mild tedium. But it is impossible to
watch the most recent developments of Miss Rehan's
style without some uneasiness. I wonder whether she is
old enough to remember the late Barry Sullivan when
he was still in his physical prime. Those who do will
recall, not an obsolete provincial tragedian, trading on
the wreck of an unaccountable reputation, but an actor
who possessed in an extraordinary degree just the imposing grace, the sensitive personal dignity of style, the force
and self-reliance into which Miss Rehan's style is settling.
Miss Rehan's exit in the second act of A Midsummer
Night's Dream, with the couplet,

> I'll follow thee, and make a heaven of hell
> To die upon the hand I love so well,

is an exact reproduction of the Barry Sullivan exit.
Again, in the first act, when Miss Rehan, prone on a
couch, raises herself on her left hand, and, with her right
raised "to heaven," solemnly declaims the lines:

> For ere Demetrius look'd on Hermia's eyne
> He hailed down oaths, that he was only mine;
> And when this hail some heat from Hermia felt,
> So he dissolved, and showers of oaths did melt,

you are, once more, not forward with Duse, but back with
Barry Sullivan, who would in just the same way, when
led into it by a touch of stateliness and sonority in the
lines, abandon his part, and become for the moment a
sort of majestic incarnation of abstract solemnity and
magnificence. His skill and intense belief in himself gave
him the dangerous power of doing so without making
himself ridiculous; and it was by this power, and by the
fascination, the grace, and the force which are implied by
it, that he gave life to old-fashioned and mutilated representations of Shakespear's plays, poorly acted and ignorantly mounted. This was all very well whilst the fascina-

tion lasted; but when his voice lost its tone, his figure its resilience and grace, and his force its spontaneity and natural dignity, there was nothing left but a mannered, elderly, truculent, and, except to his old admirers, rather absurd tragedian of the palmy school. As I was a small boy when I first saw Barry Sullivan, and as I lost sight of him before his waning charm had quite vanished, I remember him, not as he is remembered by those who saw him only in the last ten years of his life, but as an actor who was in his day much further superior in pictorial, vocal, and rhetorical qualities to his next best rival than any actor or actress can easily be nowadays. And it strikes me forcibly that unless Miss Rehan takes to playing Imogen instead of such comparatively childish stuff as Julia or even Helena, and unless she throws herself into sympathy with the contemporary movement by identifying herself with characteristically modern parts of the Magda or Nora type, she may find herself left behind in the race by competitors of much less physical genius, just as Barry Sullivan did. Miss Rehan is clearly absolute mistress of the situation at Daly's Theatre: nobody can persuade me that if she says Cymbeline, Mr. Daly can say The Two Gentlemen of Verona, or that if she says Sudermann or Ibsen, Mr. Daly can insist on the author of Dollars and Cents. But the self-culture which has produced her superb graces of manner and diction seems to have isolated her instead of quickening her sympathy and drawing closer her contact with the world. Every woman who sees Duse play Magda feels that Duse is acting and speaking for her and for all women as they are hardly ever able to speak and act for themselves. The same may be said of Miss Achurch as Nora. But no woman has ever had the very faintest sensation of that kind about any part that Miss Rehan has yet played. We admire, not what she is doing, but the charm with which she does it. That sort of admiration will not last. Miss Rehan's voice is not henceforth going to grow fresher, nor her dignity less conscious, nor her grace of gesture less studied and mannered, nor her movements swifter and more spontaneous. Already I find that young people who see her for the first time cannot quite agree that our raptures about her Katharine and her Rosalind are borne out by her Julia

and Helena. Five years hence she will be still more rhetorical and less real: further ahead I dare not look with
Barry Sullivan in my mind. There is only one way to
defy Time; and that is to have young ideas, which may
always be trusted to find youthful and vivid expression.
I am afraid this means avoiding the company of Mr.
Daly; but it is useless to blink the fact that unless a modern actress can and will force her manager, in spite of his
manly prejudices, to produce plays with real women's
parts in them, she had better, at all hazards, make shift to
manage for herself. With Grandfather Daly to choose her
plays for her, there is no future for Ada Rehan.

Writing as music critic of The Star, *under the name of
Corno di Bassetto, Shaw discussed a production of* A Midsummer Night's Dream *on January 10, 1890.*

PRETTY LOT of fellows, these dramatic critics. Do you
remember Cousin Feenix, in Dombey and Son, who spoke
of Shakespear as "man not for an age but for all time, with
whom your great grandfather was probably acquainted"?
That is much the manner in which the dramatic critics
have treated the performance of A Midsummer Night's
Dream at the Globe. They have sat it out; yawned; put
in a good word for Mr. Benson as an Archbishop's
nephew and for old William; and then set to work in
earnest over their beloved penny dreadful equestrian
lions and half-crown dreadful Toscas, and forty thousandth night of Sweet Simpering Lavender, and stale dramatic dog biscuit generally. However, it is an ill wind
that blows nobody any good. When I entered the pit at
the Globe on Monday evening, just as the overture was
getting under way, I found only four rows occupied, and
so had practically a choice of positions and an easy view
for my hard-earned two shillings. But the stalls were full;
and I noticed that several of the occupants had brought
sacred-looking books, and that the men were unusually
particular about removing their hats when they came in.
    Now, I am loth to spoil such excellent business; but I
am bound to avow that I found myself next a gentleman
who is an old acquaintance of the manager's, and he as-

sured me (and I have since verified his assurance) that the archiepiscopal connection is a pure invention of the Press, and that Mr. F. R. Benson is neither an archbishop, nor an archbishop's son, nor an archbishop's nephew, nor even, so far as can be ascertained, his remotest cousin-german. My first impulse on hearing this was, I own, to demand my money back. But just then Miss Kate Rorke's draperies floated through the arcades; and when she said

> O happy fair!
> Your eyes are lodestars, and your tongue's sweet air
> More tunable than lark to shepherd's ear

Lambeth Palace might have been dynamited across into Millbank for all I cared. Reader: do you remember Shield's three-part song; and have you ever yourself lent a hand with

> O——h! hap-pee hap-pee hap-pee hap-pee fai-air
> Your eyes, are lodestars and your tongue, sweet air.

Which, I frankly admit, spoils the sense of the verse, but not its music. This generation, I sometimes think, has no sense of word music. They will go to the Arts and Crafts Exhibition, and admire tissues of cottons, wools, and silks; but give them a beautiful tissue of words, and they have no more sense of the art of it than if it was the Post Office Directory. For instance, William Morris has been weaving words into an article on the art and industry of the fourteenth century in Time. Now watch the reviews, and see whether one of them will draw the slightest distinction between the beauty of this article's verbal fabric and the literary kamptulicon of Mr. Blank of the Sterile Club, situate in the region between Dan and Beersheba. But if William Morris had woven a carpet instead, how everybody would have pretended to admire it!

The confounded thing about it is that actors, whose business it is to be experts in word music, are nearly as deaf to it as other people. At the Globe they walk in thick darkness through Shakespear's measures. They do not even seem to know that Puck may have the vivacity of a street Arab, but not his voice: his bite, but never his bark; that Theseus should know all Gluck's operas by heart, and in their spirit deliver his noble lines; that

Oberon must have no Piccadilly taint in his dialect to betray him into such utterances as

> Be it ahnce, aw cat, aw bea-ah
> Pahd, aw boa-ah with b'istled hai-ah
> In thy eye that shall appea-ah
> When thou wak'st, it is thy dea-ah.

By this time I should be converted to the device of joining consecutive vowels with r's, if conversion were possible. I know that it is easy to say Mariar Ann, and cruelly hard to say Maria Ann. But the thing is possible with courage and devotion. When Mr. Benson schools himself to say

> Not Hermia but Helena I love

instead of

> Not Hermia but Helenar I love

I shall be spared a pang when next thereafter I hear him play Lysander. Helenar sounds too like cockney for Eleanor.

On the whole, I fear I must declare sweepingly that Miss Kate Rorke is the only member of the company who is guiltless of verse murder. She is by no means the gentle Helena of Shakespear. The soul of that damsel was weak; but none of Miss Kate Rorke's organs, I take it, is stronger than her soul. Yet by this very strength she forces herself on the part; and I accept her with joy and gratitude. Artist in one thing, artist in all things. The sense of beauty that guides Miss Rorke through the verse, guides her movements, her draperies, her eyes, and everything about her. She has charms in her fingers and charms in her toes; and she shall have music (by Mendelssohn) wherever she goes.

Miss Maud Milton, who played Hermia, took the part at such short notice that she evidently had to learn it during the intervals; for in the first act she left out all about the simplicity of Venus' doves, and a good deal more beside. Later in the evening she was comparatively letter-perfect; and she played with intelligence and force. But she was melodramatic: the indispensable classic grace was wanting: she looked persecuted, and seemed to be struggling through the toils of some forger villain towards a reconciliation with a long lost husband in the fifth act. As to Bully Bottom, I have no doubt he was more Athenian than Shakespear made him; but his stupidity lacked the true unction, and his voice had not caught the Stratford-on-Avon diapason. The rest of the company must excuse me. I never trespass on the province of a colleague. The criticism of acting is Arthur Walkley's business.

MUCH ADO ABOUT NOTHING

Shaw discussed the play in a review of February 26, 1898, in The Saturday Review.

MUCH ADO is perhaps the most dangerous actor-manager trap in the whole Shakespearean repertory. It is not a safe play like The Merchant of Venice or As You Like It, nor a serious play like Hamlet. Its success depends on the way it is handled in performance; and that, again, depends on the actor-manager being enough of a critic to discriminate ruthlessly between the pretension of the author and his achievement.

The main pretension in Much Ado is that Benedick and Beatrice are exquisitely witty and amusing persons. They are, of course, nothing of the sort. Benedick's pleasantries might pass at a sing-song in a public-house parlor; but a gentleman rash enough to venture on them in even the very mildest £52-a-year suburban imitation of polite society today would assuredly never be invited again. From his first joke, "Were you in doubt, sir, that you asked her?" to his last, "There is no staff more reverend than one tipped with horn," he is not a wit, but a blackguard. He is not Shakespear's only failure in that genre. It took the Bard a long time to grow out of the provincial conceit that made him so fond of exhibiting his accomplishments as a master of gallant badinage. The very thought of Biron, Mercutio, Gratiano, and Benedick must, I hope, have covered him with shame in his later years. Even Hamlet's airy compliments to Ophelia before the court would make a cabman blush. But at least Shakespear did not value himself on Hamlet's indecent jests as he evidently did on those of the four merry gentlemen of the earlier plays. When he at last got conviction of sin, and saw this sort of levity in its proper light, he made masterly amends by presenting the blackguard *as* a blackguard in the person of Lucio in Measure for Measure. Lucio, as a character study, is worth forty Benedicks and Birons. His obscenity is not only inoffensive, but irresistibly entertaining, because it is drawn with perfect skill, offered at its true value, and given its proper interest, without any complicity of the author in its lewdness. Lucio is much more of a gentleman than Benedick, because he keeps his coarse sallies for coarse people. Meeting one woman, he says humbly, "Gentle and fair: your brother kindly greets you. Not to be weary with you, he's in prison." Meeting another, he hails her sparkingly with "How now? which of your hips has the more profound sciatica?" The one woman is a lay sister, the other a prostitute. Benedick or Mercutio would have cracked their low jokes on the lay sister, and been held up as gentlemen of rare wit and excellent discourse for it. Whenever they approach a woman or an old man, you shiver with apprehension as to what brutality they will come out with.

Precisely the same thing, in the tenderer degree of her sex, is true of Beatrice. In her character of professed wit she has only one subject, and that is the subject which a really witty woman never jests about, because it is too serious a matter to a woman to be made light of without indelicacy. Beatrice jests about it for the sake of the indelicacy. There is only one thing worse than the Elizabethan "merry gentleman," and that is the Elizabethan "merry lady."

Why is it then that we still want to see Benedick and Beatrice, and that our most eminent actors and actresses still want to play them? Before I answer that very simple question let me ask another. Why is it that Da Ponte's "dramma giocosa," entitled Don Giovanni, a loathsome story of a coarse, witless, worthless libertine, who kills an old man in a duel and is finally dragged down through a trapdoor to hell by his twaddling ghost, is still, after more than a century, as "immortal" as Much Ado? Simply because Mozart clothed it with wonderful music, which turned the worthless words and thoughts of Da Ponte into a magical human drama of moods and transitions of feeling. That is what happened in a smaller way with Much Ado. Shakespear shews himself in it a commonplace librettist working on a stolen plot, but a great musician. No matter how poor, coarse, cheap, and obvious the thought may be, the mood is charming, and the music of the words expresses the mood. Paraphrase the encounters of Benedick and Beatrice in the style of a bluebook, carefully preserving every idea they present, and it will become apparent to the most infatuated Shakespearean that they contain at best nothing out of the common in thought or wit, and at worst a good deal of vulgar naughtiness. Paraphrase Goethe, Wagner, or Ibsen in the same way, and you will find original observation, subtle thought, wide comprehension, far-reaching intuition, and serious psychological study in them. Give Shakespear a fairer chance in the comparison by paraphrasing even his best and maturest work, and you will still get nothing more than the platitudes of proverbial philosophy, with a very occasional curiosity in the shape of a rudiment of some modern idea, not followed up. Not until the Shakespearean music is added by replacing the paraphrase with the original lines does the enchantment begin. Then you are in another world at once. When a flower-girl tells a coster to hold his jaw, for nobody is listening to him, and he retorts, "Oh, youre there, are you, you beauty?" they reproduce the wit of Beatrice and Benedick exactly. But put it this way. "I wonder that you will still be talking, Signior Benedick: nobody marks you." "What! my dear Lady Disdain, are you yet living?" You are miles away from costerland at once. When I tell you that Benedick and the coster are equally poor in thought, Beatrice and the flower-girl equally vulgar in repartee, you reply that I might as well tell you that a nightingale's love is no higher than a cat's. Which is exactly what I do tell you, though the nightingale is the better musician. You will admit, perhaps, that the love of the worst human singer in the world is accompanied by a higher degree of intellectual consciousness than that of the most ravishingly melodious nightingale. Well, in just the same way, there are plenty of quite second-rate writers who are abler thinkers and wits than William, though they are unable to weave his magic into the expression of their thoughts.

It is not easy to knock this into the public head, because comparatively few of Shakespear's admirers are at all conscious that they are listening to music as they hear

his phrases turn and his lines fall so fascinatingly and
memorably; whilst we all, no matter how stupid we are,
can understand his jokes and platitudes, and are flattered
when we are told of the subtlety of the wit we have
relished, and the profundity of the thought we have
fathomed. Englishmen are specially susceptible to this
sort of flattery, because intellectual subtlety is not their
strong point. In dealing with them you must make them
believe that you are appealing to their brains when you
are really appealing to their senses and feelings. With
Frenchmen the case is reversed: you must make them believe that you are appealing to their senses and feelings
when you are really appealing to their brains. The
Englishman, slave to every sentimental ideal and dupe of
every sensuous art, will have it that his great national
poet is a thinker. The Frenchman, enslaved and duped
only by systems and calculations, insists on his hero being
a sentimentalist and artist. That is why Shakespear is
esteemed a master-mind in England, and wondered at
as a clumsy barbarian in France.

However indiscriminate the public may be in its
Shakespear worship, the actor and actress who are to
make a success of Much Ado must know better. Let them
once make the popular mistake of supposing that what
they have to do is to bring out the wit of Benedick and
Beatrice, and they are lost. Their business in the "merry"
passages is to cover poverty of thought and coarseness
of innuendo by making the most of the grace and dignity
of the diction. The sincere, genuinely dramatic passages
will then take care of themselves. Alas! Mr. Alexander
and Miss Julia Neilson have made the plunge without
waiting for my advice. Miss Neilson, throwing away
all her grace and all her music, strives to play the merry
lady by dint of conscientious gambolling. Instead of
uttering her speeches as exquisitely as possible, she rattles
through them, laying an impossible load of archness on
every insignificant conjunction, and clipping all the
important words until there is no measure or melody left
in them. Not even the wedding scene can stop her: after
an indignant attitude or two she redoubles her former
skittishness. I can only implore her to give up all her

deep-laid Beatricisms, to discard the movements of Miss
Ellen Terry, the voice of Mrs. Patrick Campbell, and the
gaiety of Miss Kitty Loftus, and try the effect of Julia
Neilson in all her grave grace taken quite seriously..
Mr. Alexander makes the same mistake, though, being
more judicious than Miss Neilson, he does not carry it
out so disastrously. His merry gentleman is patently a
dutiful assumption from beginning to end. He smiles,.
rackets, and bounds up and down stairs like a quiet man
who has just been rated by his wife for habitual dullness.
before company. It is all hopeless: the charm of Benedick cannot be realized by the spryness of the actor's legs,.
the flashing of his teeth, or the rattle of his laugh: nothing
but the music of the words—above all, not their meaning
—can save the part. I wish I could persuade Mr. Alexander that if he were to play the part exactly as he played
Guy Domville, it would at once become ten times more
fascinating. He should at least take the revelation of
Beatrice's supposed love for him with perfect seriousness.
The more remorsefully sympathetic Benedick is when she
comes to bid him to dinner after he has been gulled into
believing she loves him, the more exquisitely ridiculous
the scene becomes. It is the audience's turn to laugh
then, not Benedick's.

Of all Sir Henry Irving's manifold treasons against
Shakespear, the most audacious was his virtually cutting
Dogberry out of Much Ado. Mr. Alexander does not go
so far; but he omits the fifth scene of the third act, upon
which the whole effect of the later scenes depends, since
it is from it that the audience really gets Dogberry's
measure. Dogberry is a capital study of parochial character. Sincerely played, he always comes out as a very real
and highly entertaining person. At the St. James's, I
grieve to say, he does not carry a moment's conviction:
he is a mere mouthpiece for malapropisms, all of which
he shouts at the gallery with intense consciousness of their
absurdity, and with open anxiety lest they should pass.
unnoticed. Surely it is clear, if anything histrionic is
clear, that Dogberry's first qualification must be a complete unconsciousness of himself as he appears to others.

Verges, even more dependent than Dogberry on that

cut-out scene with Leonato, is almost annihilated by its excision; and it was hardly worth wasting Mr. Esmond on the remainder.

When I have said that neither Benedick nor Beatrice have seen sufficiently through the weakness of Shakspear's merriments to concentrate themselves on the purely artistic qualities of their parts, and that Dogberry is nothing but an excuse for a few laughs, I have made a somewhat heavy deduction from my praises of the revival. But these matters are hardly beyond remedy; and the rest is excellent. Miss Fay Davis's perfect originality contrasts strongly with Miss Neilson's incorrigible imitativeness. Her physical grace is very remarkable; and she creates her part between its few lines, as Hero must if she is to fill up her due place in the drama. Mr. Fred Terry is a most engaging Don Pedro; and Mr. H. B. Irving is a striking Don John, though he is becoming too accomplished an actor to make shift with that single smile which is as well known at the St. James's by this time as the one wig of Mr. Pinero's hero was at "The Wells." Mr. Vernon and Mr. Beveridge are, of course, easily within their powers as Leonato and Antonio; and all the rest come off with credit—even Mr. Loraine, who has not a trace of Claudio in him. The dresses are superb, and the scenery very handsome, though Italy contains so many palaces and chapels that are better than handsome that I liked the opening scenes best. If Mr. Alexander will only make up his mind that the piece is irresistible as poetry, and hopeless as epigrammatic comedy, he need not fear for its success. But if he and Miss Neilson persist in depending on its attempts at wit and gallantry, then it remains to be seen whether the public's sense of duty or its boredom will get the upper hand.

On the occasion of Beerbohm Tree's production of Much Ado *Shaw took Tree to task for his manner with Shakespeare. The article appeared in* The Saturday Review *on February 11, 1905, and was called "The Dying Tongue of Great Elizabeth."*

MUCH AS THE SHAKESPEAREAN orgies at His Majesty's Theatre have interested and amused me from the first, it was not until I witnessed Much Ado the other night that it struck me that Mr. Tree's detachment from Shakespear was a phenomenon less personal and more national —or, at least, more metropolitan—than I had supposed. That detachment is certainly very complete. We all know the actor-managers to whom Shakespear is an august convention, conferring intellectual eminence, scholarship, and professional primacy on his exponents; but however honorary the degree, however imaginary the scholarship, however precarious the primacy, there has always been between the author and actor a genuine bond of stage method, of rhetoric, of insistence on exceptionally concentrated personal force and skill in execution, of hammering the play in by ceaseless point-making. Far be it from me to pretend that these things were achieved always, or even often; but they were aimed at; and the result was a performance which, on its technical side, had at least some relation to Shakespear, even when it was only the relation of failure.

But even that bond is now broken. Among the managers who are imaginative and capable enough to count seriously, Mr. Tree is the first within my experience for whom Shakespear does not exist at all. Confronted with a Shakespearean play, he stares into a ghastly vacuum, yet stares unterrified, undisturbed by any suspicion that his eyesight is failing, quite prepared to find the thing simply an ancient, dusty, mouldy, empty house which it is his business to furnish, decorate, and housewarm with an amusing entertainment. And it is astonishing how well he does it. Totally insensible to Shakespear's qualities, he puts his own qualities into the work. When he makes one of Shakespear's points—which he does extremely seldom—it is only because at that particular moment Shakespear's wit happens to coincide with his own: for instance, in Much Ado he makes a point of the famous "Love me! Why, it must be requited"; but you can see by his colloquial alteration of the line to "Love me! Oh! This must be requited," that he did not feel the point in the original more rhetorical version, and that it was his own dramatic instinct that prompted him to re-invent it and introduce it as a pure interpolation, ingeniously using as much of the bard's language as

could be made to convey anything to himself or the
audience. He is always papering the naked wall, helping
the lame dog over the stile, putting a gorgeous livery on
the man in possession, always, like Nature, abhorring a
vacuum, and filling it with the treasures of his own ingenuity and imagination and fun, and then generously
giving our Shakespear the credit. Think back a little on
his achievements in Shakespear's characters. Can you
not remember some telling stroke in all of them? But
it is never one of Shakespear's strokes. No doubt his
Falstaff, being a sin against nature, had all the atrocity
peculiar to such sins: still, one remembers, as an audacious but quite credible character-quip, the knight who
was impecunious enough to take fifteen pence from Pistol
as his share of the price of the stolen fan, yet riding up
to his pothouse on a valuable white nag. Shakespear
never thought of that. You remember Caliban taking a
huge bite out of a raw gurnet, catching flies to prevent
them teasing his god Stephano, and lying on a promon-
tory with heaven knows what melancholy at his heart,
watching the ship that is taking away Prospero and Prospero's daughter for ever into the unknown. You remember Richard the Second, though moved only to
futile sarcasm by Bolingbroke's mastery of him, turning
away with a stifled sob when his dog deserts him and
licks Bolingbroke's hand. You remember, too, how Richard munches sweetmeats whilst his peers are coming to
blows in his presence, and how, after his disgrace in Westminster Hall, instead of making the conventional pathetic
exit, he clasps his hands affectedly behind him, cocks his
chin pettishly in the air, and struts out, not as an accomplished actor would go out, but—he convinces you—
as Richard himself probably did go out on that occasion.
And you will remember his Benedick up a tree, shying
oranges at the three conspirators, and finally shaking the
whole crop down on them when they accuse him of "a
contemptible spirit," quite content to exploit the phrase
in its modern sense, though Shakespear means, not contemptible, but contemptuous.

Now some of these indelible remembrances are of
strokes of genius, and some are of inconsiderate tom-

fooleries (for you really should not, like Crummles's comic countryman, catch flies when another actor is try-ing to hold the audience); but they are all pure original Tree and not Shakespear. They could only have occurred to one whose mind was completely free from all preoccu-pation with Shakespear. And that is only possible to one who can see nothing in Shakespear except what must be obvious to any person of normal senses.

Now I am quite aware that I here seem to be con-demning Mr. Tree in the most severe manner. Mr. Chur-ton Collins, Mr. Sidney Lee, Mr. Swinburne will say that if all this be true, then Mr. Tree is not papering a blank wall but barbarously whitewashing a fresco, not helping a lame dog over a stile, but breaking the leg of a lion. And they would be partly right. It cannot be denied that Mr. Tree takes unheard-of pains to manu-facture "business" to help out scenes that positively bristle with missed Shakespearean points. His occasional crimes against literature are positively blasphemous. Let me give one example from Much Ado. In the masked ball scene, when the Prince flits across the stage with Hero, the little scrap of their conversation that reaches us is exquisitely caught up at the end into a little trill of verse.

PRINCE: My visor is Philemon's roof;
        Within the house of Jove.
HERO: Why then your visor should be thatched.
PRINCE: Speak low if you speak love.

When, at His Majesty's, the first two lines were omitted, and "Speak low if you speak love" tacked suddenly on to "God defend, the lute should be like the case," I stag-gered to my seat as if a dart had been struck through my liver. Had I not been under a strong and recent per-sonal obligation to Mr. Tree for a service rendered to me in the production of a play of my own, I declare I should have risen and addressed the audience, and moved a resolution. Only once before in my life have I had such a shock. That was at Covent Garden one night at the end of Don Giovanni, when the statue, without a word of warning, lit on a note so utterly foreign to the key, that I sprang to my feet in the midst of the stalls and uttered a most fearful imprecation, as remote from the ordinary channel of my conversation as the statue's error was from the score of Mozart.

Now it is clear that Mr. Tree's valuation of Shakespear's graces of language must be widely different from my own, or he would not make cuts of this kind, or modernize and interpolate as he does so freely throughout the play. And this brings me to the main object of my criticism, which is to defend Mr. Tree by calling attention to a phenomenon which is being acted on in practice before we have learnt to allow for it.

Some time ago I received a copy of a book called The Twentieth Century Bible. It was a copy of the New Testament translated into such modern English as we find in the leading article of a respectable newspaper. Nobody who remembers the outcry that arose against our official revised version of the Scriptures—the very corrections of the errors of the authorized version being denounced as sacrilegious, and as exposing their makers to the curse in the last chapter of Revelation—can doubt that this Twentieth Century version would never have been undertaken by a body of devout Protestant believers (in America, too, of all countries) under any pressure short of daily experience of the fact that the authorized version is no longer intelligible to the common people: in short, that Jacobean English is a dead language. And I confess, not without an afterblush of amazement and humiliation, that I myself, who have never lost touch with the Jacobean language, who, as an Irishman, have for my mother tongue an English two centuries earlier than twentieth century cockney; who have all my life had my head full of the Bible and Shakespear, did nevertheless find that as I read this new vernacular Testament (quite with the proper amused contempt at first for its Philistine journalese) I gathered at once from it numbers of important points that I had never got from the authorized version, and saw others in quite a new and highly suggestive light. And I said, "If this is the case with me, who found George Eliot's English thirty years ago a jargon of awkward neologisms, how must it be with cockneys who might be my sons and daughters, and to

whom George Eliot is now quainter and more old-
fashioned than ever Fielding has been to me?"

Now let us return to Much Ado.

The performance went on in the usual manner up
to the point at which Shakespear rescues the play from
collapse through the exhaustion of its wretched plot,
and through the impossibility of keeping up the pretence
that Beatrice and Benedick are delightfully witty and
genuine creatures, by falling back on his old joke, a male
Malaprop, and making Dogberry the savior of the play.
Before Mr. Louis Calvert was half through Dogberry's
charge to the watch, I felt that something had begun
which was quite on a new plane. Mr. Calvert, as I have
some special reason to know, is an extraordinarily good
actor; but after all, there were other actors in the cast.
If you come to that, Mr. Tree can act, and sometimes,
when the work in hand suits his genius, act very well
indeed. No: the difference was not the difference between
good and ordinary acting: it was a difference in kind.
And it flashed on me presently that the secret was that the
language of Shakespear was a live language to Mr. Calvert, whereas to Mr. Tree and the rest it was more or less
a dead one. Allowing as much as possible for the difference between a steady professional skill that never blurs
a syllable nor drops the end of a line into the orchestra,
and a whimsical carelessness that lets even such a line
as "Come! I will have thee; but by this light I take thee
for pity" fall flat because the word "pity" does not reach
even the third row of the stalls, much less the gaping
bardolatrous pit, still, no mere technical accomplishment
on Mr. Calvert's part could have dug the huge gulf that
separated his utterance from that of the others. It is not
perfect articulation, but perfect intelligence that finds the
nail in every phrase and hits it on the head unerringly.
Now there is nothing to tax anybody's intelligence in
Much Ado. Like all Shakespear's comedies it contains
nothing beyond the capacity of a child except the indecencies which constitute the staple of its badinage.
Mr. Tree is as capable of understanding it as Mr. Calvert,
if only he knew the language of the seventeenth century
as Mr. Calvert does. But he only knows it as a scholar

knows Coptic: he cannot really speak it. When he can
neither frankly modernize it, as in his "Oh! This must
be requited," nor confine his acting to those phrases
which still survive in our speech, he is beaten by it. To
Mr. Calvert it is as natural as his native speech: he makes
it clear, expressive, and vivid without the least preoccupa-
tion; whereas to Mr. Tree, and indeed to all the rest, more
or less, it is a continual embarrassment.

Now we are in a position to do Mr. Tree justice. Here
he is, confronted with a play in a dead language. What
the language is to him, it is, *a fortiori,* to a public much
inferior to him in culture. One has only to open a spare
ear to hear the occupants of the stalls, presumably not
the least literate section of the audience, giggling at such
phrases as "Fair and softly" and the like, evidently taking
them to be Dogberryisms, as if John Gilpin himself was
too archaic for them. What can the manager do, playing
to please such an audience at the huge hazards that a
vast theatre involves, but treat Shakespear's language as
a drawback only feebly counterbalanced by its reputation? The consequences are startling to those who have
not analytic faculty enough to understand how much of
Shakespear's magic is created by the beauty and fancy of
his word-music. Paraphrase the dialogue of Much Ado
in mere utilitarian prose, and you will find speech after
speech awkward, superfluous, dragged in by the ears,
and consequently irritating and tedious, fatal to the
crispness of the action. The characters lose their glamor:
one sees that the creator of the merry lady with her
barmaidenly repartees and the facetious bachelor with
his boarding-house funny man's table talk, was no Oscar
Wilde. The three gallant companions in arms no longer
bear thinking of in comparison with Athos, Aramis, and
d'Artagnan. Dogberry is seen to be a cheap performance
in comparison with the best comic figures of Cervantes,
Scott, and Dickens. The subtler strokes of character are
wasted because they could be made amusing and intelligible only by the method of comedy; and Shakespear,
great at "drama," farce, and fairy extravaganza, had no
idea of comedy. For instance, Claudio is a well-observed
and consistent character; childishly selfish, cruel, and
affectionate; without judgment or reflection; always rush-

ing at a word of suggestion from one extreme of infatuation and credulity to the other. Labiche would have
made him irresistibly amusing and interestngly instructive by the modern comedic method. Shakespear, for want
of comedic faculty, gets no dramatic value out of him
whatever, and fails to convey to the audience anything
except a disagreeable impression of a conventional hero
who is driven by the mere letter of the plot into an
unconvincing misunderstanding and a dastardly revenge,
in the meanness of which his gallant friends grovel as
vulgarly as himself. The story is a hopeless one, pleasing
only to lovers of the illustrated police papers. It was all
very well for Shakespear to say "It does not matter what
the story is, provided I tell it; and it does not matter what
the characters say provided I turn the phrase for them."
He could make that boast good only to people with an
ear for his music and a born habit of thinking in his
language. That habit once lost, the garden of Klingsor
withers; Much Ado becomes what Don Giovanni or Die
Zauberflöte would become if Mozart's music were burnt
and the libretto alone preserved.

Mr. Tree has to find substitutes for the lost charm;
and he does so with a fertility that would do credit to
a professed playwright. Much Ado is not only bearable
at His Majesty's, it is positively pleasant to the disillusioned, and, I should think, enchantng to the young.
All the lovely things that Shakespear dispensed with
are there in bounteous plenty. Fair ladies, Sicilian sea-
scapes, Italian gardens, summer nights and dawns (com-
pressed into five minutes), Renascential splendors, danc-
ing, singing, masquerading, architecture, orchestration
tastefully culled from Wagner, Bizet, and German, and
endless larks in the way of stage business devised by Mr.
Tree, and carried out with much innocent enjoyment,
which is fairly infectious on the other side of the footlights. And then, since Shakespear's words are still the
basis of the dialogue, there are moments when the bard
enjoys his own again; for all the players are not as
completely swanproof as Mr. Tree; and sometimes the
star dances and silence is *not* the perfectst herald of joy.
On the whole, my advice is, go and see it: you will never
again have the chance of enjoying such an entertainment.

The company is a strong one. Mr. Henry Neville, as Leonato, is of course hampered at first by the violent make-believe which is necessary to face out the enormous lie that Beatrice and Benedick are providing (I am going to quote the program—a shameless document) "a brilliant encounter of wits by which the audience is perpetually confronted but never wearied." He has also to pretend that the trick on Benedick is credible in proportion to its over-acting. So far Mr. Neville is rather the benevolently mellow veteran, helping the play and the young people, than the deeply stirred actor; but in the church scene he will be remembered longer than most of our Leonatos. Mr. Sidney Brough, agreeably to Mr. Tree's historical conception of Don Pedro as a Spanish prince, makes up as Philip II, but repudiates the character of that gloomy monarch by a levity of deportment which verges on the comic relief to which Mr. Brough's early years were dedicated. His luckless kinsman, Mr. Lionel Brough, has been given the part of Verges after Mr. Tree had first erased Verges from the book of life. The really exasperating stupidity of cutting out the scene of the visit of Dogberry and Verges to Leonato has been made traditional on the London stage ever since Sir Henry Irving (who will have an extremely unpleasant quarter of an hour if he is unlucky enough to come across the Bard in the heavenly Pantheon) ingeniously discovered that means of reducing Dogberry to a minor part. In the omitted scene we become acquainted with Verges as an intelligent old man enfeebled by age, whose straightforward attempts to explain things are baffled by the lusty pigheadedness of Dogberry. Deprived of that opportunity, poor Mr. Lionel Brough can do nothing but echo Dogberry's words, and pretend to be a greater fool than he. It is infuriating to see a good actor treated in this fashion. How would Mr. Tree like it himself? Mr. Basil Gill cannot make Claudio a man to be thought about sympathetically; but he makes him pleasant and poetic to look at and listen to; and Mr. Haviland, an admirable speaker, is irreproachable as the friar. Mr. Laurence Irving, as Don John, wallows in wickedness as only a very amiable man can, and makes this most costive of villains inappropriately exuberant. It is when his part is over, in the church scene, that he suddenly begins to play silently, thoughtfully, and well.

As to Benedick, I defy anybody not to be amused by him. When he is not amusingly good from Mr. Tree's point of view he is amusingly bad from the classical Shakespearean point of view; and when you add that arboreal personality of which I for one never tire, you get a total result which it would be mere pedantry to cavil at, and which I would not change for the most perfectly classical Benedick the School of Dramatic Art will ever turn out. It is, in its way, colossal.

Miss Miriam Clements, quite unconsciously, perhaps, and all the better for that, is a classic Hero. I have never seen the interrupted wedding played with such perfect discretion. Anybody else would have torn it to pieces. Really a most excellent piece of work. Miss Winifred Emery plays Beatrice. I am afraid I was guilty of the impertinence of being prepared to sympathize with her on account of her late illness; but the first glimpse of her corrected that. I never saw anybody look so well. She was not like a sixteenth century Italian, nor, thank goodness, a Shakespearean merry lady. She was like an eighteenth-century queen. Her acting struck me as capricious and even grudging. Her unbending walk across the choir before the altar in the church scene was almost an anti-Ritualist demonstration. There were moments, notably in the overhearing scene, when she seemed quite in earnest. There were other moments when she seemed to stand aloof from the play with infinite disparagement, and to be on the point of losing her patience and going home, leaving us to finish our nonsense as best we might without her. Then she would take a sudden fancy to a passage and dash into the play like a bird into a fountain; and a delightful minute would ensue. It was better, far better, than the usual hard-working Beatrice, desperately determined to be "piercingly keen and exquisitely apt" (program again) at all hazards, and saying things that a flower-girl would spare a busdriver as if they were gems of delicate intuition. In short, she was clever enough to play Lady Disdain instead of playing for sentimental sympathy; and the effect was keenly good and original. And, happier than Verges, she had the *carduus benedictus* scene restored, to the great benefit of the play.

The scenery—for once, we have Italian scenery adequately lighted—is a vital organ, the only failure being the commonplace church, which will not bear comparison with Mr. Gordon Craig's suggestion of a lofty nave. On the whole, a very bad play, but a very enjoyable entertainment.

When Ellen Terry went into theatrical management in 1903 one of her productions was Much Ado About Nothing; *her son, Gordon Craig, who was called Ted, had a hand in the production. Shaw expressed his reactions in a letter of June 3, 1903.*

I went to see Much Adoodle-do yesterday evening. It is a shocking bad play, and can only be saved by Dogberry picking it up at the end, when Beatrice and Benedick are worn out after the church scene. But Dogberry *cannot* pick it up unless he has his scene before the wedding, because without that the audience is unprepared for the examination scene and does not find him out until too late. Why don't you believe me when I tell you these things? You believe everyone else; but nobody else tells you the truth.

You shouldn't fidget in the scene of the masks. In the other scenes it doesn't matter, because you are supposed to be provoking and inscrutable and cant-tell-whether-you're-serious-or-not. But here you should be *demure* and *most sincere,* as if you were telling a dear friend what a dull fool the poor man is. In other respects your Beatrice is a rather creditable performance, considering that I didn't stage-manage it.

Why don't you tell that young man how to say "Silence is the perfect'st herald of joy"? A little fluttering flower of a line which he makes a turnip of.

As usual Ted has the best of it. I have never seen the church scene go before—didnt think it *could* go, in fact. He should have done something better with the monument scene or else left it alone altogether; but still, when all is said, nothing quite like it has been done before;

and if only the extra people were trained dancers instead
of athletic amateurs, and Asche were Dogberry with his
first scene left in, and the choir were complete instead of
having one twopenny tenor and no basses, and the stalls
were abolished and replaced with a comfortable half
crown parterre right up to the orchestra, why, something
might be done with it all, especially if the public were
born over again and born different, and the guillotine
freely used in Trafalgar Square for a few months beforehand. But as it is I tell you for the thousandth time, do
no more unless Ted finds the money as well as the scenery.

In a Saturday Review *article on March 12, 1898, Shaw
compared Don John as a villain to Iago in* Othello.

. . . We have lately had our respected William Shakespear intemperately scolded by his disciples for making
Don John in Much Ado a stage villain. Now if ever there
was a villain who was not a stage villain it is Don John.
What is a stage villain? Clearly, not a real villain, but
a mere machine impelled by some interested motive to
keep the plot of a play in action. He wants to succeed
to a property; or he must have twenty thousand pounds
instantly to save him from ruin; or he is in love with
some woman who wants to marry the hero. Shakespear,
with all his superficiality, knew that villainy is something
simpler and deeper than a mere means to an end. Don
John is a true natural villain: that is to say, a malevolent
person. Only, he is un-English, because he is quite
conscious of his villainy, and disguises it neither from
himself nor his accomplices. Iago is also a true villain;
but he is English to the backbone. That is why English
commentators are so careful to expatiate on his Italianate-
ness. Having no motive in the world except sheer love of
evil, he is for ever explaining that Othello has probably
made love to his wife; that Cassio is lowering the standard
of practical soldiership by arithmetic pedantry; that
Roderigo is a fool who deserves to lose his money, and the
like transparently flimsy pretexts. Further, he has a
steady eye to the main chance, and tries to combine
money-gain and promotion with the luxury of mischief.

Thus he is English in the mode of his villainy. It is so effective a mode that it is rather fortunate for humanity that the English as a nation are not particularly villainous: villainy for villainy's sake attracts them as little as art for art's sake. All one can say, therefore, is that if an Englishman were a villain he would talk like Iago, not like Don John. Being what he is, he usually stops doing mischief when there is nothing more to be got by it, and has even a distinct preference for virtue when it costs nothing. In short, he has, properly speaking, no moral character at all: he is in the first place a utilitarian and in the second a pious romanticist; and this, I take it, is the reason why the villains and heroes of the everyday English theatre are all stage villains and heroes, not real ones. Also, why on the appearance of a real villain like Don John, he is unanimously denounced in England as an unnatural and impossible stage convention.

OTHELLO

In addition to his remarks comparing Iago to Don John, in the preceding section, Shaw wrote extensively on the characters in Othello *in other places, including a piece called "A Dressing Room Secret," found elsewhere in the book. Shaw reviewed a production of the play in* The Saturday Review *of May 29, 1897.*

. . . Othello at the Lyric was a much less trying experience. Antony and Cleopatra is an attempt at a serious drama. To say that there is plenty of bogus characterization in it—Enobarbus, for instance—is merely to say that it is by Shakespear. But the contrast between Cæsar and Antony is true human drama; and Cæsar himself is deeper than the usual Shakespearean stage king. Othello, on the other hand, is pure melodrama. There is not a touch of character in it that goes below the skin; and the fitful attempts to make Iago something better than a melodramatic villain only make a hopeless mess of him and his motives. To anyone capable of reading the play with an open mind as to its merits, it is obvious that Shakespear plunged through it so impetuously that he had it finished before he had made up his mind as to the character and motives of a single person in it. Probably it was not until he stumbled into the sentimental fit in which he introduced the willow song that he saw his way through without making Desdemona enough of the "supersubtle Venetian" of Iago's description to strengthen the case for Othello's jealousy. That jealousy, by the way, is purely melodramatic jealousy. The real article is to be found later on in A Winter's Tale, where Leontes is an unmistakeable study of a jealous man from life. But when the worst has been said of Othello that can be provoked by its superficiality and staginess, it remains magnificent by the volume of its passion and the splendor of its word-music, which sweep the scenes up to a plane on which sense is drowned in sound. The words do not

convey ideas: they are streaming ensigns and tossing
branches to make the tempest of passion visible. In this
passage, for instance:

> Like to the Pontic sea,
> Whose icy current and compulsive course
> Ne'er feels retiring ebb, but keeps due on
> To the Propontic and the Hellespont,
> E'en so my bloody thoughts, with violent pace,
> Shall ne'er look back, ne'er ebb to humble love
> Till that a capable and wide revenge
> Swallow them up,

if Othello cannot turn his voice into a thunder and surge
of passion, he will achieve nothing but a ludicrously misplaced bit of geography. If in the last scene he cannot
throw the darkness of night and the shadow of death over
such lines as

> I know not where is that Promethean heat
> That can thy light relume,

he at once becomes a person who, on his way to commit a pettish murder, stops to philosophize foolishly
about a candle end. The actor cannot help himself by
studying his part acutely; for there is nothing to study
in it. Tested by the brain, it is ridiculous: tested by the
ear, it is sublime. He must have the orchestral quality in
him; and as that is a matter largely of physical endowment, it follows that only an actor of certain physical
endowments can play Othello. Let him be as crafty as
he likes without that, he can no more get the effect than
he can sound the bottom C on a violoncello. The note is
not there, that is all; and he had better be content to
play Iago, which is within the compass of any clever
actor of normal endowments.

When I have said that Mr. Wilson Barrett has not this
special musical and vocal gift, I have said everything
needful; for in this matter a miss is as good as a mile. It
is of no use to *speak* "Farewell the tranquil mind"; for
the more intelligently and reasonably it is spoken the
more absurd it is. It must affect us as "Ora per sempre
addio, sante memorie" affects us when sung by Tamagno.
Mr. Wilson Barrett is an unmusical speaker except when

he is talking Manx. He chops and drives his phrases like
a smart carpenter with a mallet and chisel, hitting all
the prepositions and conjunctions an extra hard tap; and
he has a positive genius for misquotation. For example:

> Of one that loved not wisely but well

and

> Drop tears down faster than the Arabian trees,

both of which appear to me to bear away the palm from
Miss Achurch's

> By the scandering of this pelleted storm.

It is a pity that he is not built to fit Othello; for he produces the play, as usual, very well. At the Lyceum everyone is bored to madness the moment Sir Henry Irving
and Miss Terry leave the stage: at the Lyric, as afore-
time at the Princess's, the play goes briskly from beginning to end; and there are always three or four successes
in smaller parts sparkling round Mr. Barrett's big part.
Thus Mr. Wigney Percyval, the first Cassio I ever saw
get over the difficulty of appearing a responsible officer
and a possible successor for Othello with nothing but a
drunken scene to do it in, divides the honors of the second
act with Iago; and Mr. Ambrose Manning is interesting
and amusing all through as Roderigo. Mr. Franklin Mc-
Leay, as Iago, makes him the hero of the performance.
But the character defies all consistency. Shakespear, as
usual, starts with a rough general notion of a certain type
of individual, and then throws it over at the first temptation. Iago begins as a coarse blackguard, whose jovial
bluntness passes as "honesty," and who is professionally
a routine subaltern incapable of understanding why a
mathematician gets promoted over his head. But the
moment a stage effect can be made, or a fine speech
brought off by making him refined, subtle, and dignified,
he is set talking like Hamlet, and becomes a godsend to
students of the "problems" presented by our divine William's sham characters. Mr. McLeay does all that an
actor can do with him. He follows Shakespear faithfully
on the rails and off them. He plays the jovial blackguard

to Cassio and Roderigo and the philosopher and mentor
to Othello just as the lines lead him, with perfect intelli-
gibility and with so much point, distinction, and fascination that the audience loads him with compliments, and
the critics all make up their minds to declare that he
shews the finest insight into the many-sided and complex
character of the prince of villains. As to Miss Maud
Jeffries, I came to the conclusion when she sat up in bed
and said, "Why I should fear, I know not," with pretty
petulance, that she did not realize the situation a bit;
but her voice was so pathetically charming and musical,
and she is so beautiful a woman, that I hasten to confess
that I never saw a Desdemona I liked better. Miss
Frances Ivor, always at her best in Shakespear, should
not on that account try to deliver the speech about "lash-
ing the rascal naked through the world" in the traditional
Mrs. Crummles manner. Emilia's really interesting
speeches, which contain some of Shakespear's curious
anticipations of modern ideas, were of course cut; but
Miss Ivor, in what was left, proved her aptitude for Shakespearean work, of which I self-denyingly wish her all
possible abundance.

Mr. Barrett's best scene is that in which he reads the
despatch brought by Lodovico. His worst—leaving out
of account those torrential outbreaks of savagery for
which he is too civilized—is the second act. The storm,
the dread of shipwreck, the darkness, the fierce riot, the
"dreadful bell that frights the isle from its propriety,"
are not only not suggested, but contradicted, by the
scenery and management. We are shewn a delightful
Mediterranean evening; the bell is as pretty as an operatic
angelus; Othello comes in like a temperance lecturer;
Desdemona does not appear; and the exclamation,

> Look, if my gentle love be not raised up—
> I'll make thee an example,

becomes a ludicrously schoolmasterly "I'll make thee an
example," twice repeated. Here Mr. Barrett makes the
Moor priggish instead of simple, as Shakespear meant
him to be in the moments when he meant anything beyond making effective stage points. Another mistake
in management is the business of the portrait in the third

act, which is of little value to Othello, and interrupts Iago's speeches in a flagrantly obvious manner.

In an article on Verdi, appearing in The Anglo-Saxon Review *of March, 1901, Shaw took up Shakespeare's* Othello.

. . . The composition of Otello was a much less Shakespearean feat; for the truth is that instead of Otello being an Italian opera written in the style of Shakespear, Othello is a play written by Shakespear in the style of Italian opera. It is quite peculiar among his works in this aspect. Its characters are monsters: Desdemona is a prima donna, with handkerchief, confidant, and vocal solo all complete; and Iago, though certainly more anthropomorphic than the Count di Luna, is only so when he slips out of his stage villain's part. Othello's transports are conveyed by a magnificent but senseless music which rages from the Propontick to the Hellespont in an orgy of thundering sound and bounding rhythm; and the plot is a pure farce plot: that is to say, it is supported on an artificially manufactured and desperately precarious trick with a handkerchief which a chance word might upset at any moment. With such a libretto, Verdi was quite at home: his success with it proves, not that he could occupy Shakespear's plane, but that Shakespear could on occasion occupy his, which is a very different matter.

RICHARD III

Shaw criticized Henry Irving's production of the play in The Saturday Review *on December 26, 1896.*

THE WORLD being yet little better than a mischievous schoolboy, I am afraid it cannot be denied that Punch and Judy holds the field still as the most popular of dramatic entertainments. And of all its versions, except those which are quite above the head of the man in the street, Shakespear's Richard III is the best. It has abundant devilry, humor, and character, presented with luxuriant energy of diction in the simplest form of blank verse. Shakespear revels in it with just the sort of artistic unconscionableness that fits the theme. Richard is the prince of Punches: he delights Man by provoking God, and dies unrepentant and game to the last. His incongruous conventional appendages, such as the Punch hump, the conscience, the fear of ghosts, all impart a spice of outrageousness which leaves nothing lacking to the fun of the entertainment, except the solemnity of those spectators who feel bound to take the affair as a profound and subtle historic study.

Punch, whether as Jingle, Macaire, Mephistopheles, or Richard, has always been a favorite part with Sir Henry Irving. The craftily mischievous, the sardonically impudent, tickle him immensely, besides providing him with a welcome relief from the gravity of his serious impersonations. As Richard he drops Punch after the coronation scene, which, in deference to stage tradition, he makes a turning-point at which the virtuoso in mischief, having achieved his ambition, becomes a savage at bay. I do not see why this should be. In the tent scene, Richard says:

> There is no creature loves me;
> And if I die no soul will pity me.

Macbeth repeats this patch of pathos, and immediately proceeds to pity himself unstintedly over it; but Richard

no sooner catches the sentimental cadence of his own
voice than the mocker in him is awakened at once, and
he adds, quite in Punch's vein,

> Nay, wherefore should they? since that I myself
> Find in myself no pity for myself.

Sir Henry Irving omits these lines, because he plays, as he
always does, for a pathetically sublime ending. But we
have seen the sublime ending before pretty often; and this
time it robs us of such strokes as Richard's aristocrati-
cally cynical private encouragement to his entourage of
peers:

> Our strong arms be our conscience, swords our law.
> March on; join bravely; let us to't pell-mell,
> If not to Heaven, then hand in hand to hell;

ιollowed by his amusingly blackguardly public address to
the rank and file, quite in the vein of the famous and
more successful appeal to the British troops in the Penin-
sula. "Will you that are Englishmen fed on beef let yourselves be licked by a lot of —— Spaniards fed on oranges?" Despair, one feels, could bring to Punch-Richard
nothing but the exultation of one who loved destruction
better than even victory; and the exclamation

> A thousand hearts are great within my bosom

is not the expression of a hero's courage, but the evil
ecstasy of the destroyer as he finds himself, after a weak,
piping time of peace, back at last in his native element.
   Sir Henry Irving's acting edition of the play is so enormously superior to Cibber's, that a playgoer brought up,
as I was, on the old version must needs find an overwhelming satisfaction in it. Not that I object to the
particular lines which are now always flung in poor Cibber's face. "Off with his head: so much for Buckingham!"
is just as worthy of Shakespear as "I'll hear no more. Die,
prophet, in thy speech," and distinctly better than "Off
with his son George's head."

> Hark! the shrill trumpet sounds. To horse! Away!
> My soul's in arms, and eager for the fray,

is ridiculed because Cibber wrote it; but I cannot for the
life of me see that it is inferior to

> Go muster men. My counsel is my shield.
> We must be brief when traitors brave the field.

"Richard's himself again" is capital of its kind. If you
object to the kind, the objection is stronger against Shakespear, who set Cibber the example, and was proclaimed
immortal for it, than against an unfortunate actor who
would never have dreamt of inventing the art of rhetorical balderdash for himself. The plain reason why the
public for so many generations could see no difference in
merit between the famous Cibber points and

> A horse! A horse! My kingdom for a horse!

was that there was no difference to see. When it came to
fustian, Jack was as good as his master.

The real objection to Cibber's version is that it is what
we call a "one man show." Shakespear, having no room
in a play so full of action for more than one real part,
surrounded it with figures whose historical titles and
splendid dresses, helped by a line or two at the right
moment, impose on our imagination sufficiently to make
us see the whole Court of Edward IV. If Hastings, Stan-
ley, the "jockey of Norfolk," the "deep revolving witty
Buckingham," and the rest, only bear themselves with
sufficient address not to contradict absolutely the dramatist's suggestion of them, the audience will receive enough
impression of their reality, and even of their importance,
to give Richard an air of moving in a Court as the King's
brother. But Cibber could not bear that anyone on the
stage should have an air of importance except himself: if
the subordinate members of the company could not act so
well as he, it seemed to him, not that it was his business
as the presenter of a play to conceal their deficiencies, but
that the first principles of justice and fair dealing de-
manded before all things that his superiority should be
made evident to the public. (And there are not half a
dozen leading actors on the stage today who would not
take precisely that view of the situation.) Consequently

he handled Richard III so as to make every other actor in it obviously ridiculous and insignificant, except only that Henry VI, in the first act, was allowed to win the pity of the audience in order that the effect might be the greater when Richard stabbed him. No actor could have produced more completely, exactly, and forcibly the effect aimed at by Cibber than Barry Sullivan, the one actor who kept Cibber's Richard on the stage during the present half-century. But it was an exhibition, not a play. Barry Sullivan was full of force, and very clever; if his power had been less exclusively of the infernal order, or if he had devoted himself to the drama instead of devoting the drama to himself as a mere means of self-assertion, one might have said more for him. He managed to make the audience believe in Richard; but as he could not make it believe in the others, and probably did not want to, they destroyed the illusion almost as fast as he created it. This is why Cibber's Richard, though it is so simple that the character plays itself as unmistakeably as the blank verse speaks itself, can only be made endurable by an actor of exceptional personal force. The second and third acts at the Lyceum, with their atmosphere of Court faction and their presentation before the audience of Edward and Clarence, make all the difference between the two versions.

But the Lyceum has by no means emancipated itself from superstition—even gross superstition. Italian opera itself could go no further in folly than the exhibition of a pretty and popular young actress in tights as Prince Edward. No doubt we were glad to see Miss Lena Ashwell—for the matter of that we should have been glad to see Mrs. John Wood as the other prince—but from the moment she came on the stage all serious historical illusion necessarily vanished, and was replaced by the most extreme form of theatrical convention. Probably Sir Henry Irving cast Miss Ashwell for the part because he has not followed her career since she played Elaine in King Arthur. She was then weak, timid, subordinate, with an insignificant presence and voice which, contrasted as it was with Miss Terry's, could only be described—if one had the heart to do it—as a squawl. Since then she has developed precipitously. If any sort of success had been possible for the plays in which she has appeared this year at the Duke of York's and Shaftsbury Theatres, she would have received a large share of the credit of it. Even in Carmen, when, perhaps for the sake of auld lang syne, she squawled and stood on the tips of her heels for the last time (let us hope), her scene with the dragoon in the first act was the one memorable moment in the whole of that disastrous business. She now returns to the Lyceum stage as an actress of mark, strong in womanly charm, and not in the least the sort of person whose sex is so little emphasized that it can be hidden by a doublet and hose. You might as well put forward Miss Ada Rehan as a boy. Nothing can be more absurd than the spectacle of Sir Henry Irving elaborately playing the uncle to his little nephew when he is obviously addressing a fine young woman in rational dress who is very thoroughly her own mistress, and treads the boards with no little authority and assurance as one of the younger generation knocking vigorously at the door. Miss Ashwell makes short work of the sleepiness of the Lyceum; and though I take urgent exception to her latest technical theory, which is, that the bridge of the nose is the seat of facial expression, I admit that she does all that can be done to reconcile us to the burlesque of her appearance in a part that should have been played by a boy.

Another mistake in the casting of the play was Mr. Gordon Craig's Edward IV. As Henry VI, Mr. Craig, who wasted his delicacy on the wrong part, would have been perfect. Henry not being available, he might have played Richmond with a considerable air of being a young Henry VII. But as Edward he was incredible: one felt that Richard would have had him out of the way years ago if Margaret had not saved him the trouble by vanquishing him at Tewkesbury. Shakespear took plenty of pains with the strong ruffian of the York family: his part in Henry VI makes it quite clear why he held his own both in and out of doors. The remedy for the misfit lay ready to the manager's hand. Mr. Cooper, his too burly Richmond, shewed what a capital Edward he would have made when he turned at the entrance to his tent, and

said, with the set air of a man not accustomed to be
trifled with,

> O Thou, whose captain I account myself,
> Look on my forces with a gracious eye,
> Or you will have me to reckon with afterwards.

The last line was not actually spoken by Mr. Cooper; but
he looked it, exactly as Edward IV might have done.

As to Sir Henry Irving's own performance, I am not
prepared to judge it, in point of execution, by what he
did on the first night. He was best in the Court scenes.
In the heavy single-handed scenes which Cibber loved,
he was not, as it seemed to me, answering his helm satis-
factorily; and he was occasionally a little out of temper
with his own nervous condition. He made some odd slips
in the text, notably by repeatedly substituting "you" for
"I"—for instance, "Shine out, fair sun, till you have
bought a glass." Once he inadvertently electrified the
house by very unexpectedly asking Miss Milton to get
further up the stage in the blank verse and penetrating
tones of Richard. Finally, the worry of playing against
the vein tired him. In the tent and battle scenes his exhaustion was too genuine to be quite acceptable as part
of the play. The fight was, perhaps, a relief to his feelings; but to me the spectacle of Mr. Cooper pretending to
pass his sword three times through Richard's body, as if a
man could be run through as easily as a cuttle-fish, was
neither credible nor impressive. The attempt to make a
stage combat look as imposing as Hazlitt's description of
the death of Edmund Kean's Richard reads, is hopeless.
If Kean were to return to life and do the combat for us,
we should very likely find it as absurd as his habit of lying
down on a sofa when he was too tired or too drunk to
keep his feet during the final scenes.

Further, it seems to me that Sir Henry Irving should
either cast the play to suit his acting or else modify his
acting to suit the cast. His playing in the scene with Lady
Anne—which, though a Punch scene, is Punch on the
Don Giovanni plane—was a flat contradiction, not only
of the letter of the lines, but of their spirit and feeling as
conveyed unmistakeably by their cadence. This, however,

we are used to: Sir Henry Irving never did and never will
make use of a play otherwise than as a vehicle for some
fantastic creation of his own. But if we are not to have
the tears, the passion, the tenderness, the transport of dis-
simulation which alone can make the upshot credible—
if the woman is to be openly teased and insulted, mocked,
and disgusted, all through the scene as well as in the first
"keen encounter of their wits," why not have Lady Anne
presented as a weak, childish-witted, mesmerized creature,
instead of as that most awful embodiment of virtue and
decorum, the intellectual American lady? Poor Miss
Julia Arthur honestly did her best to act the part as she
found it in Shakespear; and if Richard had done the
same she would have come off with credit. But how could
she play to a Richard who would not utter a single tone
to which any woman's heart could respond? She could
not very well box the actor-manager's ears, and walk off;
but really she deserves some credit for refraining from
that extreme remedy. She partly had her revenge when
she left the stage; for Richard, after playing the scene
with her as if he were a Houndsditch salesman cheating
a factory girl over a pair of second-hand stockings, naturally could not reach the raptures of the tremendous outburst of elation beginning

> Was ever woman in this humor wooed?
> Was ever woman in this humor won?

One felt inclined to answer, "Never, I assure you," and
make an end of the scene there and then. I am prepared
to admit that the creations of Sir Henry Irving's imagination are sometimes—in the case of his Iachimo, for example—better than those of the dramatists whom he is
supposed to interpret. But what he did in this scene, as
well as in the opening soliloquy, was child's play compared to what Shakespear meant him to do.

The rest of the performance was—well, it was Lyceum
Shakespear. Miss Geneviève Ward was, of course, a very
capable Margaret; but she missed the one touchstone passage in a very easy part—the tenderness of the appeal to
Buckingham. Mr. Macklin, equally of course, had no
trouble with Buckingham; but he did not give us that
moment which makes Richard say:

None are for me
That look into me with considerate eyes.

Messrs. Norman Forbes and W. Farren (junior) played
the murderers in the true Shakespearean manner: that is,
as if they had come straight out of the pantomime of The
Babes in the Wood; and Clarence recited his dream as if
he were an elocutionary coroner summing up. The rest
were respectably dull, except Mr. Gordon Craig, Miss
Lena Ashwell, and, in a page's part, Miss Edith Craig, the
only member of the company before whom the manager
visibly quails.

*In a letter to Forbes Robertson dated December 21 and
22, 1903, Shaw suggested that the actor play Richard III.
(The letter is reproduced in Hesketh Pearson's* G.B.S.: A
Full Length Portrait.*)*

. . . Have you ever thought of Richard III as a possible successor to your Hamlet? Nobody now alive has
seen what can be done with Richard. The provinces have
by this time forgotten Barry Sullivan; and Irving's Richard does not count. A really brilliant Nietzschean Richard would be fresh and delightful. I believe I could fill
it with the most captivating business for you, and practically get rid of the old-fashioned fight at the end. No
actor has ever done the curious recovery by Richard of
his old gaiety of heart in the excitement of the battle. It
whirls him up out of his vulgar ambition to be a king
(which makes the middle acts rather tedious after the
fantastic superhumanity of the first), and he is again the
ecstatic prince of mischief of the 'Shine out, fair sun, till
I have bought a glass' phase which makes the first act so
rapturous. All Nietzsche is in the lines:

Conscience is but a word that cowards use
Devised at first to keep the strong in awe.
Our strong arms be our conscience, swords our law!

And after all the pious twaddle of Richmond, his charging order is delicious:

Upon them! To't pell mell,
If not to heaven, then hand in hand to hell.

The offer of his kingdom for a horse is part of the same
thing: any means of keeping up the ecstasy of the fight
is worth a dozen kingdoms. In the last scene he should
have a bucket of rose pink thrown in his face, and then
reel on; all cut to pieces, killed already six times over,
with a broken sword and his armour all in splinters,
wrenching off the battered crown which is torturing his
poor split head. Being hunted down just then by the
Rev. Pecksniff Richmond and his choir, he is just able,
after an impulse to hold on to the crown tooth and nail,
to pitch it gaily to him and die like a gentleman. That
would be real Shakespear too; for William's villains are
all my eye: neither Iago, Edmund, Richard nor Macbeth
have any real malice in them. When William did a really
malicious creature, like Don John, he couldnt take any
real interest in him. Now you would be a charming Richard; and though the production might or might not be a
financial success in London, it would be a good invest-
ment, as it would last your life in the provinces as a
repertory play.

*Urged by the drama critic A. B. Walkley to see a produc-
tion of Richard III when he was music critic for The Star,
Shaw attended and, under the name of Corno di Bassetto,
wrote about it on March 23, 1889.*

. . . As a matter of fact, I did go to the Globe, not because Walkley wished me to hear "Mr. Edward German's
fine music, with its *leitmotivs* after Wagner's plan" (ha!
ha! ha!), but because a musician only has the right to
criticize works like Shakespear's earlier histories and tragedies. The two Richards, King John, and the last act of
Romeo and Juliet, depend wholly on the beauty of their
music. There is no deep significance, no great subtlety
and variety in their numbers; but for splendor of sound,
magic of romantic illusion, majesty of emphasis, ardor,
elation, reverberation of haunting echoes, and every poetic quality that can waken the heart-stir and the imaginative fire of early manhood, they stand above all recorded

music. These things cannot be spectated (Walkley signs himself Spectator): they must be heard. It is not enough to see Richard III: you should be able to *whistle* it.

However, to the music! Mr. Mansfield's execution of his opening *scena* was, I must say, deeply disappointing. When I heard his rendering of the mighty line—

> In the deep bosom of the ocean buried,

which almost rivals "the multitudinous seas incarnadine" I perceived that Richard was not going to be a musical success. And when in that deliberate staccato—

> I am determinéd to be a villain,

he actually missed half a bar by saying in modern prose fashion, "I am determin'd to be a villain," I gave him up as earless. Only in such lines as—

> Framed in the prodigality of nature,

which simply cannot be put out of joint, was his delivery admirable. And yet his very worst achievement was—

> Bound with triumphant garlands will I come,
> And lead your daughter to a conqueror's bed.

Spectator, with reckless frivolity, has left his readers to infer that the magnificent duet with Miss Mary Rorke in which these lines occur, with the famous section beginning,

> Send to her, by the man that slew her brothers,
> A pair of bleeding hearts,

is by Cibber. *"Ecce iterum!* this scene is Cibber again" says Spectator. And this, mind, not that he does not know as well as I do that the lines are Shakespear's, but simply because, as Cibber was a sort of dramatic critic (he was an actor who wrote an apology, by no means uncalled for, for his own existence, though in justice I must add that it is still the best book on the English theatre in existence, just as Boswell's Journey to the Hebrides is still the best guidebook), Spectator wishes to prove him superior to Shakespear!

To return to Mr. Mansfield. It is a positive sin for a man

with such a voice to give the words without the setting, like a Covent Garden libretto. Several times he made fine music for a moment, only to shew in the next line that he had made it haphazard. His acting version of the play, though it is an enormous improvement on the traditional Cibberesque, notably in the third and fourth acts, yet contains some wanton substitutions of Cibber's halting, tinpot, clinking stuff for noble and beautiful lines by Shakespear, which would occupy no longer time in delivery. Why, for instance, is this passage avoided?

> RICHARD'S MOTHER: . . . I prithee hear me speak;
> For I shall never speak to thee again.
> RICHARD: So.
> HIS MOTHER: Either thou wilt die, by God's just ordinance,
> Ere from this war thou turn a conqueror;
> Or I with grief and extreme age shall perish,
> And never more behold thy face again.

And so on. Is Mr. Mansfield deaf, that he allows the dead hand of Cibber to filch this passage from Miss Leclercq and the audience? Or is a gentleman connected with this paper, who has shown a suspicious familiarity with the Globe arrangements, the real author of the Mansfield version? If I were playing Richard I would sacrifice anything else in the play sooner than that monosyllable "So"; which tells more of Richard than a dozen stabbings and baby smotherings.

The last act also presents some unaccountable inconsistencies. Mr. Mansfield valiantly gives every word of the striking solo following the nightmare scene; and he rejects "Richard's himself again" with the contempt it deserves. But instead of finishing the scene in mystery and terror by stealing off into the gloom to eavesdrop with Ratcliff, he introduces that vulgar Cibberian coda in the major key:—

> Hark! the shrill trumpet sounds. To horse! Away!
> My soul's in arms, and eager for the fray.

Imagine a man at dead midnight, hours before the battle, with cold, fearful drops still on his trembling flesh, suddenly gasconading in this fashion. Shakespear waits until

Richard is in the field, and the troops actually in motion. That is the magnetic moment when all the dreadful joy of the fighting man surges up in him, and he exclaims—

A thousand hearts are great within my bosom.

ROMEO AND JULIET

A review of the Forbes Robertson production of the play appeared in The Saturday Review *on September 28, 1895.*

How WE LAVISH our money and our worship on Shakespear without in the least knowing why! From time to time we ripen for a new act of homage. Great preparations are made; high hopes are raised; everyone concerned, from the humblest *persona muta* on the stage to the sworn first-nighter in the gallery, is full of earnest belief that the splendor of the Swan will be revealed at last, like the Holy Grail. And yet the point of the whole thing is missed every time with ludicrous ineptitude; and often a ruined actor-manager spends the rest of his life, like the Ancient Mariner, in telling the tale of what it cost, and how So-and-So got his (or her) first chance in it, and how such and such other eminent people debated that nothing like it had ever been done before, and so on and so forth. Still, there is nothing for it but to try and try and try again. Every revival helps to exhaust the number of possible ways of altering Shakespear's plays unsuccessfully, and so hastens the day when the mere desire for novelty will lead to the experiment of leaving them unaltered. Let us see what there is to learn from Mr. Forbes Robertson's revival of Romeo and Juliet, before that goes the way of all other revivals. I hardly like to call Mr. Forbes Robertson an artist, because he is notoriously a gentleman with a taste for painting, and the two things are usually incompatible. Your Englishman always conceives that to be romantic and to have a susceptible imagination is to be potentially a painter. His eye for form may be that of a carpenter, his sense of color that of a haberdasher's window-dresser in the Old Kent Road: no matter, he can still imagine historical scenes—"King James receiving the news of the landing of William of Orange" or the like—and draw them and color them, or he can dress up his wife as Zenobia or Dante's Beatrice or Dolly Varden, according to her style, and copy her. I do not level these disparaging observations at Mr. Forbes Robertson: I only wish to make it clear that I approach his latest enterprise completely free from the common assumption that he is likely to stage Romeo and Juliet better than anyone else because he paints pictures and sends them to the exhibitions occasionally. To be quite frank, I am rather prejudiced against him by that fact, since I learnt in the days when I criticized pictures that his sense of color is essentially and Britannically an imaginative and moral one: that is, he associates low tones ("quiet colors" they call them in Marshall & Snellgrove's) with dignity and decency, and white linen with cleanliness and respectability. I am therefore not surprised to find the dresses at the Lyceum, though handsome and expensive, chastened by the taste of a British gentleman; so that the stalls can contemplate the fourteenth century and yet feel at home there—a remarkable result, and a very desirable one for those who like it. "Mrs. Patrick Campbell's dresses," says the program, "have been carried out by Mrs. Mason, of New Burlington Street." I can only say that I wish they had been carried out and buried. They belong to Mrs. Mason, and are her triumph, instead of to Mrs. Campbell. I know how to value an actress who is an artist in dressing fashionably, like Miss Gertrude Kingston; and I delight in one who is an artist in dressing originally, like Miss Ellen Terry; but a lady who is dressed by somebody else, according to somebody else's ideas, like any dressmaker-made woman of fashion, is artistically quite out of the question; and I can only excuse the Lyceum Juliet costumes on the supposition that Mrs. Campbell deliberately aimed at suggesting by them the tutelage of a girl of fourteen who is not yet allowed to choose her own dresses.

The scenery is excellent. Mr. William Harford's "public place in Verona" has only one defect, and that a very English one. The sky is too cold, and the cypresses too pale: better have painted them with dabs of warm brown on an actually gold sky in the beautiful old fashion, than have risked that Constablesque suggestion, faint as it is, of English raininess and chill. But for the rest, it is easy to imagine that the flood of the Adige is really hurrying along behind that embankment as Mercutio leans idly over it. Friar Laurence's cell, too, is good: one can feel the shadowed cloisters outside, with the sunlight and the well in the middle of the quadrangle; and though I do not believe that a simple friar's cell often ran to the luxury of a couple of frescoes by Giotto, yet the touch is suggestive and pardonable. Mr. Ryan's corner of Mantua in the last act would be perfect if the light could only be forced to Italian pitch: in fact it surpasses the real thing in respect of its freedom from the atrocious Mantuan stenches and huge mosquitoes from the marshes. Mr. Harker has only one scene, that of Capulet's ball, a beautiful fourteenth-century loggia; whilst Mr. Harford, having to do another scene in Capulet's house, has jumped forward to genteelly elegant Renascence work in carved white marble, in the manner of the Miracoli at Venice. It will be inferred, and rightly inferred, that the scenery is enormously in advance of that to which Mr. Augustin Daly treated us for The Two Gentlemen of Verona. No doubt Mr. Daly paid as much as Mr. Forbes Robertson; but Mr. Daly's scene-painters copied bad work, and Mr. Forbes Robertson's have copied good. That makes all the difference.

Of course, in criticizing the general effect, the play and the acting cannot be altogether left out of account, though it would be unfair to lay too much stress on them. Perhaps the most difficult character in the play as far as finesse of execution goes is Mercutio. We see Mercutio in his first scene as a wit and fantasist of the most delicate order. In his next, apparently without any shock to the Elizabethan sense of congruity, he is a detestable and intolerable cad, the exact prototype of our modern 'Arry. The change gives such another glimpse into the manners of that time as you get in Much Ado from the astonishment which Benedick creates by taking to washing his face every day. By stage tradition, Mercutio is as much a leading part as Romeo, if not more so. Therefore, when the manager chooses Romeo, he should be particularly careful to choose a good Mercutio, lest he should appear to have that part purposely underplayed. Perhaps this was why Mr. Forbes Robertson went so far out of his way as to cast Mr. Coghlan for the part. If so, he overreached himself; for he could not possibly have made a worse choice. I really cannot express myself politely on the subject of Mr. Coghlan's performance. He lounges, he mumbles, he delivers the Queen Mab speech in a raffish patter which takes, and is apparently deliberately meant to take, all beauty of tone and grace of measure out of it. It may be that Mr. Coghlan has studied the part carefully, and come to the conclusion that since the visit of the Montagues to Capulet's ball is a young blood's escapade, Mercutio should be represented as coming half drunk and lolling on the stone seat outside to repeat a tipsy rigmarole about nothing. In that case I must express my entire disagreement with Mr. Coghlan's reading. Shakespear never leaves me in any doubt as to when he means an actor to play Sir Toby Belch and when to play Mercutio, or when he means an actor to speak measured verse and when slipshod colloquial prose.

Far better than Mr. Coghlan's Mercutio, and yet quite the worst impersonation I have ever seen of a not very difficult old woman's part, was Miss Dolores Drummond's Nurse. Tybalt's is such an unmercifully bad part that one can hardly demand anything from its representative except that he should brush his hair when he comes to his uncle's ball (a condition which he invariably repudiates) and that he should be so consummate a swordsman as to make it safe for Romeo to fall on him with absolute abandonment, and annihilate him as Jean de Reszke used to annihilate Montariol. This is one of the great sensations of the play: unless an actor is capable of a really terrible explosion of rage, he had better let Romeo alone. Unfortunately, the "fire-eyed fury" before which Tybalt falls lies outside the gentlemanly limits of Mr. Forbes Robertson's stage instinct; and it may be that his skill as an actor is not equal to the task of working-up the audience to the point at which they will imagine an explosion which cannot, of course, be real. At all events the duel scene has none of the murderous excitement which is the whole dramatic point of it: it is tamed down to a mere formal pretext for the banishment of Romeo. Mr. Forbes Robertson has evidently no sympathy with Shakespear's love of a shindy: you see his love of law and order coming out

in his stage management of the fighting scenes. Nobody
is allowed to enjoy the scrimmage: Capulet and Mon-
tague are silenced; and the spectators of the duel are
women—I should say ladies—who look intensely shocked
to see gentlemen of position so grossly forgetting themselves. Mr. Forbes Robertson himself fights with uncon-
cealed repugnance: he makes you feel that to do it in that
disorderly way, without seconds, without a doctor, shewing temper about it, and actually calling his adversary
names, jars unspeakably on him. Far otherwise have we
seen him as Orlando wrestling with Charles. But there
the contest was in the presence of a court, with measured
ground and due formality—under Queensbury rules, so
to speak. For the rest, Mr. Forbes Robertson is very handsome, very well dressed, very perfectly behaved. His assortment of tones, of gestures, of facial expressions, of
attitudes, are limited to half a dozen apiece; but they are
carefully selected and all of the best. The arrangements
in the last scene are exceedingly nice: the tomb of the
Capulets is beautifully kept, well lighted, and conven-
iently accessible by a couple of broad steps—quite like a
new cathedral chapel. Indeed, when Romeo, contemplating the bier of Juliet (which reflected the utmost credit
on the undertaker), said:

> I still will stay with thee,
> And never from this palace of dim night
> Depart again,

I felt that the sacrifice he was making in doing without a
proper funeral was greatly softened. Romeo was a gentleman to the last. He laid out Paris after killing him as
carefully as if he were folding up his best suit of clothes.
One remembers Irving, a dim figure dragging a horrible
burden down through the gloom "into the rotten jaws of
death," and reflects on the differences of imaginative temperament that underlie the differences of acting and stage-
managing.

As to Juliet, she danced like the daughter of Herodias.
And she knew the measure of her lines to a hairsbreadth.
Did I not say, long ago, that Mrs. Tanqueray's piano-
playing was worth all the rest of her? And yet I was taken
in by Mrs. Tanqueray—also by Mrs. Ebbsmith, as we all

were. Woman's great art is to lie low, and let the imagination of the male endow her with depths. How Mrs.
Patrick Campbell must have laughed at us whilst we were
giving her all the credit—if credit it were—for our silly
psychologizing over those Pinero parts! As Juliet she still
fits herself into the hospitable manly heart without effort,
simply because she is a wonderful person, not only in
mere facial prettiness, in which respect she is perhaps not
superior to the bevy of "extra ladies" in the fashionable
scenes in the new Drury Lane play, not even in her light,
beautifully proportioned figure, but in the extraordinary
swiftness and certainty of her physical self-command. I
am convinced that Mrs. Patrick Campbell could thread a
needle with her toes at the first attempt as rapidly, as
smoothly, as prettily, and with as much attention to spare
for doing anything else at the same time as she can play
an arpeggio. This physical talent, which is seldom consciously recognized except when it is professedly specialized in some particular direction (as in the cast, for
instance, of Miss Letty Lind), will, when accompanied by
nimbleness of mind, quick observation, and lively theatrical instinct, carry any actress with a rush to the front
of her profession, as it has carried Mrs. Patrick Campbell.
Her Juliet, nevertheless, is an immature performance at
all the exceptional points which, please remember, are
not very numerous, much of Juliet's business being of a
kind that no "leading lady" of ordinary ability could possibly fail in. All the conscious ideas gathered by her from
the part and carried out in planned strokes of her own
are commonplace. There is not a touch of tragedy, not a
throb of love or fear, temper instead of passion: in short,
a Juliet as unawakened as Richard III, one in whose
death you dont believe, though you would not cry over it
if you did believe. Nothing of it is memorable except the
dance—the irresistible dance.

It should never be forgotten in judging an attempt to
play Romeo and Juliet that the parts are made almost
impossible, except to actors of positive genius, skilled to
the last degree in metrical declamation, by the way in
which the poetry, magnificent as it is, is interlarded by
the miserable rhetoric and silly logical conceits which
were the foible of the Elizabethans. When Juliet comes

out on her balcony and, having propounded the question, "What's in a name?" proceeds to argue it out like an amateur attorney in Christmas-card verse of the "rose by any other name" order, no actress can make it appear natural to a century which has discovered the art of giving prolonged and intense dramatic expression to pure feeling alone, without any skeleton of argument or narrative, by means of music. Romeo has lines that tighten the heart or catch you up into the heights, alternately with heartless fustian and silly ingenuities that make you curse Shakespear's stagestruckness and his youthful inability to keep his brains quiet. It needs a great flowing tide of passion, an irresistibly impetuous march of music, to carry us over these pitfalls and stumbling-blocks, even when we are foolish enough to mistake the good for the bad, and to reverently accept Mr. Coghlan as an authority on the subject of Mercutio. It would be folly to hold out any such hopes of rescue at the Lyceum. Of the whole company there is only one member who achieves artistic respectability as a Shakespearean player, and that is Mr. Warde as Capulet. For the most part, one has to listen to the music of Shakespear—in which music, I repeat again and again, the whole worth and charm of these early plays of his lies—as one might listen to a symphony of Beethoven's with all the parts played on the bones, the big drum, and the Jew's harp. But the production is an unsparing effort, and therefore as honorable to Mr. Forbes Robertson's management as the highest artistic success could make it. The more efforts of that kind we have, the sooner we shall have the artistic success.

An amateur production at Oxford was the subject of Shaw's Saturday Review *article of March 5, 1898.*

. . . It is characteristic of the authorities at Oxford that they should consider a month too little for the preparation of a boat-race, and grudge three weeks to the rehearsals of one of Shakespear's plays. The performance of Romeo and Juliet by the Oxford University Dramatic Society naturally did not, under these circumstances, approach the level of skill attained on the Thames. The

one advantage that amateurs have over professionals—
and it is such an overwhelming advantage when exhaus-
tively used that the best amateur performances are more
instructive than the most elaborate professional ones—is
the possibility of unlimited rehearsal. An amateur company prepared to rehearse Romeo and Juliet for six
months would in some respects easily beat an ordinary
London company. But there is a still better way within
the reach of amateurs. Everyone who has seen the annual
performances of Latin plays at Westminster School must
have been struck by the absence of that feebleness and
futility of utterance which makes the ordinary amateur so
obnoxious. Yet the Westminster plays get no such extraordinary measure of rehearsals. Again, if we watch the
amateur performances of Elizabethan drama with which
Mr. William Poel does such good work, we find that those
performers who are members of the Shakespear Reading
Society, or of the little private circles formed by inveterate
Elizabethan readers, acquit themselves much better, in
point of delivery, than average professional actors. This
gives us the secret of the Westminster play. The schoolboy is well practised in the utterance of Latin, not col-
loquially as he utters English, but as a task in the nature
of a performance to be submitted to the approval of his
master, just as the Elizamaniac utters Shakespearean
verse every week at least for the delectation of his circle.
Here, surely, is the clue to the right course for the O.U.D.S.
Let the members devote two nights a week all the year
round to reading Elizabethan plays, and let it be a rule
that no member shall be allotted a principal part without
a very high average of attendances. A tradition of skill
and practice in what is one of the finest of physical accomplishments will soon be established; and the O.U.D.S.
will in course of time become popular as a club of artistic
athletes instead of being ridiculed, as I fear it is to some
extent at present, as a set of unrepresentative æsthetes.
To play Shakespear without considerable technical skill
and vocal power is, frankly, to make an ass of oneself;
and the contempt of the average undergraduate for such
exhibits is by no means mere Philistinism. If the boat-
race were rowed by men who never took an oar in their
hands until the middle of February, and only did so then

because they were vain enough to want to figure in some footling imitation of the Olympian games, the University would not care two straws about the boat-race. I am bound to say that it has had much the same reason for not concerning itself about the late performance of Romeo and Juliet. If the performers had been able to handle their vowels and consonants as bats and balls and sculls are handled at Oxford in the racket-courts and cricket-fields and on the river, then, whether they were able to act or not, the performance would have been full of technical interest; the gallery would have seethed with youthful hero-worship; and the performers, doing something that every undergraduate would like to do if he could, would now be holding their heads high even among the athletes. On no other lines is there the smallest chance of a dramatic club becoming a really vital organ of an English University, or forcing the authorities, by sheer weight of public opinion, to build a University theatre as an indispensable part of their educational equipment.

The amateur company which performed Romeo and Juliet was under-trained and under-rehearsed to a degree of which, I think, it has itself no suspicion. Consequently, though its intentions were excellent, it had very little power of carrying them out: ideas and taste were not lacking; but executive power was at a huge premium. Romeo had cultivated a pretty *mezza voce,* which carried him in a sentimentally lyrical way through a performance which certainly maintained a distinctly artistic character and style all through, though it was deficient in variety and power. Mercutio, when illustrating Tybalt's accomplishments as a fencer, fell and put his knee out. He rose, with his knee-cap visibly in that excruciating condition, and continued his performance with undiminished dash. He did not faint; but I should certainly have done so if the dislocation had not fortunately reduced itself in the slow course of about two minutes. I protest against these exhibitions of fortitude: the Spartans may have considered them good manners; but a really considerate modern should frankly yell when he is hurt, and thereby give the sympathetic spectators an opportunity to relieve their feelings with equal demonstrativeness. Except for his

hypocrisy in this matter, Mercutio deserved well of the
Club. The part is a puzzling one; and his notion of
handling it was by no means an unhappy one. Juliet was
a convincing illustration of the advantages of practice.
The balcony scene and the phial scene—that is to say, the
two scenes which she had probably often recited—were
quite presentable. The rest, got up merely for the occasion, was uncertain and helpless. Friar Laurence got on
tolerably well; and the effect of playing the last scene in
its entirety was decidedly good. But I desire to dwell on
the weak parts in the performance rather than on the
passable ones. It was not worth doing for its own immedi-
ate sake; and as the candid friend of the O.U.D.S., I advise
them to drop Shakespear unless they are prepared to
work continuously at the Elizabethan drama all the year
round, in the way I have suggested. They have not yet
qualified themselves to split the ears of the groundlings,
which they should all be able to do, in the style of the
apprentice, in The Knight of the Burning Pestle, to begin
with. Later on they can keep within the modesty of
nature; but it is the business of youth "to fetch up a
couraging part" valiantly, and master all the technical
difficulties and audacities of art, just as the pianist, at
eighteen, dazzles us with transcendent execution, though
he cannot play a Mozart sonata. The secret of art's humanity will come later, when the university has been
exchanged for the real world.

THE TAMING OF THE SHREW

Assuming the guise of a protesting lady, Shaw wrote The
Pall Mall Gazette *a letter which appeared on June 8,
1888. (It is reprinted in Archibald Henderson's* George
Bernard Shaw: Man of the Century.)

Sir

They say that the American woman is the most advanced woman to be found at present on this planet.
I am an Englishwoman, just come up, frivolously enough,
from Devon to enjoy a few weeks of the season in London,
and at the very first theatre I visit I find an American
woman playing Katharine in The Taming of the Shrew—
a piece which is one vile insult to womanhood and manhood from the first word to the last. I think no woman
should enter a theatre where that play is performed; and
I should not have stayed to witness it myself, but that,
having been told that the Daly Company has restored
Shakespear's version to the stage, I desired to see with
my own eyes whether any civilized audience would stand
its brutality.

Of course, it was not Shakespear: it was only Garrick
adulterated by Shakespear. Instead of Shakespear's
coarse, thick-skinned money hunter, who sets to work to
tame his wife exactly as brutal people tame animals or
children—that is, by breaking their spirit by domineering cruelty—we had Garrick's fop who tries to "shut up"
his wife by behaving worse than she—a plan which is
often tried by foolish and ill-mannered young husbands
in real life, and one which invariably fails ignominiously,
as it deserves to. The gentleman who plays Petruchio at
Daly's—I neither know nor desire to know his name—
does what he can to persuade the audience that he is not
in earnest, and that the whole play is a farce, just as
Garrick before him found it necessary to do; but in spite
of his fine clothes, even at the wedding, and his winks
and smirks when Katharine is not looking, he cannot

make the spectacle of a man cracking a heavy whip at a starving woman other than disgusting and unmanly. In an age when woman was a mere chattel, Katharine's degrading speech about

> "Thy husband is thy lord, thy life, thy keeper,
> Thy head, thy sovereign: one that cares for thee
> [with a whip]
> And for thy maintenance; commits his body
> To painful labour, both by sea and land," etc.

might have passed with an audience of bullies. But imagine a parcel of gentlemen in the stalls at the Gaiety Theatre, half of them perhaps living idly on their wives' incomes, grinning complacently through it as if it were true or even honourably romantic. I am sorry that I did not come to town earlier that I might have made a more timely protest. In the future I hope all men and women who respect one another will boycott The Taming of the Shrew until it is driven off the boards.

Yours truly,
HORATIO RIBBONSON

St. James's Hotel, and Fairheugh Rectory, North Devon, June 7th.

On one occasion Shaw passed up an opportunity to see Garrick's Katherine and Petruchio explaining in his Saturday Review article of November 6, 1897, that he preferred Shakespeare's Taming of the Shrew.

. . . Up to a late hour on Monday night I persuaded myself that I would hasten from the Globe to Her Majesty's, and do my stern duty by Katharine and Petruchio. But when it came to the point I sacrificed duty to personal considerations. The Taming of the Shrew is a remarkable example of Shakespear's repeated attempts to make the public accept realistic comedy. Petruchio is worth fifty Orlandos as a human study. The preliminary scenes in which he shews his character by pricking up his ears at the news that there is a fortune to be got by any man who will take an ugly and ill-tempered woman off her father's hands, and hurrying off to strike the bargain before somebody else picks it up, are not romantic; but they give an honest and masterly picture of a real man, whose like we have all met. The actual taming of the woman by the methods used in taming wild beasts belongs to his determination to make himself rich and comfortable, and his perfect freedom from all delicacy in using his strength and opportunities for that purpose. The process is quite bearable, because the selfishness of the man is healthily goodhumored and untainted by wanton cruelty, and it is good for the shrew to encounter a force like that and be brought to her senses. Unfortunately, Shakespear's own immaturity, as well as the immaturity of the art he was experimenting in, made it impossible for him to keep the play on the realistic plane to the end; and the last scene is altogether disgusting to modern sensibility. No man with any decency of feeling can sit it out in the company of a woman without being extremely ashamed of the lord-of-creation moral implied in the wager and the speech put into the woman's own mouth. Therefore the play, though still worthy of a complete and efficient representation, would need, even at that, some apology. But the Garrick version of it, as a farcical afterpiece!—thank you: no.

On November 20, 1897, Shaw wrote in The Saturday Review *that he had been in the country and had found the surroundings quite soothing, although not soothing enough to make him forgive Beerbohm Tree for preferring Garrick's* Katherine and Petruchio *to Shakespeare's play.*

. . . However, a man is something more than an omelette; and no extremity of battery can tame my spirit to the point of submitting to the sophistry by which Mr. Beerbohm Tree has attempted to shift the guilt of Katharine and Petruchio from his shoulders and Garrick's to those of Shakespear. I have never hesitated to give our immortal William as much of what he deserves as is possible considering how far his enormities transcend my powers of invective; but even William is entitled to fair play. Mr. Tree contends that as Shakespear wrote the scenes which Garrick tore away from their context, they form a genuine Shakespearean play; and he outdares even this audacity by further contending that since the play was performed for the entertainment of Christopher Sly the tinker, the more it is debauched the more appropriate it is. This line of argument is so breath-bereaving that I can but gasp out an inquiry as to what Mr. Tree understands by the one really eloquent and heartfelt line uttered by Sly: "Tis a very excellent piece of work: would twere done!"

This stroke, to which the whole Sly interlude is but as the handle to the dagger, appears to me to reduce Mr. Tree's identification of the tastes of his audiences at Her Majesty's with those of a drunken tinker to a condition distinctly inferior to that of my left eye at present. The other argument is more seriously meant, and may even impose upon the simplicity of the Cockney playgoer. Let us test its principle by varying its application. Certain anti-Christian propagandists, both here and in America, have extracted from the Bible all those passages which are unsuited for family reading, and have presented a string of them to the public as a representative sample of Holy Writ. Some of our orthodox writers, though intensely indignant at this controversial ruse, have nevertheless not scrupled to do virtually the same thing with the Koran. Will Mr. Tree claim for these collections the full authority, dignity, and inspiration of the authors from whom they are culled? If not, how does he distinguish Garrick's procedure from theirs? Garrick took from a play of Shakespear's all the passages which served his baser purpose, and suppressed the rest. Had his object been to discredit Shakespear in the honest belief that Shakespearolatry was a damnable error, we might have respected Katharine and Petruchio even whilst deploring it. But he had no such conviction: in fact, he was a professed Shakespearolater, and no doubt a sincere one, as far as his wretched powers of appreciation went. He debased The Taming of the Shrew solely to make money out of the vulgarity of the taste of his time. Such a transaction can be defended on commercial grounds: to defend it on any other seems to me to be either an artistic misdemeanor or a profession of Philistinism. If Mr. Tree were to declare boldly that he thinks Katharine and Petruchio a better play than The Taming of the Shrew, and that Garrick, as an actor-manager, knew his business better than a mere poet, he would be within his rights. He would not even strain our credulity; for a long dynasty of actor-managers, from Cibber to Sir Henry Irving, have been unquestionably sincere in preferring their own acting versions to the unmutilated master-pieces of the genius on whom they have lavished lip-honor. But Mr. Tree pretends to no such preference: on the contrary, he openly stigmatizes the Garrick version as tinker's fare, and throws the responsibility on Shakespear because the materials were stolen from him.

THE TEMPEST

A performance of The Tempest *by William Poel's semi-professional group dedicated to the production of Shake-speare in the Elizabethan style, without elaborate scenery and scene shifts, was reviewed by Shaw on November 13, 1897, in* The Saturday Review.

. . . The poetry of The Tempest is so magical that it would make the scenery of a modern theatre ridiculous. The methods of the Elizabethan Stage Society (I do not commit myself to their identity with those of the Eliza-bethan stage) leave to the poet the work of conjuring up the isle "full of noises, sounds and sweet airs." And I do not see how this plan can be beaten. If Sir Henry Irving were to put the play on at the Lyceum next season (why not, by the way?), what could he do but multiply the expenditure enormously, and spoil the il-lusion? He would give us the screaming violin instead of the harmonious viol; "characteristic" music scored for wood-wind and percussion by Mr. German instead of Mr. Dolmetsch's pipe and tabor; an expensive and absurd stage ship; and some windless, airless, changeless, sound-less, electric-lit, wooden-floored mockeries of the haunts of Ariel. They would cost more; but would they be an improvement on the Mansion House arrangement? Mr. Poel says frankly, "See that singers' gallery up there! Well, lets pretend that it's the ship." We agree; and the thing is done. But how could we agree to such a pretence with a stage ship? Before it we should say, "Take that thing away: if our imagination is to create a ship, it must not be contradicted by something that apes a ship so vilely as to fill us with denial and repudiation of its im-posture." The singing gallery makes no attempt to im-pose on us: it disarms criticism by unaffected submission to the facts of the case, and throws itself honestly on our fancy, with instant success. In the same way a rag doll is fondly nursed by a child who can only stare at a waxen simulacrum of infancy. A superstitious person left to himself will see a ghost in every ray of moonlight on the wall and every old coat hanging on a nail; but make up a really careful, elaborate, plausible, picturesque, blood-curdling ghost for him, and his cunning grin will proclaim that he sees through it at a glance. The reason is, not that a man can *always* imagine things more vividly than art can present them to him, but that it takes an altogether extraordinary degree of art to compete with the pictures which the imagination makes when it is stimulated by such potent forces as the maternal instinct, superstitious awe, or the poetry of Shakespear. The dialogue between Gonzalo and that "bawling, blasphemous, incharitable dog" the boatswain, would turn the House of Lords into a ship: in less than ten words—"What care these roarers for the name of king?"—you see the white horses and the billowing green mountains playing football with crown and purple. But the Elizabethan method would not do for a play like The White Heather, excellent as it is of its kind. If Mr. Poel, on the strength of the Drury Lane dialogue, were to leave us to imagine the singers' gallery to be the bicycling ring in Battersea Park, or Boulter's Lock, we should flatly decline to imagine anything at all. It requires the nicest judgment to know exactly how much help the imagination wants. There is no general rule, not even for any particular author. You can do best without scenery in The Tempest and A Midsummer Night's Dream, because the best scenery you can get will only destroy the illusion created by the poetry; but it does not at all follow that scenery will not improve a representation of Othello. Maeterlinck's plays, requiring a mystical inscenation in the style of Fernand Knopf, would be nearly as much spoiled by Elizabethan treatment as by Drury Lane treatment. Modern melodrama is so dependent on the most realistic scenery that a representation would suffer far less by the omission of the scenery than of the dialogue. This is why the manager who stages every play in the same way is a bad manager, even when he is an adept at his one way. A great deal of the distinction of the Lyceum productions is due to the fact that Sir Henry Irving, when the work in hand is at all within the limits of his sympathies, knows exactly how far to go in the matter of scenery. When he makes mistakes, they are almost always mistakes in stage management, by which he sacrifices the effect of some unappreciated passage of dialogue of which the charm has escaped him.

Though I was sufficiently close to the stage at The Tempest to hear, or imagine I heard, every word of the dialogue, yet it was plain that the actors were not eminent after-dinner speakers, and had consequently never received in that room the customary warning to speak to the second pillar on the right of the door, on pain of not being heard. Though they all spoke creditably, and some of them remarkably well, they took matters rather too easily, with the result that the quieter passages were inaudible to a considerable number of the spectators. I mention the matter because the Elizabethan Stage Society is hardly yet alive to the acoustic difficulties raised by the lofty halls it performs in. They are mostly troublesome places for a speaker; for if he shouts, his vowels make such a roaring din that his consonants are indistinguishable; and if he does not, his voice does not travel far enough. They are too resonant for noisy speakers and too vast for gentle ones. A clean, athletic articulation, kept up without any sentimental or indolent relaxations, is indispensable as a primary physical accomplishment for the Elizabethan actor who "takes to the halls."

The performance went without a hitch. Mr. Dolmetsch looked after the music; and the costumes were worthy of the reputation which the Society has made for itself in this particular. Ariel, armless and winged in his first incarnation, was not exactly a tricksy sprite; for as the wing arrangement acted as a strait waistcoat, he had to be content with the effect he made as a living picture. This disability on his part was characteristic of the whole performance, which had to be taken in a somewhat low key and slow tempo, with a minimum of movement. If any attempt had been made at the impetuosity and liveliness for which the English experts of the sixteenth century were famous throughout Europe, it would have not only failed, but prevented the performers from attaining what they did attain, very creditably, by a more modest ambition.

TROILUS AND CRESSIDA

On February 29, 1884, a paper by Shaw on Troilus and Cressida *was presented to the scholarly New Shakespeare Society, headed by F. J. Furnivall. A report of the paper from the Society's* Transactions *is reprinted in R. F. Rattray's* Bernard Shaw: A Chronicle. *While it is not in Shaw's own words there is no reason to assume that it is not accurate.*

SHAW ASKED what attraction could so uncongenial a story have had for Shakespear. He held that Shakespear treated the story as an iconoclast treats an idol. He had long suspected Chapman and the ancient poets, and on reading Chapman's "Iliad" saw he was right; and hence Troilus and Cressida. It was Shakespear's protest against Homer's attempt to impose upon the world and against Chapman in upholding him. Shakespear, when he wrote the play, had ceased to believe in Romeo and Juliet and in bullies like Petruchio and Faulconbridge; he had passed on to maturer work—to All's Well and Much Ado; he had written Henry V and achieved a great popular success, and had then asked himself, in weariness of spirit, was this the best he could do? Chapman's "Homer" appeared and he saw it was only his Henry V; and it was to expose and avenge his mistake and failure in writing Henry V that he wrote Troilus and Cressida. Shaw drew attention to Shakespear's treatment of the class of professional swordsmen, so common in his time. These had hitherto been caricatured by Jonson, Beaumont and Fletcher and others; Shakespear first saw the value of these paradoxes and gave their several virtues to Ajax, Hector, etc. Hector was admirably just, wise and magnanimous. Ulysses, eminently "respectable," imposed by his gravity on the rest, as he imposed on his commentators, who had taken him to be "Shakespear drawn by Shakespear himself." Cressida Shaw thought to be most enchanting; Shakespear was indulgent to women, and he thought Cressida to be Shakespear's first real woman. The question of the existence of an earlier drama on the same subject was to be considered. Was it some stock piece founded on Chaucer, Lydgate or Caxton which was replaced by a new one by Shakespear, which would not infringe on anyone's rights and possibly preserved some of the original characters, such as Pandarus? Certain lines looked like survivals from the old play. In conclusion, Shaw, summing up, placed Troilus and Cressida between Henry V and Hamlet; its date was 1600; it was a historical play; it was Shakespear's all but about twenty lines.

TWELFTH NIGHT

In The Saturday Review *of July 20, 1895, Shaw discussed a performance of* Twelfth Night *by William Poel's Elizabethan Stage Society.*

I WELCOME the advent of The Elizabethan Stage Society, founded "to give practical effect to the principle that Shakespear should be accorded the build of stage for which he designed his plays." Last month the Society played Twelfth Night in the Burlington Hall: next December they will give us The Comedy of Errors in Gray's Inn Hall, where it was originally acted in 1594. It is only by such performances that people can be convinced that Shakespear's plays lose more than they gain by modern staging. I do not, like the E.S.S., affirm it as a principle that Shakespear's plays should be accorded the build of stage for which he designed them. I simply affirm it as a fact, personally observed by myself, that the modern pictorial stage is not so favorable to Shakespearean acting and stage illusion as the platform stage. Years ago, comparing the effect of Much Ado as performed at the Lyceum and as read through by a number of amateurs seated in evening dress on the platform at the London Institution, I found that the amateur performance was more vivid and enjoyable, and that the illusion, though flatly contradicted by the costumes and surroundings, was actually stronger. I happened to witness, too, a performance of Browning's Luria under circumstances still more apparently ludicrous. It was acted—not merely read—in a lecture theatre at University College, against a background of plain curtains, by performers also in evening dress. The effect was so satisfactory in comparison to the ordinary pictorial stage effect that I have ever since regarded the return to the old conditions of stage representation for old plays as perfectly practical and advisable. The success of the combinations of platform action with stage scenery at the Ober Ammergau Passion

Play, and of the Maeterlinckian treatment of Pelléas et Mélisande by the Théâtre de l'Œuvre, shews that the staging of the poetic drama may be modified in various directions with much greater boldness than I or anyone else could have supposed safe if our prejudices had not been broken up by these little amateur tentatives, which so many of us make the fatal mistake of passing by as not worth attention. The performance of Twelfth Night now in question brought out another point with remarkable distinctness, and that was the immense advantage of the platform stage to the actor. It places him in so intimate a relation to the spectators that the difficulty of getting delicate play "across the footlights," and of making vehement play forcible enough to overcome the remoteness of the "living picture" stage, all but vanishes. Is there not some story to the effect that Garrick, when it was proposed to alter the stage in the modern direction in his time, replied that if he were ten feet further from his audience there would be no difference between him and any of his rivals. After the Twelfth Night performance I can quite believe this. I am convinced that if Burbage were to rise from the dead and accept an invitation from Sir Henry Irving to appear at the Lyceum, he would recoil beaten the moment he realized that he was to be looked at as part of an optical illusion through a huge hole in the wall, instead of being practically in the middle of the theatre. The acting at Burlington Hall was for the most part bad acting, done by amateurs who were acutely conscious of themselves and of Shakespear, and very feebly conscious, indeed, of the reality and humanity of the characters they represented. Sir Toby Belch, Sir Andrew Aguecheek, and the rest of the comic personages, with the honorable exception of Malvolio, grinned continuously at the humor of their own parts. The clown made no pretence of understanding a single sentence he uttered: it sufficed for him that he *was* a clown. Orsino was an inhumanly well-conducted, well-spoken, well-dressed, considerate, and reasonable lover. Olivia, played by a young lady of obvious possibilities as an actress, will not realize those possibilities unless she promptly abandons the artificial rhetorical drama, and never touches it again until she

is able to play a modern comedy and a modern melodrama with frankness and conviction. Viola spoke some
of her lines very prettily; but she was not—well, all that is
necessary for my argument is to say that she was not as
good as Miss Rehan. Antonio, a very handsome young
man with a sensitive style and, like Olivia, unmistakeable
possibilities, had not experience enough to make the most
of himself. In short, nobody can pretend that the Society
had any advantage over Mr. Daly or Sir Henry Irving
in the histrionic talent at its disposal. But what it had
went so much further under the Elizabethan conditions
that everyone present took the acting to be much better
than it really was; whereas at Daly's, or the Lyceum, only
the most gifted players can make any considerable effect,
the other parts invariably seeming colorless and unduly
subordinate. With skilful and rapid declamation, which
would have rendered the curtailment of the play unnecessary, the performance would have beaten its modern rivals completely, especially as Mr. Dolmetsch with his viol
and lute, and Miss Helen Dolmetsch with her viola da
gamba, were there with their little party of viol and virginal players to give us some of the music of the days
when England really could produce music. On the whole,
though I will not urge Sir Henry Irving to rebuild the
Lyceum on the old inn yard model, I do seriously suggest that our leading actors might occasionally come
down and take a turn on the stage of the E.S.S., at Gray's
Inn Hall or elsewhere, just to shew us what they could
do on the sort of stage which helped Burbage to become
famous.

Seeing a production of Twelfth Night *while serving as a
music critic provoked Shaw to make some remarks on the
transposition of songs in Shakespeare's plays in an article
in* The World *on January 24, 1894.*

. . . The musical side of Mr. Daly's revival of Twelfth
Night is a curious example of the theatrical tradition that
any song written by Shakespear is appropriate to any
play written by him, except, perhaps, the play in which
it occurs. The first thing that happens in the Daly

version is the entry of all the lodging-house keepers (as
I presume) on the sea-coast of Illyria to sing Ariel's song
from The Tempest, Come unto these yellow sands. After
this absurdity I was rather disappointed that the sea captain did not strike up Full fathom five thy brother lies, in
the course of his conversation with Viola.

Since no protest has been made, may I lift up my voice
against the notion that the moment music is in question
all common sense may be suspended, and managers may
take liberties which would not be allowed to pass if they
affected the purely literary part of the play. Come unto
these yellow sands is no doubt very pretty; but so is the
speech made by Ferdinand when he escapes, like Viola,
from shipwreck. Yet if Mr. Daly had interpolated that
speech in the first act of Twelfth Night, the leading
dramatic critics would have denounced the proceeding
as a literary outrage, whereas the exactly parallel case
of the interpolation of the song is regarded as a happy
thought, wholly unobjectionable. Later on in the play
Shakespear has given the clown two songs: one, Come
away, Death, to sing to the melancholy Orsino, and the
other, O mistress mine, quite different in character, to
sing to his boon companions.

Here is another chance of shewing the innate superiority of the modern American manager to Shakespear;
and Mr. Daly jumps at it accordingly. Come away, Death,
is discarded altogether; and in its place we have O mistress mine, whilst, for a climax of perverse disorder, the
wrong ballad is sung, not to its delightful old tune, unrivalled in humorous tenderness, but to one which is so
far appropriate to Come away, Death, that it has no
humor at all. On the other hand, the introduction of
the serenade from Cymbeline at the end of the third act,
with Who is Sylvia? altered to Who's Olivia? seems to
me to be quite permissible, as it is neither an interpolation nor an alteration, but a pure interlude, and a very
seductive one, thanks to Schubert and to the conductor,
Mr. Henry Widmer, who has handled the music in such
a fashion as to get the last drop of honey out of it.

Two Gentlemen of Verona

A review of Augustin Daly's production appeared on July 6, 1895, in The Saturday Review.

THE PIECE founded by Augustin Daly on Shakespear's Two Gentlemen of Verona, to which I looked forward last week, is not exactly a comic opera, though there is plenty of music in it, and not exactly a serpentine dance, though it proceeds under a play of changing colored lights. It is something more old-fashioned than either: to wit, a vaudeville. And let me hasten to admit that it makes a very pleasant entertainment for those who know no better. Even I, who know a great deal better, as I shall presently demonstrate rather severely, enjoyed myself tolerably. I cannot feel harshly towards a gentleman who works so hard as Mr. Daly does to make Shakespear presentable: one feels that he loves the bard, and lets him have his way as far as he thinks it good for him. His rearrangement of the scenes of the first two acts is just like him. Shakespear shews lucidly how Proteus lives with his father (Antonio) in Verona, and loves a lady of that city named Julia. Mr. Daly, by taking the scene in Julia's house between Julia and her maid, and the scene in Antonio's house between Antonio and Proteus, and making them into one scene, convinces the unlettered audience that Proteus and Julia live in the same house with their father Antonio. Further, Shakespear shews us how Valentine, the other gentleman of Verona, travels from Verona to Milan, the journey being driven into our heads by a comic scene in Verona, in which Valentine's servant is overwhelmed with grief at leaving his parents, and with indignation at the insensibility of his dog to his sorrow, followed presently by another comic scene in Milan in which the same servant is welcomed to the strange city by a fellow-servant. Mr. Daly, however, is ready for Shakespear on this point too. He just represents the two scenes as occurring in the

200

same place; and immediately the puzzle as to who is who is complicated by a puzzle as to where is where. Thus is the immortal William adapted to the requirements of a nineteenth-century audience.

In preparing the text of his version Mr. Daly has proceeded on the usual principles, altering, transposing, omitting, improving, correcting, and transferring speeches from one character to another. Many of Shakespear's lines are mere poetry, not to the point, not getting the play along, evidently stuck in because the poet liked to spread himself in verse. On all such unbusinesslike superfluities Mr. Daly is down with his blue pencil. For instance, he relieves us of such stuff as the following, which merely conveys that Valentine loves Silvia, a fact already sufficiently established by the previous dialogue:

My thoughts do harbor with my Silvia nightly;
   And slaves they are to me, that send them flying:
Oh, could their master come and go as lightly,
   Himself would lodge where senseless they are lying.
My herald thoughts in thy pure bosom rest them,
   While I, their king, that thither them importune,
Do curse the grace that with such grace hath blessed them,
   Because myself do want my servant's fortune.
I curse myself, for they are sent by me,
   That they should harbor where their lord would be.

Slaves indeed are these lines and their like to Mr. Daly, who "sends them flying" without remorse. But when he comes to passages that a stage manager can understand, his reverence for the bard knows no bounds. The following awkward lines, unnecessary as they are under modern stage conditions, are at any rate not poetic, and are in the nature of police news. Therefore they are piously retained:

What halloing, and what stir, is this today?
These are my mates, that make their wills their law,
Have some unhappy passenger in chase.
They love me well; yet I have much to do,
To keep them from uncivil outrages.
Withdraw thee, Valentine: whos this comes here?

The perfunctory metrical character of such lines only makes them more ridiculous than they would be in prose. I would cut them out without remorse to make room for all the lines that have nothing to justify their existence except their poetry, their humor, their touches of character—in short, the lines for whose sake the play survives, just as it was for their sake it originally came into existence. Mr. Daly, who prefers the lines which only exist for the sake of the play, will doubtless think me as great a fool as Shakespear; but I submit to him, that he is, after all, only a man with a theory of dramatic composition, going with a blue pencil over the work of a great dramatist, and striking out everything that does not fit his theory. Now, as it happens, nobody cares about Mr. Daly's theory; whilst everybody who pays to see what is, after all, advertised as a performance of Shakespear's play entitled The Two Gentlemen of Verona, and not as a demonstration of Mr. Daly's theory, does care more or less about the art of Shakespear. Why not give them what they ask for, instead of going to great trouble and expense to give them something else?

In those matters in which Mr. Daly has given the rein to his own taste and fancy: that is to say, in scenery, costumes, and music, he is for the most part disabled by a want of real knowledge of the arts concerned. I say for the most part, because his pretty fifteenth-century dresses, though probably inspired rather by Sir Frederic Leighton than by Benozzo Gozzoli, may pass. But the scenery is insufferable. First, for "a street in Verona" we get a Bath bun colored operatic front cloth with about as much light in it as there is in a studio in Fitzjohn's Avenue in the middle of October. I respectfully invite Mr. Daly to spend his next holiday looking at a real street in Verona, asking his conscience meanwhile whether a manager with eyes in his head and the electric light at his disposal could not advance a step on the Telbin (senior) style. Telbin was an admirable scene painter; but he was limited by the mechanical conditions of gas illumination; and he learnt his technique before the great advance made during the Impressionist movement in the painting of open-air effects, especially of brilliant sunlight.

Of that advance Mr. Daly has apparently no conception. The days of Macready and Clarkson Stanfield still exist for him; he would probably prefer a water-color drawing of a foreign street by Samuel Prout to one of Mr. T. M. Rooke; and I daresay every relic of the original tallow candlelight that still clings to the art of scene-painting is as dear to him as it is to most old playgoers, including, unhappily, many of the critics.

As to the elaborate set in which Julia makes her first entrance, a glance at it shews how far Mr. Daly prefers the Marble Arch to the loggia of Orcagna. All over the scene we have Renaissance work, in its genteelest stages of decay, held up as the perfection of romantic elegance and beauty. The school that produced the classicism of the First Empire, designed the terraces of Regent's Park and the façades of Fitzroy Square, and conceived the Boboli Gardens and Versailles as places for human beings to be happy in, ramps all over the scenery, and offers as much of its pet colonnades and statues as can be crammed into a single scene, by way of a compendium of everything that is lovely in the city of San Zeno and the tombs of the Scaligers. As to the natural objects depicted, I ask whether any man living has ever seen a pale green cypress in Verona or anywhere else out of a toy Noah's Ark. A man who, having once seen cypresses and felt their presence in a north Italian landscape, paints them lettuce color, must be suffering either from madness, malice, or a theory of how nature should have colored trees, cognate with Mr. Daly's theory of how Shakespear should have written plays.

Of the music let me speak compassionately. After all, it is only very lately that Mr. Arnold Dolmetsch, by playing fifteenth-century music on fifteenth-century instruments, has shewn us that the age of beauty was true to itself in music as in pictures and armor and costumes. But what should Mr. Daly know of this, educated as he no doubt was to believe that the court of Denmark should always enter in the first act of Hamlet to the march from Judas Maccabæus? Schubert's setting of Who is Silvia? he knew, but had rashly used up in Twelfth Night as Who's Olivia. He has therefore had to fall back on another modern setting, almost supernaturally devoid of any particular merit. Besides this, all through the drama the most horribly common music repeatedly breaks out on the slightest pretext or on no pretext at all. One dance, set to a crude old English popular tune, sundry eighteenth and nineteenth century musical banalities, and a titivated plantation melody in the first act which produces an indescribably atrocious effect by coming in behind the scenes as a sort of coda to Julia's curtain speech, all turn the play, as I have said, into a vaudeville. Needless to add, the accompaniments are not played on lutes and viols, but by the orchestra and a guitar or two. In the forest scene the outlaws begin the act by a chorus. After their encounter with Valentine they go off the stage singing the refrain exactly in the style of La Fille de Madame Angot. The wanton absurdity of introducing this comic opera convention is presently eclipsed by a thunderstorm, immediately after which Valentine enters and delivers his speech sitting down on a bank of moss, as an outlaw in tights naturally would after a terrific shower. Such is the effect of many years of theatrical management on the human brain.

Perhaps the oddest remark I have to make about the performance is that, with all its glaring defects and blunders, it is rather a handsome and elaborate one as such things go. It is many years now since Mr. Ruskin first took the Academicians of his day aback by the obvious remark that Carpaccio and Giovanni Bellini were better painters than Domenichino and Salvator Rosa. Nobody dreams now of assuming that Pope was a greater poet than Chaucer, that Mozart's Twelfth Mass is superior to the masterpieces of Orlandus Lassus and Palestrina, or that our "ecclesiastical Gothic" architecture is more enlightened than Norman axe work. But the theatre is still wallowing in such follies; and until Mr. Comyns Carr and Sir Edward Burne-Jones, Baronet, put King Arthur on the stage more or less in the manner natural to men who know these things, Mr. Daly might have pleaded the unbroken conservatism of the playhouse against me. But after the Lyceum scenery and architecture I decline to accept a relapse without protest. There is no reason why cheap photographs of Italian architecture (sixpence apiece in infinite variety at the book-

stall in the South Kensington Museum) should not rescue
us from Regent's Park Renaissance colonnades on the
stage just as the electric light can rescue us from Telbin's
dun-colored sunlight. The opera is the last place in the
world where any wise man would look for adequate stage
illusion; but the fact is that Mr. Daly, with all his
colored lights, has not produced a single Italian scene
comparable in illusion to that provided by Sir Augustus
Harris at Covent Garden for Cavalleria Rusticana.

Of the acting I have not much to say. Miss Rehan
provided a strong argument in favor of rational dress
by looking much better in her page's costume than in
that of her own sex; and in the serenade scene, and that
of the wooing of Silvia for Proteus, she stirred some
feeling into the part, and reminded us of what she was
in Twelfth Night, where the same situations are fully
worked out. For the rest, she moved and spoke with imposing rhythmic grace. That is as much notice as so cheap
a part as Julia is worth from an artist who, being absolute
mistress of the situation at Daly's Theatre, might and
should have played Imogen for us instead. The two
gentlemen were impersonated by Mr. Worthing and Mr.
Craig. Mr. Worthing charged himself with feeling without any particular reference to his lines; and Mr. Craig
struck a balance by attending to the meaning of his
speeches without taking them at all to heart. Mr. Clarke,
as the Duke, was emphatic, and worked up every long
speech to a climax in the useful old style; but his tone
is harsh, his touch on his consonants coarse, and his accent
ugly, all fatal disqualifications for the delivery of Shakespearean verse. The scenes between Launce and his dog
brought out the latent silliness and childishness of the
audience as Shakespear's clowning scenes always do: I
laugh at them like a yokel myself. Mr. Lewis hardly made
the most of them. His style has been formed in modern
comedies, where the locutions are so familiar that their
meaning is in no danger of being lost by the rapidity of
his quaint utterance; but Launce's phraseology is another
matter: a few of the funniest lines missed fire because the
audience did not catch them. And with all possible allow-
ance for Mr. Daly's blue pencil, I cannot help suspecting
that Mr. Lewis's memory was responsible for one or two

of his omissions. Still, Mr. Lewis has always his comic force, whether he makes the most or the least of it; so that he cannot fail in such a part as Launce. Miss Maxine Elliot's Silvia was the most considerable performance after Miss Rehan's Julia. The whole company will gain by the substitution on Tuesday next of a much better play, A Midsummer Night's Dream, as a basis for Mr. Daly's operations. No doubt he is at this moment, like Mrs. Todgers, "a dodgin' among the tender bits with a fork, and an eatin' of 'em"; but there is sure to be enough of the original left here and there to repay a visit.

THE MAN

From the beginning, those interested in Shakespeare, scholarly or not, have felt an irresistible urge to discover the man behind the plays. This form of detective work was particularly prevalent at the time Shaw was doing most of his writing about Shakespeare. While this type of criticism is usually irrelevant and always hazardous, it is nevertheless of some interest to know Shaw's ideas about the life of his predecessor.

His most complete statements are found in the preface to The Dark Lady of the Sonnets *and a review of Mr. Frank Harris's book,* Shakespeare and his Love. *Both pieces are reactions to Harris's theories on Shakespeare which Harris had expressed not only in his book but also in a play on the same subject.*

Shaw had developed his own ideas about Shakespeare's life from his reading and from discussions with others, including a little known scholar named Thomas Tyler whom Shaw saw frequently in the British Museum.

Shaw wrote The Dark Lady of the Sonnets *for a program pleading the cause of a National Theatre in England. The chief characters in this short play are Shakespeare, Queen Elizabeth, and the Dark Lady. One of the running jokes of the piece is that other people constantly speak lines from Shakespeare's plays whereupon he takes the words down: Shaw's way of suggesting that Shakespeare did not make up all that poetry but stole it from others. In the preface to* The Dark Lady *Shaw challenged Harris's theories, using Harris's own method of treating the plays as autobiography. Typical of Shaw's conclusions is his idea on Shakespeare's social standing.*

. . . On the vexed question of Shakespear's social standing Mr. Harris says that Shakespear "had not had the advantage of a middle-class training." I suggest that Shakespear missed this questionable advantage, not because he was socially too low to have attained to it, but because he conceived himself as belonging to the upper class from which our public school boys are now drawn. . . .

. . . The whole range of Shakespear's foibles: the snobbishness, the naughtiness, the contempt for tradesmen and mechanics, the assumption that witty conversation can only mean smutty conversation, the flunkeyism towards social superiors and insolence towards social inferiors, the easy ways with servants which is seen not only between The Two Gentlemen of Verona and their valets, but in the affection and respect inspired by a great servant like Adam: all these are the characteristics of Eton and Harrow, not of the public elementary or private adventure school. They prove, as everything we know about Shakespear suggests, that he thought of the Shakespears and Ardens as families of consequence, and regarded himself as a gentleman under a cloud through his father's ill luck in business, and never for a moment as a man of the people. This is at once the explanation of and excuse for his snobbery. He was not a parvenu trying to cover his humble origin with a purchased coat of arms: he was a gentleman resuming what he conceived to be his natural position as soon as he gained the means to keep it up.

In discussing Harris's book and play in his review in The Nation *on December 10, 1910, Shaw went into other aspects of Shakespeare's personal life.*

. . . Coming to the play itself, the first thing one looks for in it is Shakespear; and that is just what one does not find. You get "the melancholy Dane" of Kemble and Mr. Wopsle; but the melancholy Dane was not even Hamlet, much less Shakespear. Mr. Harris's theory of Shakespear as a man with his heart broken by a love affair will not wash. That Shakespear's soul was damned (I really know no other way of expressing it) by a barren pessimism is undeniable; but even when it drove him to the blasphemous despair of Lear and the Nihilism of Macbeth, it did not break him. He was not crushed by it: he wielded it Titanically, and made it a sublime quality in his plays. He almost delighted in it: it never made him bitter: to the end there was mighty music in him, and outrageous gaiety. To represent him as a snivelling brokenhearted swain, dying because he was jilted, is not only an intolerable and wanton belittlement of a great spirit, but a flat contradiction of Mr. Harris's own practice of treating the plays as autobiography. Nobody has carried that practice to wilder extremes than he; and far be it from me to blame him, because nobody has discovered, or divined, more interesting and suggestive references. But why does he throw it over when he attempts to put Shakespear on the stage for us? He says that Hamlet is Shakespear. Well, what is Hamlet's attitude towards women? He is in love with Ophelia. He writes her eloquent love letters; and when he has fascinated her, he bullies her and overwhelms her with bitter taunts, reviles her painted face, bids her to get her to a nunnery, and tells her she was a fool to believe him, speaking with even more savage contempt of his own love than of her susceptibility to it. . . .

. . . If Hamlet is Shakespear, then Mr. Harris's hero is not Shakespear, but, in the words of Dickens, whom Mr. Harris despises, "so far from it, on the contrary, quite the reverse." "Men have died from time to time; and worms have eaten them; but not for love," says Shakespear. And again, "I am not so young, sir, to love a woman for her singing"—the only thing, by the way, that could move him. "Her voice was ever soft, gentle, and low" is his tenderest praise.

Add to this the evidence of the sonnets. Shakespear treated the dark lady as Hamlet treated Ophelia, only worse. He could not forgive himself for being in love with her; and he took the greatest care to make it clear that he was not duped: that there was not a bad point in her personal appearance that was lost on him even in his most amorous moments. He gives her a list of her blemishes: wiry hair, bad complexion, and so on (he does not even spare her an allusion to the "reek" of her breath); and his description of his lust, and his revulsion from it, is the most merciless passage in English literature. . . .

. . . One crowning intrusion of commonplace sentiment is the exhibition of Shakespear as sentimentally
devoted to his mother. I ask Mr. Harris, in some desperation, what evidence he has for this. Even if we
assume with him that Shakespear was a perfect monster
of conventional sentiment, filial sentimentality is not an
English convention, but a French one. Englishmen
mostly quarrel with their families, especially with their
mothers. Shakespear has drawn for us one beautiful and
wonderful mother; but she shews all her maternal tenderness and wisdom for an orphan who is no kin to her,
whilst to her son she is shrewd, critical, and without
illusions. I mean, of course, the Countess of Rousillon
in All's Well that Ends Well. . . .

. . . Yet Mr. Harris will have it that Shakespear
idolized his mother, and that this comes out repeatedly
in his plays. In the names of all the mothers that ever
were adored by their sons, where? Hamlet, for instance?
Are his relations with his mother a case in point? Or
Falconbridge's, or Richard the Third's, or Cloten's, or
Juliet's? The list is becoming thin, because, out of
thirty-eight plays, only ten have mothers in them; and of
the ten five may be struck out of the argument as histories. Nobody but Mr. Harris would cite the story of
Volumnia and Coriolanus as Shakespearean autobiography; and nobody at all would cite Margaret of Anjou,
the Duchess of York, or Constance. There are, for the
purposes of Mr. Harris's argument, just two sympathetic
mothers in the whole range of the plays. One is the
Countess of Rousillon and the other is Hermione. Both
of them are idealized noblewomen of the same type,
which is not likely to have been the type of Mrs. John
Shakespear. Both of them are tenderer as daughters'
mothers than as sons' mothers. The great Shakespearean
heroes are all motherless, except Hamlet, whose scene
with his mother is almost unbearably shameful: we endure it only because it is "Shakespear" to us instead of
an effective illusion of reality. Never do we get from
Shakespear, as between son and mother, that unmistakeable tenderness that touches us as between Lear and
Cordelia and between Prospero and Miranda. Mr.
Harris insists on Prospero and Miranda in his book;

but in his play, Shakespear's daughter is a Puritan Gor-
gon who bullies him. This may be good drama; but it is
not good history if Mr. Harris's own historical tests are
worth anything.

*Later in the article Shaw wrote his own summary of
Shakespeare the man.*

. . . Everything we know about Shakespear can be got
into a half-hour sketch. He was a very civil gentleman
who got round men of all classes; he was extremely
susceptible to word-music and to graces of speech; he
picked up all sorts of odds and ends from books and
from the street talk of his day and welded them into
his work; he was so full of witty sallies of all kinds,
decorous and indecorous, that he had to be checked even
at the Mermaid suppers; he was idolized by his admirers
to an extent which nauseated his most enthusiastic and
affectionate friends; and he got into trouble by treating
women in the way already described. Add to this that
he was, like all highly intelligent and conscientious
people, business-like about money and appreciative of
the value of respectability and the discomfort and discredit of Bohemianism; also that he stood on his social
position and desired to have it affirmed by the grant of
a coat of arms, and you have all we know of Shakespear
beyond what we gather from his plays. And it does not
carry us to a tragedy.

In a letter to Hesketh Pearson, reprinted in Pearson's
G.B.S.: A Full Length Portrait, *Shaw noted that Shakespeare had not lived long enough to have a "third
period" and speculated on what the results of such a
period might have been. Pearson had asked Shaw if he
had anything to add to his strong criticism of Shakespeare in past years and this was Shaw's reply.*

. . . Of course I have. But first get out of your head
the superstition that I am a young man, and Shakespear
an old one who has written himself out and retired to
Stratford as William Shakespear, Gent. The truth is that
Shakespear died prematurely: perhaps he drank too

much, as Ibsen did. I know you are an old Bardolator and think the comparison with him is hard on me; but as a matter of fact it is grossly unfair to Shakespear. Do you realise that I have lived more than thirty years longer than he did, and that my biggest works were written at an age he never attained? All the great artists who have lived long enough have had a juvenile phase, a middle phase, and a Third Manner, as we say when we are talking of Beethoven. Well, Beethoven composed the Ninth Symphony and the Mass in D at the age at which Shakespear was dead. The enormous talent of Handel did not produce Messiah, which still enchants listeners who, like myself, do not believe a word of it, until Handel was six years older than Shakespear was at his death. Ibsen was sixteen years older than Shakespear ever was when he wrote The Master Builder. I was respectively thirteen and fifteen years older when I wrote Methuselah and St. Joan. All these works are Third Manner works; and Shakespear had no Third Manner. I do not pretend that Shakespear at sixty would have written Prometheus Unbound or Emperor or Galilean or The Niblung's Ring or Back to Methuselah; but Gonzalo might have gone further than stealing a few lines from Montaigne and Prospero done something better with his cloudcapt towers than knock them down. There was Saint Thomas More to be surpassed and John Bunyan to be anticipated. As it is he can claim that we are all standing on his shoulders. Whose shoulders had he to stand on? Marlow and Chapman, the best of his rivals, were mere blatherskites compared to him. And he was on the brink of the appalling *dégringolade* of the British drama which followed his death, and went on for three hundred years until my time. That is why I have to compare him with giants like Handel and Beethoven. There were no giants in the British theatre to compare with him. And his plays were so abominably murdered and mutilated until Harley Granville-Barker, twenty years my junior, restored them to the stage, that it was shamefully evident that the clergymen who knelt down and kissed Ireland's forgeries and the critics who made him ridiculous by their senseless idolatries had never read a line of his works and never intended to.

THE PHILOSOPHER

Shakespeare wrote plays, not treatises on philosophy, but this did not deter Shaw: his chief complaint against Shakespeare was his deficiency as a philosopher, particularly a moral philosopher. It is the basis for Shaw's famous essay, "Better than Shakespear?", an essay which appeared as the preface to Caesar *and* Cleopatra *in* Three Plays for Puritans.

"BETTER THAN SHAKESPEAR?"

As TO the other plays in this volume, the application of my title is less obvious, since neither Julius Cæsar, Cleopatra, nor Lady Cicely Waynflete have any external political connexion with Puritanism. The very name of Cleopatra suggests at once a tragedy of Circe, with the horrible difference that whereas the ancient myth rightly represents Circe as turning heroes into hogs, the modern romantic convention would represent her as turning hogs into heroes. Shakespear's Antony and Cleopatra must needs be as intolerable to the true Puritan as it is vaguely distressing to the ordinary healthy citizen, because, after giving a faithful picture of the soldier broken down by debauchery, and the typical wanton in whose arms such men perish, Shakespeare finally strains all his huge command of rhetoric and stage pathos to give a theatrical sublimity to the wretched end of the business, and to persuade foolish spectators that the world was well lost by the twain. Such falsehood is not to be borne except by the real Cleopatras and Antonys (they are to be found in every public house) who would no doubt be glad enough to be transfigured by some poet as immortal lovers. Woe to the poet who stoops to such folly! The lot of the man who sees life truly and thinks about it romantically is Despair. How well we know the cries

of that despair! Vanity of vanities, all is vanity! moans
the Preacher, when life has at last taught him that
Nature will not dance to his moralist-made tunes.
Thackeray, scores of centuries later, was still baying the
moon in the same terms. Out, out, brief candle; cries
Shakespear, in his tragedy of the modern literary man
as murderer and witch consulter. Surely the time is past
for patience with writers who, having to choose between
giving up life in despair and discarding the trumpery
moral kitchen scales in which they try to weigh the uni-
verse, superstitiously stick to the scales, and spend the
rest of the lives they pretend to despise in breaking
men's spirits. But even in pessimism there is a choice
between intellectual honesty and dishonesty. Hogarth
drew the rake and the harlot without glorifying their
end. Swift, accepting our system of morals and religion,
delivered the inevitable verdict of that system on us
through the mouth of the king of Brobdingnag, and
described Man as the Yahoo, shocking his superior the
horse by his every action. Strindberg, the only genuinely
Shakespearean modern dramatist, shews that the female
Yahoo, measured by romantic standards, is viler than her
male dupe and slave. I respect these resolute tragi-
comedians: they are logical and faithful: they force you
to face the fact that you must either accept their conclusions as valid (in which case it is cowardly to continue
living) or admit that their way of judging conduct is
absurd. But when your Shakespears and Thackerays
huddle up the matter at the end by killing somebody
and covering your eyes with the undertaker's handkerchief, duly onioned with some pathetic phrase, as The
flight of angels sing thee to they rest, or Adsum, or the
like, I have no respect for them at all: such maudlin
tricks may impose on tea-drunkards, not on me.

Besides, I have a technical objection to making sexual
infatuation a tragic theme. Experience proves that it is
only effective in the comic spirit. We can bear to see
Mrs. Quickly pawning her plate for love of Falstaff, but
not Antony running away from the battle of Actium
for love of Cleopatra. Let realism have its demonstration, comedy its criticism, or even bawdry its horse-
laugh at the expense of sexual infatuation, if it must;

but to ask us to subject our souls to its ruinous glamor, to worship it, deify it, and imply that it alone makes our life worth living, is nothing but folly gone mad erotically—a thing compared to which Falstaff's unbeglamored drinking and drabbing is respectable and rightminded. Whoever, then, expects to find Cleopatra a Circe and Cæsar a hog in these pages, had better lay down my book and be spared a disappointment.

In Cæsar, I have used another character with which Shakespear has been beforehand. But Shakespear, who knew human weakness so well, never knew human strength of the Cæsarian type. His Cæsar is an admitted failure: his Lear is a masterpiece. The tragedy of disillusion and doubt, of the agonized struggle for a foothold on the quicksand made by an acute observation striving to verify its vain attribution of morality and respectability to Nature, of the faithless will and the keen eyes that the faithless will is too weak to blind: all this will give you a Hamlet or a Macbeth, and win you great applause from literary gentlemen; but it will not give you a Julius Cæsar. Cæsar was not in Shakespear, nor in the epoch, now fast waning, which he inaugurated. It cost Shakespear no pang to write Cæsar down for the merely technical purpose of writing Brutus up. And what a Brutus! A perfect Girondin, mirrored in Shakespear's art two hundred years before the real thing came to maturity and talked and stalked and had its head duly cut off by the coarser Antonys and Octaviuses of its time, who at least knew the difference between life and rhetoric.

It will be said that these remarks can bear no other construction than an offer of my Cæsar to the public as an improvement on Shakespear's. And in fact, that is their precise purport. But here let me give a friendly warning to those scribes who have so often exclaimed against my criticisms of Shakespear as blasphemies against a hitherto unquestioned Perfection and Infallibility. Such criticisms are no more new than the creed of my Diabolonian Puritan or my revival of the humors of Cool as a Cucumber. Too much surprise at them betrays an acquaintance with Shakespear criticism so limited as not to include even the prefaces of Dr. Johnson and the utterances of Napoleon. I have merely repeated in the dialect of my own time and in the light of its philosophy what they said in the dialect and light of theirs. Do not be misled by the Shakespear fanciers who, ever since his own time, have delighted in his plays just as they might have delighted in a particular breed of pigeons if they had never learnt to read. His genuine critics, from Ben Jonson to Mr. Frank Harris, have always kept as far on this side idolatry as I.

As to our ordinary uncritical citizens, they have been slowly trudging forward these three centuries to the point which Shakespear reached at a bound in Elizabeth's time. Today most of them have arrived there or thereabouts, with the result that his plays are at last beginning to be performed as he wrote them; and the long line of disgraceful farces, melodramas, and stage pageants which actor-managers, from Garrick and Cibber to our own contemporaries, have hacked out of his plays as peasants have hacked huts out of the Coliseum, are beginning to vanish from the stage. It is a significant fact that the mutilators of Shakespear, who never could be persuaded that Shakespear knew his business better than they, have ever been the most fanatical of his worshippers. The late Augustin Daly thought no price too extravagant for an addition to his collection of Shakespear relics; but in arranging Shakespear's plays for the stage, he proceeded on the assumption that Shakespear was a botcher and he an artist. I am far too good a Shakespearean ever to forgive Henry Irving for producing a version of King Lear so mutilated that the numerous critics who had never read the play could not follow the story of Gloster. Both these idolators of the Bard must have thought Forbes Robertson mad because he restored Fortinbras to the stage and played as much of Hamlet as there was time for instead of as little. And the instant success of the experiment probably altered their minds no further than to make them think the public mad. Mr. Benson actually gives the play complete at two sittings, causing the aforesaid numerous critics to remark with naïve surprise that Polonius is a complete and interesting character. It was the age of gross ignorance of Shakespear and incapacity for his works that produced the indiscriminate eulogies with which we are familiar. It was the revival of serious attention to those works that coincided with the movement for giving genuine instead of spurious and silly representations of his plays. So much for Bardolatry!

It does not follow, however, that the right to criticize Shakespear involves the power of writing better plays. And in fact—do not be surprised at my modesty—I do not profess to write better plays. The writing of practicable stage plays does not present an infinite scope to human talent; and the playwrights who magnify its difficulties are humbugs. The summit of their art has been attained again and again. No man will ever write a better tragedy than Lear, a better comedy than Le Festin de Pierre or Peer Gynt, a better opera than Don Giovanni, a better music drama than The Niblung's Ring, or, for the matter of that, better fashionable plays and melodramas than are now being turned out by writers whom nobody dreams of mocking with the word immortal. It is the philosophy, the outlook on life, that changes, not the craft of the playwright. A generation that is thoroughly moralized and patriotized, that conceives virtuous indignation as spiritually nutritious, that murders the murderer and robs the thief, that grovels before all sorts of ideals, social, military, ecclesiastical, royal and divine, may be, from my point of view, steeped in error; but it need not want for as good plays as the hand of man can produce. Only, those plays will be neither written nor relished by men in whose philosophy guilt and innocence, and consequently revenge and idolatry, have no meaning. Such men must rewrite all the old plays in terms of their own philosophy; and that is why, as Stuart-Glennie has pointed out, there can be no new drama without a new philosophy. To which I may add that there can be no Shakespear or Goethe without one either, nor two Shakespears in one philosophic epoch, since, as I have said, the first great comer in that epoch reaps the whole harvest and reduces those who come after to the rank of mere gleaners, or, worse than that, fools who go laboriously through all the motions of the reaper and binder in an empty field. What is the use of writing plays or painting frescoes if you have nothing more to say or shew than was said and shewn by Shakespear, Michael Angelo, and Raphael? If these had not seen things differently, for better or worse, from the dramatic poets of the Townley mysteries, or from Giotto, they could not have produced their works: no, not though their skill of pen and hand had been double what it was. After them there was no need (and *need* alone nerves men to face the persecution in the teeth of which new art is brought to birth) to redo the already done, until in due time, when their philosophy wore itself out, a new race of nineteenth century poets and critics, from Byron to William Morris, began, first to speak coldly of Shakespear and Raphael, and then to rediscover, in the medieval art which these Renascence masters had superseded, certain forgotten elements which were germinating again for the new harvest. What is more, they began to discover that the technical skill of the masters was by no means superlative. Indeed, I defy anyone to prove that the great epoch makers in fine art have owed their position to their technical skill. It is true that when we search for examples of a prodigious command of language and of graphic line, we can think of nobody better than Shakespear and Michael Angelo. But both of them laid their arts waste for centuries by leading later artists to seek greatness in copying their technique. The technique was acquired, refined on, and elaborated over and over again; but the supremacy of the two great exemplars remained undisputed. As a matter of easily observable fact, every generation produces men of extraordinary special faculty, artistic, mathematical and linguistic, who for lack of new ideas, or indeed of any ideas worth mentioning, achieve no distinction outside music halls and class rooms, although they can do things easily that the great epoch makers did clumsily or not at all. The contempt of the academic pedant for the original artist is often founded on a genuine superiority of technical knowledge and aptitude: he is sometimes a better anatomical draughtsman than Raphael, a better hand at triple counterpoint than Beethoven, a better versifier than Byron. Nay, this is true not merely of pedants, but of men who have produced works of art of some note. If technical facility were the

secret of greatness in art, Swinburne would be greater
than Browning and Byron rolled into one, Stevenson
greater than Scott or Dickens, Mendelssohn than Wagner, Maclise than Madox Brown. Besides, new ideas
make their technique as water makes its channel; and
the technician without ideas is as useless as the canal
constructor without water, though he may do very skilfully what the Mississippi does very rudely. To clinch
the argument, you have only to observe that the epoch
maker himself has generally begun working professionally before his new ideas have mastered him sufficiently
to insist on constant expression by his art. In such
cases you are compelled to admit that if he had by
chance died earlier, his greatness would have remained
unachieved, although his technical qualifications would
have been well enough established. The early imitative
works of great men are usually conspicuously inferior to
the best works of their forerunners. Imagine Wagner
dying after composing Rienzi, or Shelley after Zastrozzi!
Would any competent critic then have rated Wagner's
technical aptitude as high as Rossini's, Spontini's, or
Meyerbeer's; or Shelley's as high as Moore's? Turn the
problem another way: does anyone suppose that if
Shakespear had conceived Goethe's or Ibsen's ideas, he
would have expressed them any worse than Goethe or
Ibsen? Human faculty being what it is, is it likely that
in our time any advance, except in external conditions,
will take place in the arts of expression sufficient to
enable an author, without making himself ridiculous,
to undertake to say what he has to say better than
Homer or Shakespear? But the humblest author, and
much more a rather arrogant one like myself, may profess to have something to say by this time that neither
Homer nor Shakespear said. And the playgoer may
reasonably ask to have historical events and persons
presented to him in the light of his own time, even
though Homer and Shakespear have already shewn them
in the light of their time. For example, Homer presented Achilles and Ajax as heroes to the world in the
Iliad. In due time came Shakespear, who said, virtually:
I really cannot accept this spoilt child and this brawny
fool as great men merely because Homer flattered them

in playing to the Greek gallery. Consequently we have, in Troilus and Cressida, the verdict of Shakespear's epoch (our own) on the pair. This did not in the least involve any pretence on Shakespear's part to be a greater poet than Homer.

When Shakespear in turn came to deal with Henry V and Julius Cæsar, he did so according to his own essentially knightly conception of a great statesman-commander. But in the XIX century comes the German historian Mommsen, who also takes Cæsar for his hero, and explains the immense difference in scope between the perfect knight Vercingetorix and his great conqueror Julius Cæsar. In this country, Carlyle, with his vein of peasant inspiration, apprehended the sort of greatness that places the true hero of history so far beyond the mere *preux chevalier,* whose fanatical personal honor, gallantry, and self-sacrifice, are founded on a passion for death born of inability to bear the weight of a life that will not grant ideal conditions to the liver. This one ray of perception became Carlyle's whole stock-in-trade; and it sufficed to make a literary master of him. In due time, when Mommsen is an old man, and Carlyle dead, come I and dramatize the by-this-time familiar distinction in Arms and the Man, with its comedic conflict between the knightly Bulgarian and the Mommsenite Swiss captain. Whereupon a great many playgoers who have not yet read Cervantes, much less Mommsen and Carlyle, raise a shriek of concern for their knightly ideal as if nobody had ever questioned its sufficiency since the middle ages. Let them thank me for educating them so far. And let them allow me to set forth Cæsar in the same modern light, taking the platform from Shakespear as he from Homer, and with no thought of pretending to express the Mommsenite view of Cæsar any better than Shakespear expressed a view which was not even Plutarchian, and must, I fear, be referred to the tradition in stage conquerors established by Marlowe's Tamerlane as much as to the chivalrous conception of heroism dramatized in Henry V.

For my own part, I can avouch that such powers of invention, humor and stage ingenuity as I have been able to exercise in Plays Pleasant and Unpleasant, and

these Three Plays for Puritans, availed me not at all
until I saw the old facts in a new light. Technically, I
do not find myself able to proceed otherwise than as
former playwrights have done. True, my plays have the
latest mechanical improvements: the action is not
carried on by impossible soliloquys and asides; and my
people get on and off the stage without requiring four
doors to a room which in real life would have only one.
But my stories are the old stories; my characters are the
familiar harlequin and columbine, clown and pantaloon
(note the harlequin's leap in the third act of Cæsar and
Cleopatra); my stage tricks and suspenses and thrills
and jests are the ones in vogue when I was a boy, by
which time my grandfather was tired of them. To the
young people who make their acquaintance for the first
time in my plays, they may be as novel as Cyrano's nose
to those who have never seen Punch; whilst to older
playgoers the unexpectedness of my attempt to substitute
natural history for conventional ethics and romantic
logic may so transfigure the eternal stage puppets and
their inevitable dilemmas as to make their identification
impossible for the moment. If so, so much the better for
me: I shall perhaps enjoy a few years of immortality.
But the whirligig of time will soon bring my audiences
to my own point of view; and then the next Shakespear
that comes along will turn these petty tentatives of mine
into masterpieces final for their epoch. By that time my
twentieth century characteristics will pass unnoticed as
a matter of course, whilst the eighteenth century artificiality that marks the work of every literary Irishman of
my generation will seem antiquated and silly. It is a
dangerous thing to be hailed at once, as a few rash
admirers have hailed me, as above all things original:
what the world calls originality is only an unaccustomed
method of tickling it. Meyerbeer seemed prodigiously
original to the Parisians when he first burst on them.
Today, he is only the crow who followed Beethoven's
plough. I am a crow who have followed many ploughs.
No doubt I seem prodigiously clever to those who have
never hopped, hungry and curious, across the fields of
philosophy, politics, and art. Karl Marx said of Stuart
Mill that his eminence was due to the flatness of the

surrounding country. In these days of Free Schools, universal reading, cheap newspapers, and the inevitable ensuing demand for notabilities of all sorts, literary, military, political and fashionable, to write paragraphs about, that sort of eminence is within the reach of very moderate ability. Reputations are cheap nowadays. Even were they dear, it would still be impossible for any public-spirited citizen of the world to hope that his reputation might endure; for this would be to hope that the flood of general enlightenment may never rise above his miserable high-watermark. I hate to think that Shakespear has lasted 300 years, though he got no further than Koheleth the Preacher, who died many centuries before him; or that Plato, more than 2000 years old, is still ahead of our voters. We must hurry on: we must get rid of reputations: they are weeds in the soil of ignorance. Cultivate that soil, and they will flower more beautifully, but only as annuals. If this preface will at all help to get rid of mine, the writing of it will have been well worth the pains.

THE ARTIST-PHILOSOPHER

In the preface to Man and Superman *Shaw criticized Shakespeare for not being an "artist-philosopher."*

. . . That the author of Everyman was no mere artist, but an artist-philosopher, and that the artist-philosophers are the only sort of artists I take quite seriously, will be no news to you. Even Plato and Boswell, as the dramatists who invented Socrates and Dr. Johnson, impress me more deeply than the romantic playwrights. Ever since, as a boy, I first breathed the air of the transcendental regions at a performance of Mozart's Zauberflöte, I have been proof against the garish splendors and alcoholic excitements of the ordinary stage combinations of Tappertitian romance with the police intelligence. Bunyan, Blake, Hogarth, and Turner (these four apart and above all the English classics), Goethe, Shelley, Schopenhauer, Wagner, Ibsen, Morris, Tolstoy, and Nietzsche are among the writers whose peculiar sense of the world I recognize as more or less akin to my own. Mark the word peculiar. I read Dickens and Shakespear without shame or stint; but their pregnant observations and demonstrations of life are not co-ordinated into any philosophy or religion; on the contrary, Dickens's sentimental assumptions are violently contradicted by his observations; and Shakespear's pessimism is only his wounded humanity. Both have the specific genius of the fictionist and the common sympathies of human feeling and thought in pre-eminent degree. They are often saner and shrewder than the philosophers just as Sancho Panza was often saner and shrewder than Don Quixote. They clear away vast masses of oppressive gravity by their sense of the ridiculous, which is at bottom a combination of sound moral judgment with lighthearted good humor. But they are concerned with the diversities of the world instead of with its unities; they are so irreligious that they exploit popular religion for profes-

sional purposes without delicacy or scruple (for example,
Sydney Carton and the ghost in Hamlet!); they are an-
archical, and cannot balance their exposures of Angelo
and Dogberry, Sir Leicester Dedlock and Mr. Tite Bar-
nacle, with any portrait of a prophet or a worthy leader;
they have no constructive ideas; they regard those who
have them as dangerous fanatics; in all their fictions there
is no leading thought or inspiration for which any man
could conceivably risk the spoiling of his hat in a
shower, much less his life. Both are alike forced to bor-
row motives for the more strenuous actions of their
personages from the common stockpot of melodramatic
plots; so that Hamlet has to be stimulated by the
prejudices of a policeman and Macbeth by the cupidities
of a bushranger. Dickens, without the excuse of having
to manufacture motives for Hamlets and Macbeths,
superfluously punts his crew down the stream of his
monthly parts by mechanical devices which I leave you
to describe, my own memory being quite baffled by the
simplest question as to Monks in Oliver Twist, or the
long lost parentage of Smike, or the relations between
the Dorrit and Clennam families so inopportunely discovered by Monsieur Rigaud Blandois. The truth is,
the world was to Shakespear a great "stage of fools" on
which he was utterly bewildered. He could see no sort of
sense in living at all; and Dickens saved himself from the
despair of the dream in The Chimes by taking the world
for granted and busying himself with its details. Neither of them could do anything with a serious positive character: they could place a human figure before
you with perfect verisimilitude; but when the moment
came for making it live and move, they found, unless
it made them laugh, that they had a puppet on their
hands, and had to invent some artificial external stim-
ulus to make it work. This is what is the matter with
Hamlet all through: he has no will except in his bursts
of temper. Foolish Bardolaters make a virtue of this
after their fashion: they declare that the play is the
tragedy of irresoluton; but all Shakespear's projections
of the deepest humanity he knew have the same defect:
their characters and manners are lifelike; but their actions are forced on them from without, and the external

force is grotesquely inappropriate except when it is quite conventional, as in the case of Henry V. Falstaff is more vivid than any of these serious reflective characters, because he is self-acting: his motives are his own appetites and instincts and humors. Richard III, too, is delightful as the whimsical comedian who stops a funeral to make love to the corpse's son's widow; but when, in the next act, he is replaced by a stage villain who smothers babies and offs with people's heads, we are revolted at the imposture and repudiate the changeling. Faulconbridge, Coriolanus, Leontes are admirable descriptions of instinctive temperaments: indeed the play of Coriolanus is the greatest of Shakespear's comedies; but description is not philosophy; and comedy neither compromises the author nor reveals him. He must be judged by those characters into which he puts what he knows of himself, his Hamlets and Macbeths and Lears and Prosperos. If these characters are agonizing in a void about factitious melodramatic murders and revenges and the like, whilst the comic characters walk with their feet on solid ground, vivid and amusing, you know that the author has much to shew and nothing to teach. The comparison between Falstaff and Prospero is like the comparison between Micawber and David Copperfield. At the end of the book you know Micawber, whereas you only know what has happened to David, and are not interested enough in him to wonder what his politics or religion might be if anything so stupendous as a religious or political idea, or a general idea of any sort, were to occur to him. He is tolerable as a child; but he never becomes a man, and might be left out of his own biography altogether but for his usefulness as a stage confidant, a Horatio or "Charles his friend": what they call on the stage a feeder.

Now you cannot say this of the works of the artist-philosophers. You cannot say it, for instance, of The Pilgrim's Progress. Put your Shakespearean hero and coward, Henry V and Pistol or Parolles, beside Mr. Valiant and Mr. Fearing, and you have a sudden revelation of the abyss that lies between the fashionable author who could see nothing in the world but personal aims and the tragedy of their disappointment or the comedy of their incongruity, and the field preacher who achieved virtue and courage by identifying himself with the purpose of the world as he understood it. The contrast is enormous: Bunyan's coward stirs your blood more than Shakespear's hero, who actually leaves you cold and secretly hostile. You suddenly see that Shakespear, with all his flashes and divinations, never understood virtue and courage, never conceived how any man who was not a fool could, like Bunyan's hero, look back from the brink of the river of death over the strife and labor of his pilgrimage, and say "yet do I not repent me"; or, with the panache of a millionaire, bequeath "my sword to him that shall succeed me in my pilgrimage, and my courage and skill to him that can get it." This is the true joy in life, the being used for a purpose recognized by yourself as a mighty one; the being thoroughly worn out before you are thrown on the scrap heap; the being a force of Nature instead of a feverish selfish little clod of ailments and grievances complaining that the world will not devote itself to making you happy. And also the only real tragedy in life is the being used by personally minded men for purposes which you recognize to be base. All the rest is at worst mere misfortune or mortality: this alone is misery, slavery, hell on earth; and the revolt against it is the only force that offers a man's work to the poor artist, whom our personally minded rich people would so willingly employ as pandar, buffoon, beauty monger, sentimentalizer, and the like.

A Void in the Elizabethan Drama

In his preface to St. Joan *Shaw took up the matter of
Shakespeare's failure to depict individuals of strength
and responsibility in his plays.*

. . . I have, however, one advantage over the Elizabethans. I write in full view of the middle ages, which
may be said to have been rediscovered in the middle of
the nineteenth century after an eclipse of about four hundred and fifty years. The renascence of antique literature and art in the sixteenth century, and the lusty
growth of capitalism, between them buried the middle
ages; and their resurrection is a second renascence.
Now there is not a breath of medieval atmosphere in
Shakespear's histories. His John of Gaunt is like a study
of the old age of Drake. Although he was a Catholic by
family tradition, his figures are all intensely Protestant,
individualist, sceptical, self-centred in everything but
their love affairs, and completely personal and selfish even
in them. His kings are not statesmen: his cardinals have
no religion: a novice can read his plays from one end to
the other without learning that the world is finally gov-
erned by forces expressing themselves in religions and
laws which make epochs rather than by vulgarly ambitious individuals who make rows. The divinity which
shapes our ends, rough hew them how we will, is mentioned fatalistically only to be forgotten immediately
like a passing vague apprehension. To Shakespear as to
Mark Twain, Cauchon would have been a tyrant and a
bully instead of a Catholic, and the inquisitor Lemaître
would have been a Sadist instead of a lawyer. Warwick
would have had no more feudal quality than his successor the king maker has in the play of Henry VI. We
should have seen them all completely satisfied that if
they would only to their own selves be true they could
not then be false to any man (a precept which represents
the reaction against medievalism at its intensest) as if

227

they were beings in the air, without public responsibilities of any kind. All Shakespear's characters are so: that is why they seem natural to our middle classes, who are comfortable and irresponsible at other people's expense, and are neither ashamed of that condition nor even conscious of it. Nature abhors this vacuum in Shakespear; and I have taken care to let the medieval atmosphere blow through my play freely. Those who see it performed will not mistake the startling event it records for a mere personal accident. They will have before them not only the visible and human puppets, but the Church, the inquisition, the feudal system, with divine inspiration always beating against their too inelastic limits: all more terrible in their dramatic force than any of the little mortal figures clanking about in plate armor or moving silently in the frocks and hoods of the order of St. Dominic.

THE MORAL ORDER IN WRITING

Shaw followed the same theme in a postscript to the preface for his novel, The Irrational Knot. *Here he established a "first order" and a "second order" of literature; as might be expected he is in the "first order" and Shakespeare is in the "second."*

. . . Since writing the above I have looked through the proof-sheets of this book, and found, with some access of respect for my youth, that it is a fiction of the first order. By this I do not mean that it is a masterpiece in that order, or even a pleasant example of it, but simply that, such as it is, it is one of those fictions in which the morality is original and not ready-made. Now this quality is the true diagnostic of the first order in literature, and indeed in all the arts, including the art of life. It is, for example, the distinction that sets Shakespear's Hamlet above his other plays, and that sets Ibsen's work as a whole above Shakespear's work as a whole. Shakespear's morality is a mere reach-me-down; and because Hamlet does not feel comfortable in it and struggles against the misfit, he suggests something better, futile as his struggle is, and incompetent as Shakespear shews himself in his effort to think out the revolt of his feeling against ready-made morality. Ibsen's morality is original all through: he knows well that the men in the street have no use for principles, because they can neither understand nor apply them; and that what they can understand and apply are arbitrary rules of conduct, often frightfully destructive and inhuman, but at least definite rules enabling the common stupid man to know where he stands and what he may do and not do without getting into trouble. Now to all writers of the first order, these rules, and the need for them produced by the moral and intellectual incompetence of the ordinary human animal, are no more invariably beneficial and respectable than the sunlight which ripens the wheat in

Sussex and leaves the desert deadly in Sahara, making the cheeks of the ploughman's child rosy in the morning and striking the ploughman brain-sick or dead in the afternoon; no more inspired (and no less) than the religion of the Andaman islanders; as much in need of frequent throwing away and replacement as the community's boots. By writers of the second order the ready-made morality is accepted as the basis of all moral judgment and criticism of the characters they portray, even when their genius forces them to represent their most attractive heroes and heroines as violating the ready-made code in all directions. Far be it from me to pretend that the first order is more readable than the second! Shakespear, Scott, Dickens, Dumas *père* are not, to say the least, less readable than Euripides and Ibsen. Nor is the first order always more constructive; for Byron, Oscar Wilde, and Larochefoucauld did not get further in positive philosophy than Ruskin and Carlyle, though they could snuff Ruskin's Seven Lamps with their fingers without flinching. Still, the first order remains the first order and the second the second for all that: no man who shuts his eyes and opens his mouth when religion and morality are offered to him on a long spoon can share the same Parnassian bench with those who make an original contribution to religion and morality, were it only a criticism.

SHAKESPEARE AND BUNYAN

Quite naturally for Shaw, Bunyan was an "artist-philosopher" and a writer in the "first order." Shaw contrasted Shakespeare with Bunyan in a review of a dramatization of The Pilgrim's Progress *which appeared in* The Saturday Review *on January 2, 1897.*

WHEN I SAW a stage version of The Pilgrim's Progress announced for production, I shook my head, knowing that Bunyan is far too great a dramatist for our theatre, which has never been resolute enough even in its lewdness and venality to win the respect and interest which positive, powerful wickedness always engages, much less the services of men of heroic conviction. Its greatest catch, Shakespear, wrote for the theatre because, with extraordinary artistic powers, he understood nothing and believed nothing. Thirty-six big plays in five blank verse acts, and (as Mr. Ruskin, I think, once pointed out) not a single hero! Only one man in them all who believes in life, enjoys life, thinks life worth living, and has a sincere, unrhetorical tear dropped over his deathbed; and that man—Falstaff! What a crew they are— these Saturday to Monday athletic stockbroker Orlandos, these villains, fools, clowns, drunkards, cowards, intriguers, fighters, lovers, patriots, hypochondriacs who mistake themselves (and are mistaken by the author) for philosophers, princes without any sense of public duty, futile pessimists who imagine they are confronting a barren and unmeaning world when they are only contemplating their own worthlessness, self-seekers of all kinds, keenly observed and masterfully drawn from the romantic-commercial point of view. Once or twice we scent among them an anticipation of the crudest side of Ibsen's polemics on the Woman Question, as in All's Well that Ends Well, where the man cuts as meanly selfish a figure beside his enlightened lady doctor wife as Helmer beside Nora; or in Cymbeline, where Post-

231

humus, having, as he believes, killed his wife for incon-
stancy, speculates for a moment on what his life would
have been worth if the same standard of continence
had been applied to himself. And certainly no modern
study of the voluptuous temperament, and the spurious
heroism and heroinism which its ecstasies produce, can
add much to Antony and Cleopatra, unless it were some
sense of the spuriousness on the author's part. But
search for statesmanship, or even citizenship, or any
sense of the commonwealth, material or spiritual, and
you will not find the making of a decent vestryman or
curate in the whole horde. As to faith, hope, courage,
conviction, or any of the true heroic qualities, you find
nothing but death made sensational, despair made stage-
sublime, sex made romantic, and barrenness covered up
by sentimentality and the mechanical lilt of blank verse.

All that you miss in Shakespear you find in Bunyan,
to whom the true heroic came quite obviously and
naturally. The world was to him a more terrible place
than it was to Shakespear; but he saw through it a path
at the end of which a man might look not only forward
to the Celestial City, but back on his life and say:—
"Tho' with great difficulty I am got hither, yet now I do
not repent me of all the trouble I have been at to arrive
where I am. My sword I give to him that shall succeed
me in my pilgrimage, and my courage and skill to him
that can get them." The heart vibrates like a bell to
such an utterance as this: to turn from it to "Out, out,
brief candle," and "The rest is silence," and "We are
such stuff as dreams are made of; and our little life is
rounded by a sleep" is to turn from life, strength, resolution, morning air and eternal youth, to the terrors of a
drunken nightmare.

Let us descend now to the lower ground where Shakespear is not disabled by his inferiority in energy and elevation of spirit. Take one of his big fighting scenes, and
compare its blank verse, in point of mere rhetorical
strenuousness, with Bunyan's prose. Macbeth's famous
cue for the fight with Macduff runs thus:—

Yet I will try the last: before my body
I throw my warlike shield. Lay on, Macduff,
And damned be him that first cries Hold, enough!

Turn from this jingle, dramatically right in feeling, but silly and resourceless in thought and expression, to Apollyon's cue for the fight in the Valley of Humiliation: "I am void of fear in this matter. Prepare thyself to die; for I swear by my infernal den that thou shalt go no farther: here will I spill thy soul." This is the same thing done masterly. Apart from its superior grandeur, force, and appropriateness, it is better claptrap and infinitely better word-music.

Shakespear, fond as he is of describing fights, has hardly ever sufficient energy or reality of imagination to finish without betraying the paper origin of his fancies by dragging in something classical in the style of Cyclops' hammer falling "on Mars's armor, forged for proof eterne." Hear how Bunyan does it: "I fought till my sword did cleave to my hand; and when they were joined together as if the sword grew out of my arm; and when the blood run thorow my fingers, then I fought with most courage." Nowhere in all Shakespear is there a touch like that of the blood running down through the man's fingers, and his courage rising to passion at it. Even in mere technical adaptation to the art of the actor, Bunyan's dramatic speeches are as good as Shakespear's tirades. Only a trained dramatic speaker can appreciate the terse manageableness and effectiveness of such a speech as this, with its grandiose exordium, followed up by its pointed question and its stern threat: "By this I perceive thou art one of my subjects; for all that country is mine, and I am the Prince and the God of it. How is it then that thou hast ran away from thy King? Were it not that I hope thou mayst do me more service, I would strike thee now at one blow to the ground." Here there is no raving and swearing and rhyming and classical allusion. The sentences go straight to their mark; and their concluding phrases soar like the sunrise, or swing and drop like a hammer, just as the actor wants them.

I might multiply these instances by the dozen; but I had rather leave dramatic students to compare the two authors at first-hand. In an article on Bunyan lately published in the Contemporary Review—the only article worth reading on the subject I ever saw (yes, thank

you: I am quite familiar with Macaulay's patronizing
prattle about The Pilgrim's Progress)—Mr. Richard
Heath, the historian of the Anabaptists, shews how Bunyan learnt his lesson, not only from his own rough
pilgrimage through life, but from the tradition of many
an actual journey from real Cities of Destruction (under
Alva), with Interpreters' houses and convoy of Great-
hearts all complete. Against such a man what chance
had our poor immortal William, with his "little Latin"
(would it had been less, like his Greek!), his heathen
mythology, his Plutarch, his Boccaccio, his Holinshed,
his circle of London literary wits, soddening their minds
with books and their nerves with alcohol (quite like us),
and all the rest of his Strand and Fleet Street surroundings, activities, and interests, social and professional,
mentionable and unmentionable? Let us applaud him,
in due measure, in that he came out of it no blackguardly Bohemian, but a thoroughly respectable snob;
raised the desperation and cynicism of its outlook to
something like sublimity in his tragedies; dramatized its
morbid, self-centred passions and its feeble and shallow
speculations with all the force that was in them; disin-
fected it by copious doses of romantic poetry, fun, and
common sense; and gave to its perpetual sex-obsession
the relief of individual character and feminine winsome-
ness. Also—if you are a sufficiently good Whig—that
after incarnating the spirit of the whole epoch which
began with the sixteenth century and is ending (I hope)
with the nineteenth, he is still the idol of all well-read
children. But as he never thought a noble life worth
living or a great work worth doing, because the commercial profit-and-loss sheet shewed that the one did
not bring happiness nor the other money, he never
struck the great vein—the vein in which Bunyan told of
that "man of a very stout countenance" who went up to
the keeper of the book of life and said, not "Out, out,
brief candle," but "Set down my name, sir," and immediately fell on the armed men and cut his way into
heaven after receiving and giving many wounds.

In the preface to Three Plays by Brieux *Shaw, following
his usual criteria, explained his preference for Brieux
over Shakespeare and Molière.*

. . . Brieux's task is thus larger than Molière's. Molière
destroyed the prestige of those conspiracies against society which we call the professions, and which thrive
by the exploitation of idolatry. He unmasked the doctor, the philosopher, the fencing master, the priest. He
ridiculed their dupes: the hypochondriac, the academi-
cian, the devotee, the gentleman in search of accomplishments. He exposed the snob: he shewed the gentleman as the butt and creature of his valet, emphasizing
thus the inevitable relation between the man who lives
by unearned money and the man who lives by weight
of service. Beyond bringing this latter point up to a
later date Beaumarchais did nothing. But Molière
never indicted society. Burke said that you cannot
bring an indictment against a nation; yet within a
generation from that utterance men began to draw in-
dictments against whole epochs, especially against the
capitalistic epoch. It is true that Molière, like Shakespear, indicted human nature, which would seem to be
a broader attack; but such attacks only make thoughtful
men melancholy and hopeless, and practical men cynical
or murderous. Le Misanthrope, which seems to me, as
a foreigner perhaps, to be Molière's dullest and worst
play, is like Hamlet in two respects. The first, which is
that it would have been much better if it had been
written in prose, is merely technical and need not de-
tain us. The second is that the author does not clearly
know what he is driving at. Le Festin de Pierre, Molière's best philosophic play, is as brilliant and arresting
as Le Misanthrope is neither the one nor the other; but
here again there is no positive side: the statue is a hollow

creature with nothing to say for himself; and Don Juan makes no attempt to take advantage of his weakness. The reason why Shakespear and Molière are always well spoken of and recommended to the young is that their quarrel is really a quarrel with God for not making men better. If they had quarrelled with a specified class of persons with incomes of four figures for not doing their work better, or for doing no work at all, they would be denounced as seditious, impious, and profligate corrupters of morality.

Brieux wastes neither ink nor indignation on Providence. The idle despair that shakes its fist impotently at the skies, uttering sublime blasphemies, such as

"As flies to wanton boys are we to the gods: They kill us for their sport,"

does not amuse Brieux. His fisticuffs are not aimed heavenward: they fall on human noses for the good of human souls. When he sees human nature in conflict with a political abuse, he does not blame human nature, knowing that such blame is the favorite trick of those who wish to perpetuate the abuse without being able to defend it. He does not even blame the abuse: he exposes it, and then leaves human nature to tackle it with its eyes open.

SHAKESPEARE AND IBSEN

The person Shaw held up most constantly in contrast to Shakespeare was Ibsen; the differences between them symbolized for Shaw the superiority of the type of playwrighting for which he waged a ceaseless war. In The Saturday Review *of March 26, 1898, he scolded William Archer for putting Shakespeare in the same class with Ibsen as a thinker.*

. . . To Mr. Archer, also, I have a remonstrance to address. He has dropped into poetry, to the extent of a column and a half in the Chronicle, over the same matter. And he has actually dragged in Shakespear! Is it kind to Shakespear? Is it polite to Ibsen? I notice how very guardedly it is done: a careful scrutiny will shew that Mr. Archer has committed himself to nothing more controversial than the statement that Ibsen will go the way that Shakespear went, which may mean no more than the way of all flesh. But I am greatly afraid that Ibsen will infer, at the first glance, that he is expected to feel complimented at being compared to Shakespear, in which case he will certainly be so unspeakably enraged that no subsequent explanations will ever restore the good understanding existing between him and his translator. It reminds one of the painful occasion when, at a musical celebration, a wreath was solemnly awarded to Gounod and Wagner as representing jointly all that was great in modern music, with the result, of course, of throwing both masters into a frenzy. Considering that the literary side of the mission of Ibsen here has been the rescue of this unhappy country from its centuries of slavery to Shakespear, it does seem a little strong to inform the creator of the Masterbuilder and Hedda Gabler that he is going the way of the creator of Prospero and the Queen in Hamlet. There is nothing that requires more discretion than the paying of compliments to great men. When an American journalist describes Sir Edward Burne-Jones as "the English Gustave Doré," or declares Madox Brown to have been "as a realist, second only to Frith," he means well; and possibly the victims of his good intentions give him credit for them. But I do most earnestly beg the inhabitants of this island to be extremely careful how they compare any foreigner to Shakespear. The foreigner can know nothing of Shakespear's power over language. He can only judge him by his intellectual force and dramatic insight, quite apart from his beauty of expression. From such a test Ibsen comes out with a double first-class: Shakespear comes out hardly anywhere. Our English deficiency in analytic power makes it extremely hard for us to understand how a man who is great in any respect can be insignificant in any other respect; and perhaps the average foreigner is not much cleverer. But when the foreigner has the particular respect in which our man is great cut off from him artificially by the change of language, as a screen of colored glass will shut off certain rays from a camera, then the deficiency which is concealed even from our experts by the splendor of Shakespear's literary gift, may be obvious to quite commonplace people who know him only through translations. In any language of the world Brand, Peer Gynt, and Emperor or Galilean prove their author a thinker of extraordinary penetration, and a moralist of international influence. Turn from them to To be or not to be, or The seven ages of man, and imagine, if you can, anybody more critical than a village schoolmaster being imposed on by such platitudinous fudge. The comparison does not honor Ibsen: it makes Shakespear ridiculous: and for both their sakes it should not be drawn. If we cannot for once let the poor Bard alone, let us humbly apologize to Ibsen for our foolish worship of a foolish collection of shallow proverbs in blank verse. Let us plead that if we compare, not the absolute Shakespear with the absolute Ibsen, but the advance from the old stage zany Hamblet to our William's Hamlet with the advance from Faust to Peer Gynt, Hamlet was really a great achievement, and might stand as an isolated feat against Peer Gynt as an isolated feat. But as it led to nothing, whereas Peer Gynt led to so much that it now ranks only as part of Ibsen's romantic wild oats—above all, as Ibsen's message nerved him to fight all Europe in the teeth of starvation, whereas Shakespear's was not proof even against the ignorance and vulgarity of the London playgoer, it only needs another turn of the discussion to shew that a comparison of the two popular masterpieces is like a comparison of the Eiffel Tower to one of the peaks in an Alpine chain. It is quite useless to attempt to flatter the great men of the nineteenth century by comparing them to the men of the decadent sixteenth. It shews a want of respect for them and for ourselves. If Ibsen had got no further than "the path that Shakespear trod," he would never have been heard of outside Norway; and as it is quite possible that he may be perfectly aware of this, I implore Mr. Archer never to mention Stratford-on-Avon to him, especially as he has already conferred the Order of the Swan on Maeterlinck. Ibsen may be as little disposed to share honors with "the Belgian Shakespear" as Wagner was with Gounod.

THE DRAMATIST

In matters of dramatic construction Shaw had the highest regard for Shakespeare. The bulk of his observations on the subject are found in his discussions of the individual plays; more references appear in the section on Shakespeare's philosophy. In addition to these, however, there are other statements by Shaw on Shakespeare's dramatic art. In The Quintessence of Ibsenism *Shaw praises Shakespeare, along with Ibsen, for avoiding the use of accidents in his plays. The passage comes from the chapter called "The Technical Novelty in Ibsen's Plays."*

. . . In short, pure accidents are not dramatic: they are only anecdotic. They may be sensational, impressive, provocative, ruinous, curious, or a dozen other things; but they have no specifically dramatic interest. There is no drama in being knocked down or run over. The catastrophe in Hamlet would not be in the least dramatic had Polonius fallen downstairs and broken his neck, Claudius succumbed to delirium tremens, Hamlet forgotten to breathe in the intensity of his philosophic speculation, Ophelia died of Danish measles, Laertes been shot by the palace sentry, and Rosencrantz and Guildenstern drowned in the North Sea. Even as it is, the Queen, who poisons herself by accident, has an air of being polished off to get her out of the way: her death is the one dramatic failure of the piece. Bushels of good paper have been inked in vain by writers who imagined they could produce a tragedy by killing everyone in the last act accidentally. As a matter of fact no accident, however sanguinary, can produce a moment of real drama, though a difference of opinion between husband and wife as to living in town or country might be the beginning of an appalling tragedy or a capital comedy.

It may be said that everything is an accident: that

Othello's character is an accident, Iago's character another accident, and the fact that they happened to come together in the Venetian service an even more accidental accident. Also that Torvald Helmer might just as likely have married Mrs. Nickleby as Nora. Granting this trifling for what it is worth, the fact remains that marriage is no more an accident than birth or death: that is, it is expected to happen to everybody. And if every man has a good deal of Torvald Helmer in him, and every woman a good deal of Nora, neither their characters nor their meeting and marrying are accidents. Othello, though entertaining, pitiful, and resonant with the thrills a master of language can produce by mere artistic sonority is certainly much more accidental than A Doll's House; but it is correspondingly less important and interesting to us. It has been kept alive, not by its manufactured misunderstandings and stolen handkerchiefs and the like, nor even by its orchestral verse, but by its exhibition and discussion of human nature, marriage, and jealousy; and it would be a prodigiously better play if it were a serious discussion of the highly interesting problem of how a simple Moorish soldier would get on with a "supersubtle" Venetian lady of fashion if he married her. As it is, the play turns on a mistake; and though a mistake can produce a murder, which is the vulgar substitute for a tragedy, it cannot produce a real tragedy in the modern sense. Reflective people are not more interested in the Chamber of Horrors than in their own homes, nor in murderers, victims, and villains than in themselves; and the moment a man has acquired sufficient reflective power to cease gaping at waxworks, he is on his way to losing interest in Othello, Desdemona, and Iago exactly to the extent to which they become interesting to the police. Cassio's weakness for drink comes much nearer home to most of us than Othello's strangling and throat cutting, or Iago's theatrical confidence trick. The proof is that Shakespear's professional colleagues, who exploited all his sensational devices, and piled up torture on murder and incest on adultery until they had far out-Heroded Herod, are now unmemorable and unplayable. Shakespear survives because he coolly treated the sensational

horrors of his borrowed plots as inorganic theatrical
accessories, using them simply as pretexts for dramatiz-
ing human character as it exists in the normal world. In
enjoying and discussing his plays we unconsciously dis-
count the combats and murders: commentators are
never so astray (and consequently so ingenious) as when
they take Hamlet seriously as a madman, Macbeth as a
homicidal Highlander, and impish humorists like Richard and Iago as lurid villains of the Renascence. The
plays in which these figures appear could be changed
into comedies without altering a hair of their beards.
Shakespear, had anyone been intelligent enough to tax
him with this, would perhaps have said that most crimes
are accidents that happen to people exactly like ourselves, and that Macbeth, under propitious circumstances, would have made an exemplary rector of Stratford, a real criminal being a defective monster, a human
accident, useful on the stage only for minor parts such
as Don Johns, second murderers, and the like. Anyhow,
the fact remains that Shakespear survives by what he
has in common with Ibsen, and not by what he has in
common with Webster and the rest. Hamlet's surprise
at finding that he "lacks gall" to behave in the ideal-
istically conventional manner, and that no extremity of
rhetoric about the duty of revenging "a dear father
slain" and exterminating the "bloody bawdy villain"
who murdered him seems to make any difference in
their domestic relations in the palace in Elsinore, still
keeps us talking about him and going to the theatre to
listen to him, whilst the older Hamlets, who never had
any Ibsenist hesitations, and shammed madness, and
entangled the courtiers in the arras and burnt them,
and stuck hard to the theatrical school of the fat boy in
Pickwick ("I wants to make your flesh creep"), are as
dead as John Shakespear's mutton.

A Dressing Room Secret

For the Haymarket Theatre program of The Dark Lady
of the Sonnets, *dated November 24, 1910, Shaw wrote
a little sketch entitled "A Dressing Room Secret." This
humorous piece involves a bust of Shakespeare and several of the characters from his plays. Shaw makes the
point that Shakespeare's characters are not psychological
entities, as many critics insist, but dramatic creations.
It is written in fun but this does not prevent its being
both serious and perceptive. (It is reprinted in Shaw's*
Short Stories, Scraps and Shavings.)

IT WAS trying-on day; and the last touches were being
given to the costumes for the Shakespear Ball as the
wearers faced the looking-glass at the costumiers.

"It's no use," said Iago discontentedly. "I dont look
right; and I don't feel right."

"I assure you, sir," said the costumier: "you are a
perfect picture."

"I may look a picture," said Iago; "but I dont look
the character."

"What character?" said the costumier.

"The character of Iago, of course. *My* character."

"Sir," said the costumier: "shall I tell you a secret that
would ruin me if it became known that I betrayed it?"

"Has it anything to do with this dress?"

"It has everything to do with it, sir."

"Then fire away."

"Well, sir, the truth is, we cannot dress Iago in character, because he is not a character."

"Not a character! Iago not a character! Are you mad?
Are you drunk? Are you hoplessly illiterate? Are you
imbecile? Or are you simply blasphemous?"

"I know it seems presumptuous, sir, after so many
great critics have written long chapters analyzing the
character of Iago: that profound, complex, enigmatic

creation of our greatest dramatic poet. But if you notice, sir, nobody has ever had to write long chapters about *my* character."

"Why on earth should they?"

"Why indeed, sir! No enigma about me. No profundity. If my character was much written about, you would be the first to suspect that I hadnt any."

"If that bust of Shakespear could speak," said Iago, severely, "it would ask to be removed at once to a suitable niche in the façade of the Shakespear Memorial National Theatre, instead of being left here to be insulted."

"Not a bit of it," said the bust of Shakespear. "As a matter of fact, I *can* speak. It is not easy for a bust to speak; but when I hear an honest man rebuked for talking common sense, even the stones would speak. And I am only plaster."

"This is a silly trick," gasped Iago, struggling with the effects of the start the Bard had given him. "You have a phonograph in that bust. You might at least have made it a blank verse phonograph."

"On my honor, sir," protested the pale costumier, all disordered, "not a word has ever passed between me and that bust—I beg pardon, me and Mr. Shakespear—before this hour."

"The reason you cannot get the dress and the make-up right is very simple," said the bust. "I made a mess of Iago because villains are such infernally dull and disagreeable people that I never could go through with them. I can stand five minutes of a villain, like Don John in—in—oh, whats its name?—*you* know—that box office play with the comic constable in it. But if I had to spread a villain out and make his part a big one, I always ended, in spite of myself, by making him rather a pleasant sort of chap. I used to feel very bad about it. It was all right as long as they were doing reasonably pleasant things; but when it came to making them commit all sorts of murders and tell all sorts of lies and do all sorts of mischief, I felt ashamed. I had no right to do it."

"Surely," said Iago, "you dont call Iago a pleasant sort of chap!"

"One of the most popular characters on the stage," said the bust.

"Me!" said Iago, stupent.

The bust nodded, and immediately fell on the floor on its nose, as the sculptor had not balanced it for nodding.

The costumier rushed forward, and, with many apologies and solicitous expressions of regret, dusted the Bard and replaced him on his pedestal, fortunately unbroken.

"I remember the play you were in," said the bust, quite undisturbed by its misadventure. "I let myself go on the verse: thundering good stuff it was: you could hear the souls of the people crying out in the mere sound of the lines. I didnt bother about the sense— just flung about all the splendid words I could find. Oh, it was noble, I tell you: drums and trumpets; and the Propontick and the Hellespont; and a malignant and a turbaned Turk in Aleppo; and eyes that dropt tears as fast as the Arabian trees their medicinal gum: the most impossible, far-fetched nonsense; but such music! Well, I started that play with two frightful villains, one male and one female."

"Female!" said Iago. "You forget. There is no female villain in Othello."

"I tell you theres no villain at all in it," said the immortal William. "But I started with a female villain."

"Who?" said the costumier.

"Desdemona, of course," replied the Bard. 'I had a tremendous notion of a supersubtle and utterly corrupt Venetian lady who was to drive Othello to despair by betraying him. It's all in the first act. But I weakened on it. She turned amiable on my hands, in spite of me. Besides, I saw that it wasnt necessary—that I could get a far more smashing effect by making her quite innocent. I yielded to that temptation: I never could resist an effect. It was a sin against human nature; and I was well paid out; for the change turned the play into a farce."

"A farce!" exclaimed Iago and the costumier simultaneously, unable to believe their ears. "Othello a farce!"

"Nothing else," said the bust dogmatically. "*You* think a farce is a play in which some funny rough-and-tumble makes the people laugh. Thats only your ignorance. What I call a farce is a play in which the misunderstandings are not natural but mechanical. By making Desdemona a decent poor devil of an honest woman, and Othello a really superior sort of man, I took away all natural reason for his jealousy. To make the situation natural I must either have made her a bad woman as I originally intended, or him a jealous, treacherous, selfish man, like Leontes in The Tale. But I couldn't belittle Othello in that way; so, like a fool, I belittled him the other way by making him the dupe of a farcical trick with a handkerchief that wouldn't have held water off the stage for five minutes. Thats why the play is no use with a thoughtful audience. It's nothing but wanton mischief and murder. I apologize for it; though, by Jingo! I should like to see any of your modern chaps write anything half so good."

"I always said that Emilia was the real part for the leading lady," said the costumier.

"But you didnt change your mind about me," pleaded Iago.

"Yes I did," said Shakespear. "I started on you with a quite clear notion of drawing the most detestable sort of man I know: a fellow who goes in for being frank and genial, unpretentious and second rate, content to be a satellite of men with more style, but who is loathsomely coarse, and has that stupid sort of selfishness that makes a man incapable of understanding the mischief his dirty tricks may do, or refraining from them if there is the most wretched trifle to be gained by them. But my contempt and loathing for the creature—what was worse, the intense boredom of him—beat me before I got into the second act. The really true and natural things he said were so sickeningly coarse that I couldn't go on fouling my play with them. He began to be clever and witty in spite of me. Then it was all up. It was Richard III over again. I made him a humorous dog. I went further: I gave him my own divine contempt for the follies of mankind and for himself, instead of his own proper infernal envy of man's divinity. That sort of thing was always happening to me. Some plays it improved; but it knocked the bottom out of Othello. It doesnt amuse really sensible people to see a woman strangled by mistake. Of course some people would go anywhere to see a woman strangled, mistake or no mistake; but such riff-raff are no use to me, though their money is as good as anyone else's."

The bust, whose powers of conversation were beginning to alarm the costumier, hard pressed as he was for time, was about to proceed when the door flew open and Lady Macbeth rushed in. As it happened, she was Iago's wife; so the costumier did not think it necessary to remind her that this was the gentlemen's dressing room. Besides, she was a person of exalted social station; and he was so afraid of her that he did not even venture to shut the door lest such an action might seem to imply a rebuke to her for leaving it open.

"I feel quite sure this dress is all wrong," she said. "They keep telling me I'm a perfect picture; but I dont feel a bit like Lady Macbeth."

"Heaven forbid you should, madam!" said the costumier. "We can change your appearance, but not your nature."

"Nonsense!" said the lady: "my nature changes with every new dress I put on. Goodness Gracious, whats that?" she exclaimed, as the bust chuckled approvingly.

"It's the bust," said Iago. "He talks like one o'clock. I really believe it's the old man himself."

"Rubbish!" said the lady. "A bust cant talk."

"Yes it can," said Shakespear. "*I* am talking; and *I* am a bust."

"But I tell you you cant," said the lady: "it's not good sense."

"Well, stop me if you can," said Shakespear. "Nobody ever could in Bess's time."

"Nothing will ever make me believe it," said the lady. "It's mere medieval superstition. But I put it to you, do I look in this dress as if I could commit a murder?"

"Dont worry about it," said the Bard. "You are another of my failures. I meant Lady Mac to be something really awful; but she turned into my wife, who

never committed a murder in her life—at least not a
quick one."

"Your wife! Ann Hathaway!! Was she like Lady Macbeth?"

"Very," said Shakespear, with conviction. "If you
notice, Lady Macbeth has only one consistent characteristic, which is, that she thinks everything her husband
does is wrong and that she can do it better. If I'd ever
murdered anybody she'd have bullied me for making a
mess of it and gone upstairs to improve on it herself.
Whenever we gave a party, she apologized to the company for my behavior. Apart from that, I defy to find
any sort of sense in Lady Macbeth. I couldnt conceive
anybody murdering a man like that. All I could do
when it came to the point was just to brazen it out that
she did it, and then give her a little touch of nature or
two—from Ann—to make people believe she was real."

"I am disillusioned, disenchanted, disgusted," said
the lady. "You might at least have held your tongue
about it until after the Ball."

"You ought to think the better of me for it," said
the bust. "I was really a gentle creature. It was so
awful to be born about ten times as clever as anyone
else—to like people and yet to have to despise their
vanities and illusions. People are such fools, even the
most likeable ones, as far as brains go. I wasnt cruel
enough to enjoy my superiority."

"Such conceit!" said the lady, turning up her nose.

"Whats a man to do?" said the Bard. "Do you suppose I could go round pretending to be an ordinary
person?"

"I believe you have no conscience," said the lady. "It
has often been noticed."

"Conscience!" cried the bust. "Why, it spoilt my best
character. I started to write a play about Henry V. I
wanted to shew him in his dissolute youth; and I
planned a very remarkable character, a sort of Hamlet
sowing his wild oats, to be always with the Prince, pointing the moral and adorning the tale—excuse the an-
achronism: Dr. Johnson, I believe: the only man that ever
wrote anything sensible about me. Poins was the name
of this paragon. Well, if youll believe me, I had hardly

got well into the play when a wretched super whom I intended for a cowardly footpad just to come on in a couple of scenes to rob some merchant and then be robbed himself by the Prince and Poins—a creature of absolutely no importance—suddenly turned into a magnificent reincarnation of Silenus, a monumental comic part. He killed Poins; he killed the whole plan of the play. I revelled in him; wallowed in him; made a delightful little circle of disreputable people for him to move and shine in. I felt sure that no matter how my other characters might go back on me, he never would. But I reckoned without my conscience. One evening, as I was walking through Eastcheap with a young friend (a young man with his life before him), I passed a fat old man, half dunk, leering at a woman who ought to have been young but wasnt. The next moment my conscience was saying in my ear: 'William: is this funny?' I preached at my young friend until he pretended he had an appointment and left me. Then I went home and spoilt the end of the play. I didnt do it well. I couldnt do it right. But I had to make that old man perish miserably; and I had to hang his wretched parasites or throw them into the gutter and the hospital. One should think before one begins things of this sort. By the way, would you mind shutting the door? I am catching cold."

"So sorry," said the lady. "My fault." And she ran to the door and shut it before the costumier could anticipate her.

Too late.

"I am going to sneeze," said the bust; "and I dont know that I can."

With an effort it succeeded just a little in retracting its nostrils and screwing up its eyes. A fearful explosion followed. Then the bust lay in fragments on the floor.

It never spoke again.

The "Shakespearean Law"

In the preface to Man and Superman *Shaw described the "Shakespearean Law" regarding the relationship between men and women in the plays.*

. . . In Shakespear's plays the woman always takes the initiative. In his problem plays and his popular plays alike the love interest is the interest of seeing the woman hunt the man down. She may do it by charming him, like Rosalind, or by stratagem, like Mariana; but in every case the relation between the woman and the man is the same: she is the pursuer and contriver, he the pursued and disposed of. When she is baffled, like Ophelia, she goes mad and commits suicide; and the man goes straight from her funeral to a fencing match. No doubt Nature, with very young creatures, may save the woman the trouble of scheming: Prospero knows that he has only to throw Ferdinand and Miranda together and they will mate like a pair of doves; and there is no need for Perdita to capture Florizel as the lady doctor in All's Well That Ends Well (an early Ibsenite heroine) captures Bertram. But the mature cases all illustrate the Shakespearean law. The one apparent exception, Petruchio, is not a real one: he is most carefully characterized as a purely commercial matrimonial adventurer. Once he is assured that Katharine has money, he undertakes to marry her before he has seen her. In real life we find not only Petruchios, but Mantalinis and Dobbins who pursue women with appeals to their pity or jealousy or vanity, or cling to them in a romantically infatuated way. Such effeminates do not count in the world scheme: even Bunsby dropping like a fascinated bird into the jaws of Mrs. MacStinger is by comparison a true tragic object of pity and terror. I find in my own plays that Woman, projecting herself dramatically by my hands (a process over which I assure you I have no more real control than I have over my wife), behaves just as Woman did in the plays of Shakespear.

A Debt to Burbage

In the preface to Great Catherine *Shaw made the interesting suggestion that the actor Richard Burbage should be given some of the credit for the great heroic roles written by Shakespeare.*

. . . Even at the risk of talking shop, an honest playwright should take at least one opportunity of acknowledging that his art is not only limited by the art of the actor, but often stimulated and developed by it. No sane and skilled author writes plays that present impossibilities to the actor or to the stage engineer. If, as occasionally happens, he asks them to do things that they have never done before and cannot conceive as presentable or possible (as Wagner and Thomas Hardy have done, for example), it is always found that the difficulties are not really insuperable, the author having foreseen unsuspected possibilities both in the actor and in the audience, whose will-to-make-believe can perform the quaintest miracles. Thus may authors advance the arts of acting and of staging plays. But the actor also may enlarge the scope of the drama by displaying powers not previously discovered by the author. If the best available actors are only Horatios, the authors will have to leave Hamlet out, and be content with Horatios for heroes. Some of the difference between Shakespear's Orlandos and Bassanios and Bertrams and his Hamlets and Macbeths must have been due not only to his development as a dramatic poet, but to the development of Burbage as an actor. Playwrights do not write for ideal actors when their livelihood is at stake: if they did, they would write parts for heroes with twenty arms like an Indian god.

Tragedy, Comedy, and Tragi-Comedy

In a piece called "Tolstoy: Tragedian or Comedian?"
Shaw discussed Shakespeare's plays in terms of tradi-
tional categories.

WAS TOLSTOY tragedian or comedian? The popular
definition of tragedy is heavy drama in which everyone
is killed in the last act, comedy being light drama in
which everyone is married in the last act. The classical
definition is, of tragedy, drama that purges the soul by
pity and terror, ar·l, of comedy, drama that chastens
morals by ridicule. These classical definitions, illustrated by Eschylus-Sophocles-Euripides *versus* Aristoph-
anes in the ancient Greek theatre, and Corneille-
Racine *versus* Molière in the French theatre, are still
much the best the critic can work with. But the British
school has always scandalized classic scholarship and
French taste by defying them: nothing will prevent the
English playwright from mixing comedy, and even
tomfoolery, with tragedy. Lear may pass for pure
tragedy; for even the fool in Lear is tragic; but Shakespear could not keep the porter out of Macbeth nor the
clown out of Antony and Cleopatra. We are incorrigible in this respect, and may as well make a merit of
it.

We must therefore recognize and examine a third
variety of drama. It begins as tragedy with scraps of
fun in it, like Macbeth, and ends as comedy without
mirth in it, the place of mirth being taken by a more
or less bitter and critical irony. We do not call the
result melodrama, because that term has come to mean
drama in which crude emotions are helped to expression
by musical accompaniment. Besides, there is at first no
true new species: the incongruous elements do not combine: there is simply frank juxtaposition of fun with
terror in tragedy and of gravity with levity in comedy.
You have Macbeth; and you have Le Misanthrope, Le

Festin de Pierre, All's Well That Ends Well, Troilus
and Cressida: all of them, from the Aristotelian and
Voltairean point of view, neither fish, fowl, nor good
red herring.

When the censorship killed serious drama in England,
and the dramatists had to express themselves in novels,
the mixture became more lawless than ever: it was
practised by Fielding and culminated in Dickens, whose
extravagances would have been severely curbed if he
had had to submit his Micawbers and Mrs. Wilfers to
the test of representation on the stage, when it would
have been discovered at once that their parts are mere
repetitions of the same joke, and have none of that
faculty of developing and advancing matters which
constitutes stage action. . . .

After Dickens, Comedy completed its development
into the new species, which has been called tragi-comedy
when any attempt has been made to define it. Tragedy
itself never developed: it was simple, sublime, and overwhelming from the first: it either failed and was not
tragedy at all or else it got there so utterly that no need
was felt for going any further. The only need felt was
for relief; and therefore, though tragedy remains un-
changed from Eschylus to Richard Wagner (Europe's
last great tragic poet), the reaction to a moment of fun
which we associate with Shakespear got the upper hand
even of Eschylus, and produced his comic sentinels who,
afraid to go to the rescue of Agamemnon, pretend that
nothing is happening, just as it got the better of Victor
Hugo, with his Don Cæsar de Bazan tumbling down
the chimney, and his Rustighello playing Wamba to
the Duke of Ferrara's Cedric the Saxon. But in the
main Tragedy remained on its summit, simple, un-
mixed, and heroic, from Sophocles to Verdi.

Not so Comedy. When the Merry Wives of Windsor
gave way to Marriage à la Mode, Romeo to Hamlet,
Punch to Don Juan, Petruchio to Almaviva, and, generally, horseplay and fun for fun's sake to serious chas-
tening of morals less and less by ridicule and more and
more by irony, the comic poet becoming less and less a
fellow of infinite jest and more and more a satirical
rogue and a discloser of essentially tragic ironies, the

road was open to a sort of comedy as much more tragic than a catastrophic tragedy as an unhappy marriage, or even a happy one, is more tragic than a railway accident. Shakespear's bitter play with a bitter title, All's Well That Ends Well, anticipates Ibsen: the happy ending at which the title sneers is less comforting than the end of Romeo and Juliet. And Ibsen was the dramatic poet who firmly established tragi-comedy as a much deeper and grimmer entertainment than tragedy. His heroes dying without hope or honor, his dead, forgotten, superseded men walking and talking with the ghosts of the past, are all heroes of comedy: their existence and their downfall are not soul-purifying convulsions of pity and horror, but reproaches, challenges, criticisms addressed to society and to the spectator as a voting constituent of society. They are miserable and yet not hopeless; for they are mostly criticisms of false intellectual positions which, being intellectual, are remediable by better thinking.

Thus Comedy has become the higher form. The element of accident in Tragedy has always been its weak spot; for though an accident may be sensational, nothing can make it interesting or save it from being irritating. Othello is spoilt by a handkerchief, as Shakespear found out afterwards when he wrote A Winter's Tale. The curtain falls on The School for Scandal just when the relations between the dishonorable Joseph Surface and the much more dishonorable Lady Teazle have become interesting for the first moment in the play. In its tragedy and comedy alike, the modern tragi-comedy begins where the old tragedies and comedies left off; and we have actually had plays made and produced dealing with what happened to Ibsen's *dramatis personae* before the first act began.

THE INTERPRETERS

*Shaw invariably took Shakespeare's side when it came to
production: again and again, in his reviews and elsewhere, Shaw denounced script cuts and productional
schemes which distorted the plays and destroyed their
integrity. In an article called "The Religion of the
Pianoforte" in* The Fortnightly Review *of February,
1894, Shaw argued for the written drama as a means of
preserving the author's original work; in support of his
position he pointed to what Shakespeare had suffered
at the hands of producers. (It should be noted that this
was written before Shaw had seen Forbes Robertson's*
Hamlet, *Poel's Elizabethan-style productions, and other
reasonably faithful presentations.)*

"BAD" SHAKESPEARE

. . . What is it that keeps Shakespear alive among us?
Is it the stage, the great actors, the occasional revivals
with new music and scenery, and agreeably mendacious
accounts of the proceedings in the newspapers after the
first night? Not a bit of it. Those who know their Shakespear at all know him before they are twenty-five: after
that there is no time—one has to live instead of to read;
and how many Shakespearean revivals, pray, has an Englishman the chance of seeing before he is twenty-five, even
if he lives in a city and not in the untheatred country,
or in a family which regards the pit of the theatre as the
antechamber to that pit which has no bottom? I myself,
born of profane stock, and with a quarter-century of
play-going, juvenile and manly, behind me, have not
seen as many as a full half of Shakespear's plays acted;
and if my impressions of his genius were based solely
on these representations I should be in darkness indeed.
For what is it that I have seen on such occasions? Take

255

the solitary play of Shakespear's which is revived more
than twice in a generation! Well, I have seen Mr. Barry
Sullivan's Hamlet, Mr. Daniel Bandmann's Hamlet,
Miss Marriott's Hamlet, Mr. Irving's Hamlet, Signor
Salvini's Hamlet, Mr. Wilson Barrett's Hamlet, Mr. Benson's Hamlet, Mr. Beerbohm Tree's Hamlet, and perhaps others which I forget. But to none of these artists
do I owe my acquaintance with Shakepear's play of
Hamlet. In proof whereof, let me announce that, for all
my Hamlet going, were I to perish this day, I should go
to my account without having seen Fortinbras, save in
my mind's eye, or watched the ghostly twilight march
(as I conceive it) of those soldiers who went to their
graves like beds to dispute with him a territory that was
not tomb enough and continent to hide the slain. When
first I saw Hamlet I innocently expected Fortinbras to
dash in, as in Sir John Gilbert's picture, with shield and
helmet, like a mediæval Charles XII., and, by right of
his sword and his will, take the throne which the fencing foil and the speculative intellect had let slip, thereby
pointing the play's most characteristically English moral.
But what was my first Hamlet to my first Romeo and
Juliet, in which Romeo, instead of dying forthwith
when he took the poison, was interrupted by Juliet, who
sat up and made him carry her down to the footlights,
where she complained of being very cold, and had to be
warmed by a love scene, in the middle of which Romeo,
who had forgotten all about the poison, was taken ill
and died? Or my first Richard III, which turned out
to be a wild *potpourri* of all the historical plays, with
a studied debasement of all the best word music in the
lines, and an original domestic scene in which Richard,
after feebly bullying his wife, observed, "If this don't
kill her, she's immortal"? Cibber's Richard III was, to
my youthful judgment, superior to Shakespear's play on
one point only, and that was the omission of the stage
direction, "Exeunt fighting," whereby Richmond and
the tyrant were enabled to have it out to the bitter end
full in my view. Need I add that it was not through this
sort of thing, with five out of every six parts pitiably ill
acted and ill uttered, that I came to know Shakespear?
Later on, when it was no longer Mr. Blank's Hamlet

and Miss Dash's Juliet that was in question, but "the Lyceum revival," the stage brought me but little nearer to the drama. For the terrible cutting involved by modern hours of performance; the foredoomed futility of the attempt to take a work originally conceived mainly as a long story told on the stage, with plenty of casual adventures and unlimited changes of scene, and to tight-lace it into something like a modern play consisting of a single situation in three acts; and the commercial relations which lead the salaried players to make the most abject artistic sacrifices to their professional consciousness that the performance is the actor-manager's "show," and by no means their own or Shakespear's: all these and many other violently anti-artistic conditions of modern theatrical enterprise still stood inexorably between the stage and the real Shakespear.

The case of Shakespear is not, of course, the whole case against the theatre: it is, indeed, the weakest part of it, because the stage certainly does more for Shakespear than for any other dramatic poet. The English drama, from Marlowe to Browning, would practically not exist if it were not printed.

A PROMPT BOOK FOR HAMLET?

Shaw took up the argument for written drama in the preface to Plays Unpleasant; *again he referred to Shakespeare.*

. . . The dramatic author has reasons for publishing his plays which would hold good even if English families went to the theatre as regularly as they take in the newspaper. A perfectly adequate and successful stage representation of a play requires a combination of circumstances so extraordinarily fortunate that I doubt whether it has ever occurred in the history of the world. Take the case of the most successful English dramatist of the first rank: Shakespear. Although he wrote three centuries ago, he still holds his own so well that it is not impossible to meet old playgoers who have witnessed public performances of more than thirty out of his thirty-seven reputed plays, a dozen of them fairly often, and half a dozen over and over again. I myself, though I have by no means availed myself of all my opportunities, have seen twenty-three of his plays publicly acted. But if I had not read them as well, my impression of them would be not merely incomplete, but violently distorted and falsified. It is only within the last few years that some of our younger actor-managers have been struck with the idea, quite novel in their profession, of performing Shakespear's plays as he wrote them, instead of using them as a cuckoo uses a sparrow's nest. In spite of the success of these experiments, the stage is still dominated by Garrick's conviction that the manager and actor must adapt Shakespear's plays to the modern stage by a process which no doubt presents itself to the adapter's mind as one of masterly amelioration, but which must necessarily be mainly one of debasement and mutilation whenever, as occasionally happens, the adapter is inferior to the author. . . .

. . . The fact that a skilfully written play is infinitely more adaptable to all sorts of acting than available acting is to all sorts of plays (the actual conditions thus exactly reversing the desirable ones) finally drives the author to the conclusion that his own view of his work can only be conveyed by himself. And since he could not act the play singlehanded even if he were a trained actor, he must fall back on his powers of literary expression, as other poets and fictionists do. So far, this has hardly been seriously attempted by dramatists. Of Shakespear's plays we have not even complete prompt copies: the folio gives us hardly anything but the bare lines. What would we not give for the copy of Hamlet used by Shakespear at rehearsal, with the original stage business scrawled by the prompter's pencil? And if we had in addition the descriptive directions which the author gave on the stage: above all, the character sketches, however brief, by which he tried to convey to the actor the sort of person he meant him to incarnate, what a light they would shed, not only on the play, but on the history of the sixteenth century! Well, we should have had all this and much more if Shakespear, instead of merely writing out his lines, had prepared the plays for publication in competition with fiction as elaborate as that of Meredith. It is for want of this elaboration that Shakespear, unsurpassed as poet, storyteller, character draughtsman, humorist, and rhetorician, has left us no intellectually coherent drama, and could not afford to pursue a genuinely scientific method in his studies of character and society, though in such unpopular plays as All's Well, Measure for Measure, and Troilus and Cressida, we find him ready and willing to start at the twentieth century if the seventeenth would only let him.

Such literary treatment is much more needed by modern plays than by Shakespear's, because in his time the acting of plays was very imperfectly differentiated from the declamation of verses; and descriptive or narrative recitation did what is now done by scenery, furniture, and stage business. Anyone reading the mere dialogue of an Elizabethan play understands all but half a dozen unimportant lines of it without difficulty; whilst many modern plays, highly successful on the stage, are not merely unreadable but positively unintelligible without visible stage business.

SHAKESPEARE AND ROMANTIC ACTING

In a review of a play named Donna Diana *in* The Saturday Review *of November 7, 1896, Shaw discussed one of the reasons why Shakespeare's plays had been altered through the years. He spoke of the "classically romantic phase" of acting which held the stage for so many years. Its appeal was its staginess and it was an art which worked against the "touches of nature" in Shakespeare.*

. . . The theatrical imagination, the love of the boards, produced this art and nursed it. When it was at its height the touches of nature in Shakespear were not endured: the passages were altered and the events reshaped until they were of a piece with the pure-bred drama engendered solely by the passion of the stage-struck, uncrossed by nature, character, poetry, philosophy, social criticism, or any other alien stock. Stage kings and queens, stage lovers, stage tyrants, stage parents, stage villains, and stage heroes were alone to be found in it; and, naturally, they alone were fit for the stage or in their proper place there. Generations of shallow critics, mostly amateurs, have laughed at Partridge for admiring the King in Hamlet more than Hamlet himself (with Garrick in the part), because "anyone could see that the King was an actor." But surely Partridge was right. He went to the theatre to see, not a real limited monarch, but a stage king, speaking as Partridges like to hear a king speaking, and able to have people's heads cut off, or to browbeat treason from behind an invisible hedge of majestically asserted divinity. Fielding misunderstood the matter because in a world of Fieldings there would be neither kings nor Partridges. It is all very well for Hamlet to declare that the business of the theatre is to hold the mirror up to nature. He is allowed to do it out of respect for the bard, just as he is allowed to say to a minor actor, "Do not saw the air thus," though he has

himself been sawing the air all the evening, and the unfortunate minor actor has hardly had the chance of
cutting a chip off with a penknife. But everybody knows
perfectly well that the function of the theatre is to
realize for the spectators certain pictures which their
imagination craves for, the said pictures being fantastic
as the dreams of Alnaschar. Nature is only brought in
as an accomplice in the illusion: for example, the
actress puts rouge on her cheek instead of burnt cork
because it looks more natural; but the moment the illusion is sacrificed to nature, the house is up in arms and
the play is chivied from the stage. I began my own
dramatic career by writing plays in which I faithfully
held the mirror up to nature. They are much admired
in private reading by social reformers, industrial in-
vestigators, and revolted daughters; but on one of them
being rashly exhibited behind the footlights, it was received with a paroxysm of execration, whilst the mere
perusal of the others induces loathing in every person,
including myself, in whom the theatrical instinct
flourishes in its integrity. Shakespear made exactly one
attempt, in Troilus and Cressida, to hold the mirror up
to nature; and he probably nearly ruined himself by it.
At all events, he never did it again; and practical experience of what was really popular in the rest of his
plays led to Venice Preserved and Donna Diana. It was
the stagey element that held the stage, not the natural
element. In this way, too, the style of execution proper
to these plays, an excessively stagey style, was evolved
and perfected, the "palmy days" being the days when
nature, except as a means of illusion, had totally vanished from both plays and acting.

Shaw wrote a great deal on the acting of Shakespeare, being careful always to point out those who were true to Shakespeare and those who were not. Among the actresses Shaw discussed in reviews and elsewhere were Ellen Terry, Janet Achurch, Ada Rehan and Mrs. Patrick Campbell. Among the actors on whom he wrote reviews was Forbes Robertson. He also contrasted the acting of an old style actor he admired, Barry Sullivan, with that of Henry Irving in several places: a review of Comedy of Errors *on December 14, 1895, the preface to* Ellen Terry and Bernard Shaw: A Correspondence, *as well as other reviews and articles. Shaw's views on Irving's Shakespearean acting were summed up in an obituary in the* Neue Freie Presse *of Vienna, reprinted in Shaw's* Pen Portraits and Reviews.

. . . He had really only one part; and that part was the part of Irving. His Hamlet was not Shakespear's Hamlet, nor his Lear Shakespear's Lear: they were both avatars of the imaginary Irving in whom he was so absorbingly interested. His huge and enduring success as Shylock was due to his absolutely refusing to allow Shylock to be the discomfited villain of the piece. The Merchant of Venice became the Martyrdom of Irving, which was, it must be confessed, far finer than the Tricking of Shylock. His Iachimo, a very fine performance, was better than Shakespear's Iachimo, and not a bit like him. On the other hand, his Lear was an impertinent intrusion of a quite silly conceit of his own into a great play. His Romeo, though a very clever piece of acting, wonderfully stage-managed in the scene where Romeo dragged the body of Paris down a horrible staircase into the tomb of the Capulets, was an absurdity, because it was impossible to accept Irving as Romeo, and he had no power of adapting himself to an author's conception: his creations were all his own; and they were all Irvings.

HERBERT BEERBOHM TREE

Shaw felt that Beerbohm Tree's Shakespearean productions were just as much desecrations as Irving's. He went into this in his review of Tree's Much Ado About Nothing; *he wrote about it again in a piece contributed to Max Beerbohm's collection of memoirs for Tree, reprinted in Shaw's* Pen Portraits and Reviews. *Shaw explained what had resulted from Tree's lack of certain technical attributes, particularly the vocal facility to do justice to Elizabethan blank verse.*

. . . The results were most marked in his Shakespearean work, and would certainly have produced curious scenes at rehearsal had the author been present. No doubt it is an exaggeration to say that the only unforgettable passages in his Shakespearean acting are those of which Tree and not Shakespear was the author. His Wolsey, which was a "straight" performance of high merit and dignity, could be cited to the contrary. But take, for examples, his Richard II and his Malvolio. One of the most moving points in his Richard was made with the assistance of a dog who does not appear among Shakespear's *dramatis personae*. When the dog—Richard's pet dog—turned to Bolingbroke and licked his hand, Richard's heart broke; and he left the stage with a sob. Next to this came his treatment of the entry of Bolingbroke and the deposed Richard into London. Shakespear makes the Duke of York describe it. Nothing could be easier with a well-trained actor at hand. And nothing could be more difficult and inconvenient than to bring horses on the stage and represent it in action. But this is just what Tree did. One still remembers that great white horse, and the look of hunted terror with which Richard turned his head as the crowd hooted him. It passed in a moment; and it flatly contradicted Shakespear's description of the saint-like patience of Richard; but the effect was intense: no one but

Chaliapin has since done so much by a single look and an appearance for an instant on horseback. Again, one remembers how Richard walked out of Westminster Hall after his abdication.

Turn now to the scenes in which Shakespear has given the actor a profusion of rhetoric to declaim. Take the famous "For God's sake let us sit upon the ground, and tell sad stories of the death of kings." My sole recollection of that scene is that when I was sitting in the stalls listening to it, a paper was passed to me. I opened it and read: "If you will rise and move a resolution, I will second it.—Murray Carson." The late Murray Carson was, above all things, an elocutionist; and the scene was going for nothing. Tree was giving Shakespear, at immense trouble and expense, and with extraordinary executive cunning, a great deal that Shakespear had not asked for, and denying him something much simpler that he did ask for, and set great store by.

As Malvolio, Tree was inspired to provide himself with four smaller Malvolios who aped the great chamberlain in dress, in manners, in deportment. He had a magnificent flight of stairs on the stage; and when he was descending it majestically, he slipped and fell with a crash sitting. Mere clowning, you will say; but no: the fall was not the point. Tree, without betraying the smallest discomfiture, raised his eyeglass and surveyed the landscape as if he had sat down on purpose. This, like the four satellite Malvolios, was not only funny but subtle. But when he came to speak those lines with which any old Shakespearean hand can draw a laugh by a simple trick of the voice, Tree made nothing of them, not knowing a game which he had never studied.

"On Cutting Shakespear"

Shaw, who had advised Ellen Terry to make cuts in
Cymbeline *and had written his own last act for it, never-*
theless maintained that as a rule Shakespeare's plays
should not be cut, particularly by those actor-managers
who did not properly understand the plays. He sum-
marized his views in a piece called "On Cutting Shake-
spear" which appeared in The Fortnightly Review *of*
August, 1919, reprinted in Shaw on Theatre, *edited by*
E. J. West.

Mr. William Archer has quoted me in support of the
practice of performing selections from Shakespear's
plays instead of the plays in their entirety as he left
them.

Everything that Mr. Archer says is very true and very
sensible. Unfortunately, the results in practice are the
productions of Cibber, Garrick, Irving, Tree, Augustin
Daly, Sir Frank Benson, and the commercial managers
generally, which may be highly entertaining productions, but are somehow not Shakespear, whereas Mr.
Granville-Barker's resolutely unreasonable shewing-up
of Shakespear's faults and follies to the uttermost comma
was at once felt to be a restoration of Shakespear to the
stage.

The moment you admit that the producer's business
is to improve Shakespear by cutting out everything that
he himself would not have written, and everything that
he thinks the audience will either not like or not understand, and everything that does not make prosaic sense,
you are launched on a slope on which there is no
stopping until you reach the abyss where Irving's Lear
lies forgotten. The reason stares us in the face. The
producer's disapprovals, and consequently his cuts, are
the symptoms of the differences between Shakespear and
himself; and his assumption that all these differences are
differences of superiority on his part and inferiority on
Shakespear's, must end in the cutting down or raising

up of Shakespear to his level. Tree thought a third-rate ballet more interesting than the colloquy of Cassio with Iago on the subject of temperance. No doubt many people agreed with him. It was certainly more expensive. Irving, when he was producing Cymbeline, cut out of his own part the lines:

" 'Tis her breathing that
Perfumes the chamber thus. The flame o' the taper
Bows towards her, and would underpeep her lids
To see the unclosed lights, now canopied
Under those windows, white and azure, laced
With blue of heaven's own tinct."

He was genuinely astonished when he was told that he must not do it, as the lines were the most famous for their beauty of all the purple patches in Shakespear. A glance at the passage will shew how very "sensible" his cut was. Mr. Archer wants to cut, "O single-soled jest, solely singular for the singleness," because it is "absolutely meaningless." But think of all the other lines that must go with it on the same ground! The gayer side of Shakespear's poetic ecstasy expressed itself in word-dances of jingling nonsense which are, from the point of view of the grave Scots commentator who demands a meaning and a moral from every text, mere delirium and echolalia. But what would Shakespear be without them? "The spring time, the only merry ring time, when birds do sing hey ding a ding ding" is certainly not good sense nor even accurate ornithological observation! Who ever heard a bird sing "hey ding a ding ding" or anything even remotely resembling it? Out with it, then; and away, too, with such absurdities as Beatrice's obviously untrue statement that a star danced at her birth, which must revolt all the obstetricians and astronomers in the audience. As to Othello's fustian about the Propontick and the Hellespont, is this senseless hullabaloo of sonorous vowels and precipitate consonants to be retained when people have trains to catch? Mr. Archer is credulous in imagining that in these orchestral passages the wit has evaporated and the meaning become inscrutable. There never was any meaning or wit in them in his sense any more than there is wit or meaning in the crash of Wagner's cymbals or the gallop of his trombones in the Valkyries' ride. The producer who has a head for syllogisms cuts such passages out. The producer who has an ear for music, like Mr. Granville-Barker, breaks his heart in trying to get them adequately executed.

Then take my own celebrated criticisms of Shakespear, written when the Bard, like all the other dramatists, was staggering under the terrible impact of Ibsen. Can men whose intellectual standards have been screwed up to Goethe's Faust, Wagner's Ring, and "deep revolving" Ibsen's soul histories, be expected to sit and listen to such penny-reading twaddle as The Seven Ages of Man, or even Hamlet's soliloquy on suicide? Out with the lot of them, then: let us cut the cackle and come to the 'osses.

I might pile Pelion on Ossa with illustrations of the passages that might very well be cut out of Shakespear's plays on Mr. Archer's grounds and on mine and on Garrick's, Irving's, etc., etc., etc. It is clear that you need only a sufficiently large and critical committee of producers instead of a single producer to cut out the entire play, a conclusion which most managers reach without the assistance of a committee. It is equally clear that to avoid this reduction to common sense the only workable plan is Mr. Barker's plan, which makes Shakespear, and not the producer, the ultimate authority. That Shakespear is a bore and even an absurdity to people who cannot listen to blank verse and enjoy it as musicians listen to an opera (Shakespear's methods are extremely like Verdi's); that Mr. George Robey, heroically trying to find jokes crude enough for an audience of rustic Tommies, would shrink from Touchstone's story about the beef and the mustard; that we who think it funny to call a man's head his nut remain joyless when Shakespear calls it his costard not knowing that a costard is an apple); that Benedick cannot amuse or fascinate the young ladies who have adored Robert Loraine and Granville-Barker as Jack Tanner; that William's puns are as dead as Tom Hood's or Farnie's; that Elizabethan English is a half-dead language and Euphuist English unintelligible and intolerable: all these undeniable facts are reasons for not performing Shakespear's plays at all, but not reasons for breaking them up and trying to jerry-build modern plays with them, as the Romans broke up the Coliseum to build hovels. Businesslike and economical as that procedure seems (for why waste good material?), experience remorselessly proves that Shakespear making a fool of himself is more interesting than the judicious producer correcting him. The people who really want Shakespear want all of him, and not merely Mr. Archer's or anyone else's favorite bits; and this not in the least because they enjoy every word of it, but because they want to be sure of hearing the words they do enjoy, and because the effect of the judiciously selected passages, not to mention injudiciously selected passages, is not the same as that of the whole play, just as the effect of the currants picked out of a bun is not the same as that of the whole bun, indigestible as it may be to people who do not like buns.

There are plenty of modern instances to go upon. I have seen Peer Gynt most judiciously and practically cut by Lugné-Poë, and The Wild Duck cut to the bone by Mr. Archer. I have seen Wagner at full length at Bayreuth and Munich, and cut most sensibly at Covent Garden. I have actually seen Il Trovatore, most swift and concise of operas, cut by Sir Thomas Beecham. My own plays, notoriously too long, have been cut with masterly skill by American managers. Mr. Henry Arthur Jones made a capital acting version of A Doll's House, entitled Breaking a Butterfly. I do not allege that the result has always been disastrous failure, though it has sometimes gone that far. A hash makes a better meal than an empty plate. But I do aver without qualification that the mutilation has always been an offence, and the effect different and worse both in degree and in kind from the effect of a remorselessly faithful performance. Wagner's remark when he heard Rossini's Barber of Seville performed for once in its integrity in Turin applies to all the works of the great masters. You get something from such a performance that the selections never give you. And I suggest that this is not wholly a mystery. It occurs only when the work is produced under the direction of a manager who understands its value and can find in every passage the charm or the function which induced the author to write it, and who can dictate or suggest the method of execution that brings out that charm or discharges that function. Without this sense and this skill the manager will cut, cut, cut, every time he comes to a difficulty; and he will put the interest of the refreshment bars and the saving of electric light and the observance of the conventional hours of beginning the performance before his duty to the author, maintaining all the time that the manager who cuts most is the author's best friend.

In short, there are a thousand more sensible reasons for cutting not only Shakespear's plays, but all plays, all symphonies, all operas, all epics, and all pictures which are too large for the dining-room. And there is absolutely no reason on earth for not cutting them except the design of the author, who was probably too conceited to be a good judge of his own work.

The sane conclusion is therefore that cutting must be dogmatically ruled out, because, as Lao-Tse said, "of the making of reforms there is no end." The simple thing to do with a Shakespear play is to perform it. The alternative is to let it alone. If Shakespear made a mess of it, it is not likely that Smith or Robinson will succeed where he failed.

"SHAKESPEAR: A STANDARD TEXT"

In a letter to the Times Literary Supplement *of March 17, 1921, Shaw wrote on "Shakespear: A Standard Text." Other letters on the subject appeared on March 31, and April 14, 1921. Portions of the first letter dealt directly with Shakespearean manuscripts.*

MAY I, as a publishing playwright, point out to Mr. William Poel (who knows it already) that it is at present impossible to write or print a play fully or exactly in ordinary script or type? And it never will be possible until we establish in popular use a fixed and complete notation, such as musicians possess. No such notation exists in a shape intelligible to the general reader. Therefore the first flat fact to be faced is that the printers of the Shakespear Folio and the Quartos could not indicate how the Elizabethan actor spoke his lines, whether they were trying to do so or not. No doubt, when the Elizabethan punctuation of plays is more than usually crazy, as where, for instance, an unaccountable colon appears where there should be no stop at all, it may not be a mere misprint: the compositor may have set up some mark made in his copy by somebody in the theatre for some purpose. It does not follow that it was a stop written by Shakespear for publication. If we found one of Shakespear's handkerchiefs with a knot on it, we might reasonably conjecture that he had knotted it to remind him of something he was afraid of forgetting; but what sane producer of Othello would tie a knot in Desdemona's fatal handkerchief on the ground that all Elizabethan handkerchiefs were worn knotted? All actors and all producers and all prompters made marks on their parts and copies to indicate emphasis, strokes of stage business, signals, calls, and the like; but except in the matter of underscoring words, which is common practice, they each make different marks according to private codes of their own. Dots, strokes,

crosses, angles indicating the position of the arms, crude
footprints mapping the position of the feet, make
memoranda perfectly intelligible to the actor who
scrawls them, and inscrutable to anyone else. Every
producer who knows his business, and does not merely
fudge along at rehearsal from entry to entry by trial
and error, sprinkles his copy of the play with a homemade shorthand which nobody but he can decipher.
Even the prompter, whose copy should serve for his
successors as well as himself, distractedly blackleads it
until it is often difficult to make out the text, and impossible to understand the directions.

Now imagine manuscript copies treated in this way
and then handed to a printer to set up, or to a scrivener
to make fair copy for the printer. How is the scrivener
to tell whether these dots and dashes and scriggles and
crosses and clockhands and queries and notes of admiration are meant for stops or not? It is easy to say that
he can use his common sense; but neither scriveners nor
compositors are highly educated enough to understand
everything they copy or set up: setting up Shakespear
must often be very like setting up Einstein or Homer
in the original. Thus what looks like a colon, and is set
up as such in the Quarto, may mean, "emphasize the
next [or previous] word," or "pause significantly," or
"don't forget to pronounce the h," or merely the Elizabethan equivalent to "Curtain warning" or "check your
floats and take your ambers out of your number one
batten." To cherish it as Shakespear's punctuation, or
pretend to greater authenticity for it than for the colons
of Rowe or Dr. Johnson or Pope or Malone or the
Cowden Clarkes or Q, or any modern editor, is next door
to Baconian cipher hunting.

Let me recapitulate the process by which the plays got
into print. First, Shakespear wrote a play. It may be
presumed that he punctuated it; but this is by no means
certain. I have on my desk a typed play by a clever
young writer whose dialogue is very vivacious, and is
that of an educated man accustomed to converse with
educated people. It bristles with mad hyphens *à tort et
à travers;* but there is not a stop in it from beginning
to end except the full stops at the ends of the speeches;

and I suspect that these were put in by the typist. Oscar Wilde sent the MS of An Ideal Husband to the Haymarket Theatre without taking the trouble to note the entrances and exits of the persons on the stage. There is no degree of carelessness that is not credible to men who know that they will be present to explain matters when serious work begins. But let us assume that Shakespear punctuated his script. From it the scrivener copied out the parts for the actors, and made a legible prompt copy. That the scrivener respected Shakespear's stops and "followed copy" exactly is against even modern experience; and in the XVI-XVII *fin de siècle*, when scriveners were proud of their clergy and tenacious of their technical authority, the scrivener would punctuate as he thought Shakespear (whom he would despise as an amateur) ought to have punctuated, and not as he did or did not punctuate. The copies so produced were then marked at rehearsal in all sorts of ways by all sorts of people for all sorts of theatrical purposes. Thus marked, they were fair-copied again by a scrivener —possibly the same, possibly another—for the printer. Now, as all authors know, the printer who does not consider that punctuation is his special business, and that authors know nothing about it (they mostly know very little), has not yet been born. Besides, the printer of that period would have the tradition that his page should look well, and that the letterpress should not be disfigured, as in modern books, by wide spaces between sentences and words and letters, or by awkward-looking stops. And so we get two opinionated scriveners, a whole company of actors and stage officials, and a tradition-ridden compositor, between Shakespear's holograph and the printed page. Such a process applied to an imperfect and inexact notation, as to the use of which authors and even grammarians are so little agreed that it cannot be used in legal documents, leaves the punctuation of the Quartos and the Folio practically void of authority. Even if it could be proved that Shakespear corrected the proofs of the best Quarto texts, I should still defy any modern editor to follow them stop for stop without publicly washing his hands of all responsibility for them.

This does not mean that there is not a case, and a very strong case, for making facsimiles of the earliest printed texts. A glance through any of the facsimiles already published will discover points at which changes made by modern editors are changes for the worse. But when the utmost has been said that can be said for the readings of the Quartos and the Folio, no middle course is open to a modern editor between a photographic reproduction and a text doctored precisely as the conventional editions have been doctored. If the editor be Mr. Granville-Barker, so much the better: he will test the questionable passages on the stage, and retain readings that a mere man of letters would tamper with. If the editor be Mr. William Poel, he will print the text in the way that best suggests his divination of its proper delivery. He will run the words together in rapid passages, and bring out keywords in ways undreamt of by Heming and Condell. Such editions would be much more valuable and interesting than superfluous repetitions of existing editions made in the study; but they would not be a whit more "standard" or authentic.

Besides, they would introduce more controversial new readings than any merely literary editor dare venture. For example, take the following ranting and redundant utterance of Macbeth:

> Hang out your banners on the outer walls.
> The cry is still they come.

Barry Sullivan cured both the rant and redundancy very simply. He entered at the back of the stage throwing an order over his shoulder to his subalterns, and then came down to the footlights to discuss the military situation. Thus we got the reading:

> Hang out your banners. On the outer walls
> the cry is still they come.

This, tested on the stage as Mr. Granville-Barker would test it, is a convincing improvement. But the authority for it is not the text as it has come down to us, but Barry Sullivan's conjecture submitted to Mr. Barker's test. And Barry Sullivan went further than that. Instead of saying, as Hamlet, "I am but mad north-north-west: when the wind is southerly, I know a hawk from a handsaw," he said, "I know a hawk from a heron. Pshaw!" This may read strainedly; but when acted with appropriate business it is so effective that Mr. Barker's stage test would favor its adoption. Such readings, however, would compel Mr. Barker to interpolate scores of stage directions for which there would be no authority but his own artistic instinct.

As to Mr. Poel, there is no living enthusiast more firmly convinced than he that he knows the mind of Shakespear; and this conviction has nerved him to do yeoman's service to his master. It would nerve him equally to feats that Dr. Johnson would have funked. The liberties he would take with the text to square it with his own original and vivid conception of character, theatrical technique, and Elizabethan political history and social structure would rouse a cry of controversy. On that very account a Poel Shakespear should be published, even if it were to consist of only a few specimen plays; and a Granville-Barker Shakespear should rival it. But neither edition could be called a standard edition except by the courtesy which allows every theatre to call itself the Theatre Royal. And the question which of the two famous Shakespearean producers were the more unscrupulous would never be settled.

Now may I be allowed a suggestion of my own? Why not try to make a record of our language as it is spoken today on the stage classically? We have in Forbes-Robertson an actor whose speech is unchallengeable in every English-speaking land, not only in Oxford and the West End of London, but in countries where the dialect of Oxford and the West End is received with shouts of derisive laughter. It does not matter how Forbes-Robertson pronounces this or that vowel: his speech will carry any Englishman anywhere. It is unquestionably proper for a king, for a chief justice, for an archbishop, or for a private gentleman; having acquired it, no one has anything more to learn to qualify himself as a speaker for the most dignified employment. Well, why not begin with an edition of Hamlet in which this Robertsonian speech shall be recorded by phonetic spelling? I am aware that this cannot be done completely except by using Bell's Visible Speech, which nobody but Mr. Graham Bell and perhaps a few others can read; but by eking out the ordinary alphabet with a few letters turned upside down, and coming to a clearly stated understanding as to the meaning of those which remain right side up, it is quite possible to make a very useful record, supplemented by the existing phonographic records of which Sir Johnston can specify the defects exactly. Such a phonetic edition of Hamlet could be fairly described as a standard Hamlet, valid for its day. The Academic Committee of the Royal Society of Literature could justify its existence by undertaking this work.

EPILOGUE

*Shaw wrote a puppet show called "Shakes Versus Shav"
which was given in the Lyttleton Hall at Malvern on
August 9, 1949, with puppets representing Shakespeare
and Shaw. In a preface to it Shaw wrote, "this in all
actuarial probability is my last play and the climax of
my eminence, such as it is." It is unquestionably the
appropriate conclusion for this volume.*

SHAKES VERSUS SHAV

*Shakes enters and salutes the audience with a flour-
ish of his hat.*

SHAKES. Now is the winter of our discontent
Made glorious summer by the Malvern sun.
I, William Shakes, was born in Stratford town,
Where every year a festival is held
To honour my renown not for an age
But for all time. Hither I raging come
An infamous impostor to chastize,
Who in an ecstasy of self-conceit
Shortens my name to Shav, and dares pretend
Here to reincarnate my very self,
And in your stately playhouse to set up
A festival, and plant a mulberry
In most presumptuous mockery of mine.
Tell me, ye citizens of Malvern,
Where I may find this caitiff. Face to face
Set but this fiend of Ireland and myself;
And leave the rest to me. [*Shav enters*]. Who art
      thou?
That rearst a forehead almost rivalling mine?
SHAV. Nay, who art thou, that knowest not these fea-
      tures

276

Pictured throughout the globe? Who should I be
But G. B. S.?

SHAKES. What! Stand, thou shameless fraud.
For one or both of us the hour is come.
Put up your hands.

SHAV. Come on.

*They spar. Shakes knocks Shav down with a straight
left and begins counting him out, stooping over him
and beating the seconds with his finger.*

SHAKES. Hackerty-backerty one, Hackerty-backerty two,
Hackerty-backerty three . . . Hackerty-backerty
nine—

*At the count of nine Shav springs up and knocks
Shakes down with a right to the chin.*

SHAV [*counting*] Hackerty-backerty one. . . . Hackerty-
backerty ten. Out.

SHAKES. Out! And by thee! Never. [*He rises*]. Younger
you are
By full three hundred years, and therefore carry
A heavier punch than mine; but what of that?
Death will soon finish you; but as for me,
Not marble nor the gilded monuments
Of princes—

SHAV.   —shall outlive your powerful rhymes.
So you have told us: I have read your sonnets.

SHAKES. Couldst write Macbeth?

SHAV. No need. He has been bettered
By Walter Scott's Rob Roy. Behold, and blush.

*Rob Roy and Macbeth appear, Rob in Highland
tartan and kilt with claymore, Macbeth in kingly
costume.*

MACBETH. Thus far into the bowels of the land
Have we marched on without impediment.
Shall I still call you Campbell?

ROB [*in a strong Scotch accent*] Caumill me no Caumills.
Ma fet is on ma native heath: ma name's Macgregor.

MACBETH. I have no words. My voice is in my sword.
Lay on, Rob Roy;
And damned be he that proves the smaller boy.

*He draws and stands on guard. Rob draws; spins
round several times like a man throwing a hammer;
and finally cuts off Macbeth's head at one stroke.*

ROB. Whaur's your Wullie Shaxper the noo?

Bagpipe and drum music, to which Rob dances off.

MACBETH [*headless*] I will return to Stratford: the hotels
Are cheaper there. [*He picks up his head, and goes off
with it under his arm to the tune of British Grena-
diers*].

SHAKES. Call you this cateran
Better than my Macbeth, one line from whom
Is worth a thousand of your piffling plays.

SHAV. Quote one. Just one. I challenge thee. One line.

SHAKES. "The shardborne beetle with his drowsy hum."

SHAV. Hast never heard of Adam Lindsay Gordon?

SHAKES. A name that sings. What of him?

SHAV.   He eclipsed
Thy shardborne beetle. Hear his mighty lines. [*Re-
citing*]
"The bettle booms adown the glooms
And bumps among the clumps."

SHAKES [*roaring with laughter*] Ha ha! Ho ho! My lungs
like chanticleer
Must crow their fill. This fellow hath an ear.
How does it run? "The beetle booms—

SHAV. Adown the glooms—

SHAKES. And bumps—

SHAV. Among the clumps." Well done, Australia!

Shav laughs.

SHAKES. Laughest thou at thyself? Pullst thou my leg?

SHAV. There is more fun in heaven and earth, sweet
William,
Than is dreamt of in your philosophy.

SHAKES. Where is thy Hamlet? Couldst thou write King
Lear?

SHAV. Aye, with his daughters all complete. Couldst thou
Have written Heartbreak House? Behold my Lear.

*A transparency is suddenly lit up, showing Captain
Shotover seated, as in Millais' picture called North-
West Passage, with a young woman of virginal beauty.*

SHOTOVER [*raising his hand and intoning*] I built a
house for my daughters and opened the doors
thereof
That men might come for their choosing, and their
betters spring from their love;

But one of them married a numskull: the other a liar
 wed;
And now she must lie beside him even as she made
 her bed.

THE VIRGIN. "Yes: this silly house, this strangely happy
 house, this agonizing house, this house without
 foundations. I shall call it Heartbreak House."

SHOTOVER. Enough. Enough. Let the heart break in
 silence.

The picture vanishes.

SHAKES. You stole that word from me: did I not write
"The heartache and the thousand natural woes
That flesh is heir to"?

SHAV. You were not the first
To sing of broken hearts. I was the first
That taught your faithless Timons how to mend them.

SHAKES. Taught what you could not know. Sing if you
 can
My cloud capped towers, my gorgeous palaces,
My solemn temples. The great globe itself,
Yea, all which it inherit, shall dissolve—

SHAV. —and like this foolish little show of ours
Leave not a wrack behind. So you have said.
I say the world will long outlast our day.
Tomorrow and tomorrow and tomorrow
We puppets shall replay our scene. Meanwhile,
Immortal William dead and turned to clay
May stop a hole to keep the wind away.
Oh that the earth which kept the world in awe
Should patch a wall t' expel the winter's flaw!

SHAKES. These words are mine, not thine.

SHAV. Peace, jealous Bard:
We both are mortal. For a moment suffer
My glimmering light to shine.

A light appears between them.

SHAKES. Out, out, brief candle! [*He puffs it out*].
Darkness. The play ends.

THE END

INDEX

(*Specific references to Shakespearean characters are located under the play in which they appear*)